The Little Slaves of the Harp

McGill-Queen's Studies in Ethnic History
Donald Harman Akenson, Editor

1 Irish Migrants in the Canadas
  A New Approach
  Bruce S. Elliott
2 Critical Years in Immigration
  Canada and Australia Compared
  Freda Hawkins
3 Italians in Toronto
  Development of a National Identity, 1875–1935
  John E. Zucchi
4 Linguistics and Poetics of Latvian Folk Songs
  Essays in Honour of the Sesquicentennial of the
  Birth of Kr. Barons
  Vaira Vikis-Freibergs
5 Johan Schrøder's Travels in Canada, 1863
  Orm Øverland
6 Class, Ethnicity, and Social Inequality
  Christopher McAll
7 The Victorian Interpretation of Racial Conflict
  The Maori, the British, and the New Zealand
  Wars
  James Belich
8 White Canada Forever
  Popular Attitudes and Public Policy toward
  Orientals in British Columbia
  W. Peter Ward
9 The People of Glengarry
  Highlanders in Transition, 1745–1820
  Marianne McLean
10 Vancouver's Chinatown
   Racial Discourse in Canada, 1875–1980
   Kay J. Anderson
11 Best Left as Indians
   Native-White Relations in the Yukon Territory,
   1840–1973
   Ken S. Coates
12 Such Hard-Working People
   Italian Immigrants in Postwar Toronto
   Franca Iacovetta
13 The Little Slaves of the Harp
   Italian Child Street Musicians in Nineteenth-
   Century Paris, London, and New York
   John E. Zucchi

The Little Slaves of the Harp

Italian Child Street Musicians in Nineteenth-Century Paris, London, and New York

JOHN E. ZUCCHI

McGill-Queen's University Press
Montreal & Kingston • London • Buffalo

© McGill-Queen's University Press 1992
ISBN 0-7735-0890-2

Legal deposit second quarter 1992
Bibliothèque nationale du Québec

∞

Printed in Canada on acid-free paper

This book has been published
with the help of a grant from the
Canadian Federation for the Humanities,
using funds provided by the
Social Sciences and Humanities
Research Council of Canada.
Publication has also been supported by
the Canada Council through its block grant program.

Canadian Cataloguing in Publication Data

Zucchi, John E., 1955–
  The little slaves of the harp: Italian child street
musicians in nineteenth century Paris, London and
New York

  (McGill-Queen's studies in ethnic history; 13)
  Includes bibliographical references and index.
  ISBN 0-7735-0890-2

  1. Street music and musicians – France – Paris –
History – 19th century. 2. Street music and musicians
– England – London – History – 19th century.
3. Street music and musicians – New York (N.Y.) –
History – 19th century. 4. Children as musicians –
History – 19th century. 5. Italy – Emigration and
immigration – History – 19th century.
I. Title. II. Series.

HD6231.Z83 1992   362.7'99   C91-090622-X

Typeset in Palatino 10.5/13 by
Caractéra production graphique inc., Quebec City.

Contents

Preface   vii

Maps   ix

Introduction   3

1 Emigration and the Street Music Trade   17

2 "Les Petits Italiens" in Paris   42

3 "The Organ Boys" in London   76

4 "The Little Slaves" in New York   111

5 Italian Legislation, 1868–1873   144

6 Conclusion   164

Appendix A   172

Appendix B   175

Notes   179

Bibliography   197

Index   206

For Ceci;
and for Giacomo, Maximilian, Maddalena,
and any one who might follow

Preface

Many people have asked me how I became interested in such a topic as child street musicians. I came on the idea in 1980 as I was researching my dissertation on Italians in Toronto (subsequently published in this series by McGill-Queen's University Press). My objective then was to study the Italian migration to Toronto as a series of migrations of people from various Italian home towns to that city. The first significant group of townspeople I came across were immigrants from Laurenzana (in the region of Basilicata). I could not understand why they were listed in municipal records as harpists and violinists. I decided to pursue the matter, and if possible to write an article on the migration of one town group or one trade. The research took on a life of its own, and this book is the result.

There are many people and institutions whom I wish to thank. My principal debt is to the late Robert F. Harney, my adviser at the University of Toronto, who instilled in me a love for migration history, and gave me the bearings for pursuing the field. I shall always miss his presence.

I am grateful also to the late Dr Giovanni Battista Cragnolini and Mrs Vera Cragnolini for kindly allowing me to use their apartment in Rome on a couple of occasions during my research period.

I have come to appreciate the help of many librarians, curators, and photographers who assisted me in this project: at the "UL" at Cambridge, the British Library, the New York Public Library, Robarts Library at the University of Toronto, McLennan Library at McGill University, the Archives de la Préfecture de Police in Paris, the Archivio Storico of the Ministero degli Affari Esteri in

Rome, and the photography departments of the J. Paul Getty Museum in Los Angeles and the Science Museum in London. Time and economic constraints prevented my consulting other pertinent archival collections (in, for example, Naples and Potenza).

This project began with funding from a postdoctoral fellowship of the Social Sciences and Humanities Research Council. As well, I received the generous encouragement of Darwin College, University of Cambridge, in the form of a junior research fellowship in 1984-85.

During my two years in Cambridge I had the very kind help and encouragement of Frank Thistlethwaite, fellow emeritus at St John's College. My colleague at McGill University, Valentin Boss, read the entire manuscript and gave me many helpful suggestions, as did Dr Gianfausto Rosoli of the Centro Studi Emigrazione. The two anonymous readers for the Press and the Aid to Scholarly Publications Programme were also very helpful, as were Philip Cercone, Don Akenson, Susanne McAdam, and Joan McGilvray of McGill-Queen's University Press. Kathy Johnson reminded me (very discreetly) how indispensable editors are. I bear the responsibility for any shortcomings in the text.

I am also grateful to the friends I met in Cambridge at the start of the project, especially Ana Lydia Sawaya. It was a new beginning.

Maria Cecilia has helped me make sense of all this, as have our children, Giacomo, Maximilian, and Maddalena.

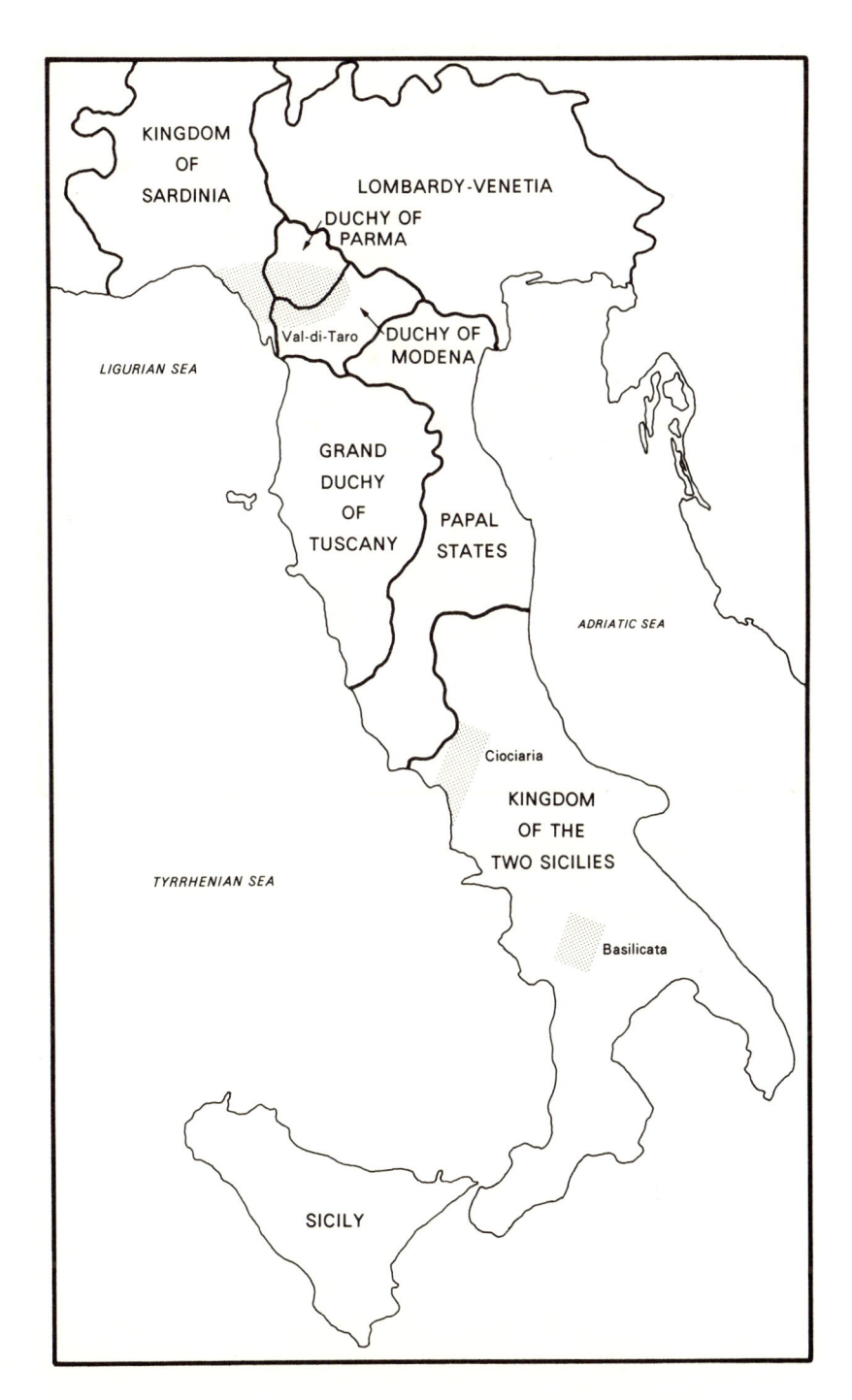

Italy, 1859. The three areas of origin of the street musicians are shaded.

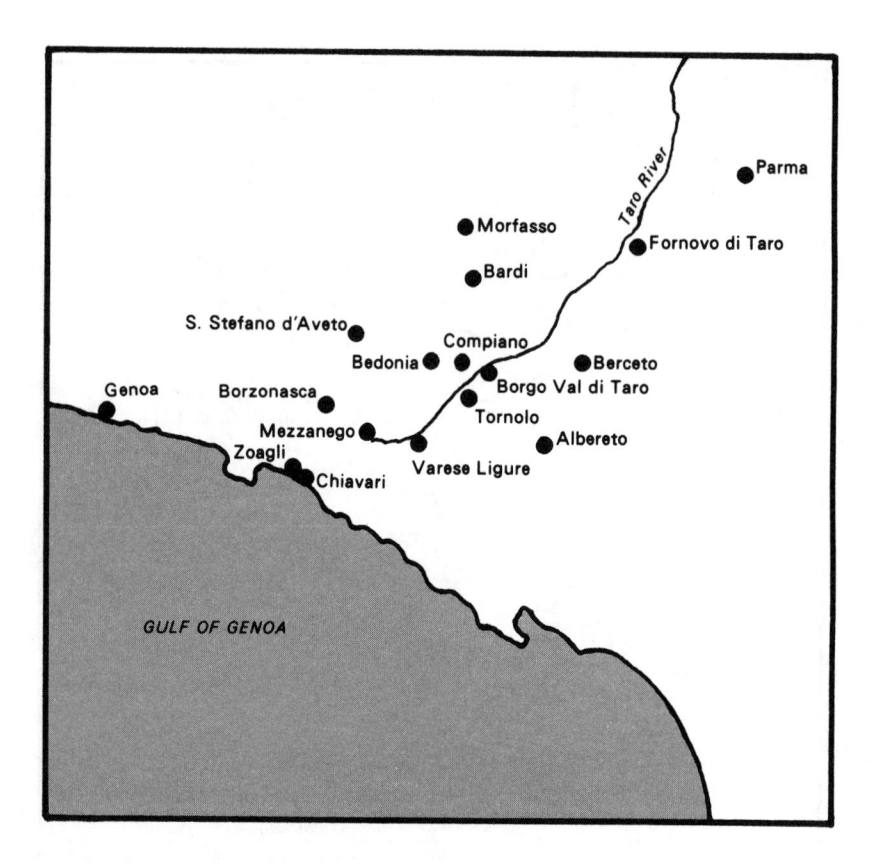

The Val-di-Taro and Ligurian sending area

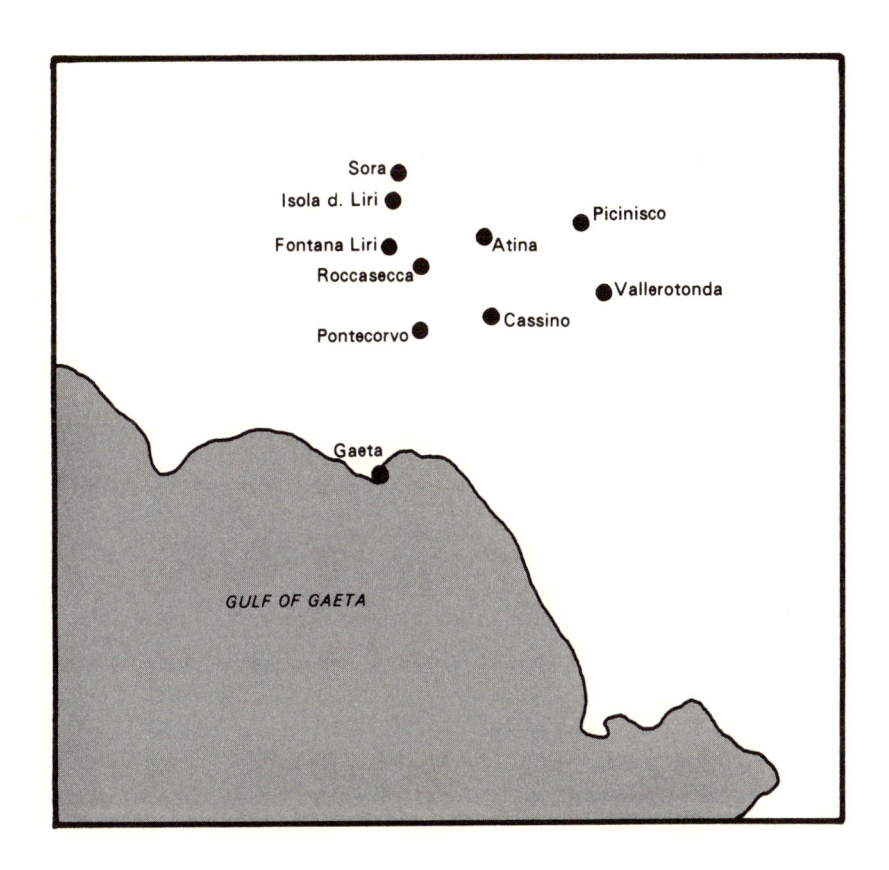

The Ciociaria sending area

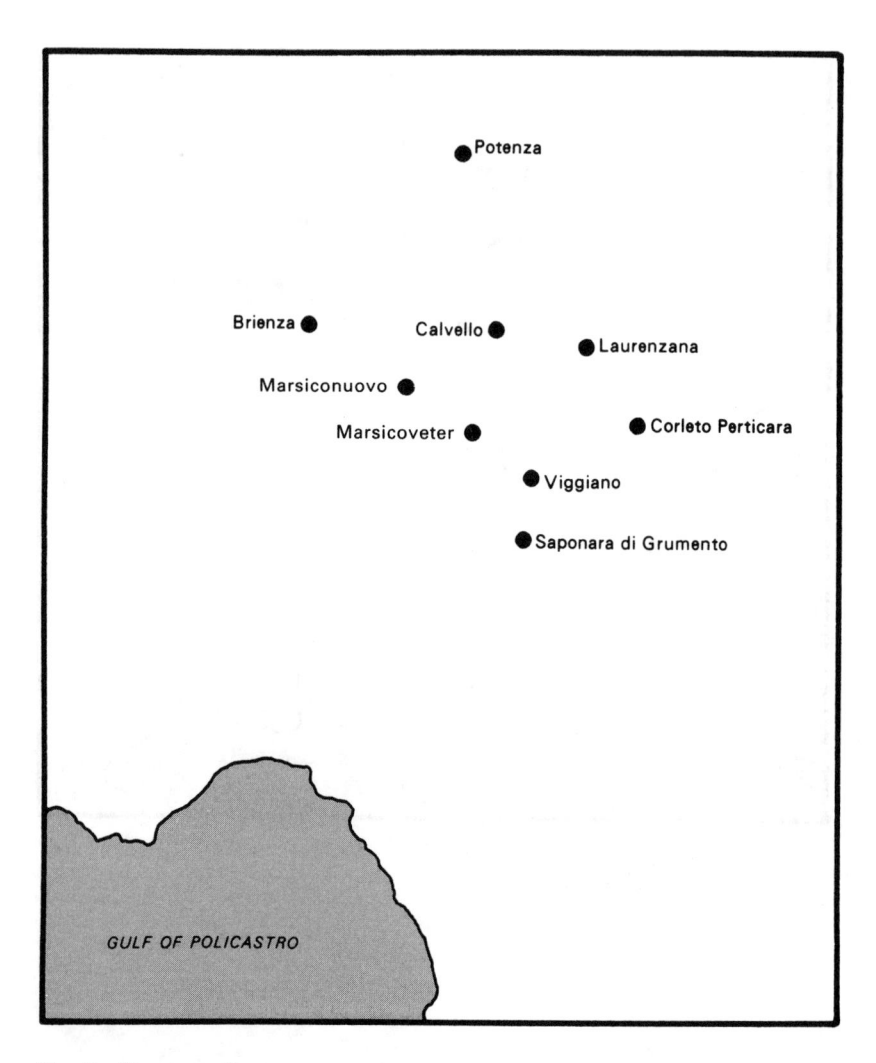

The Basilicata sending area

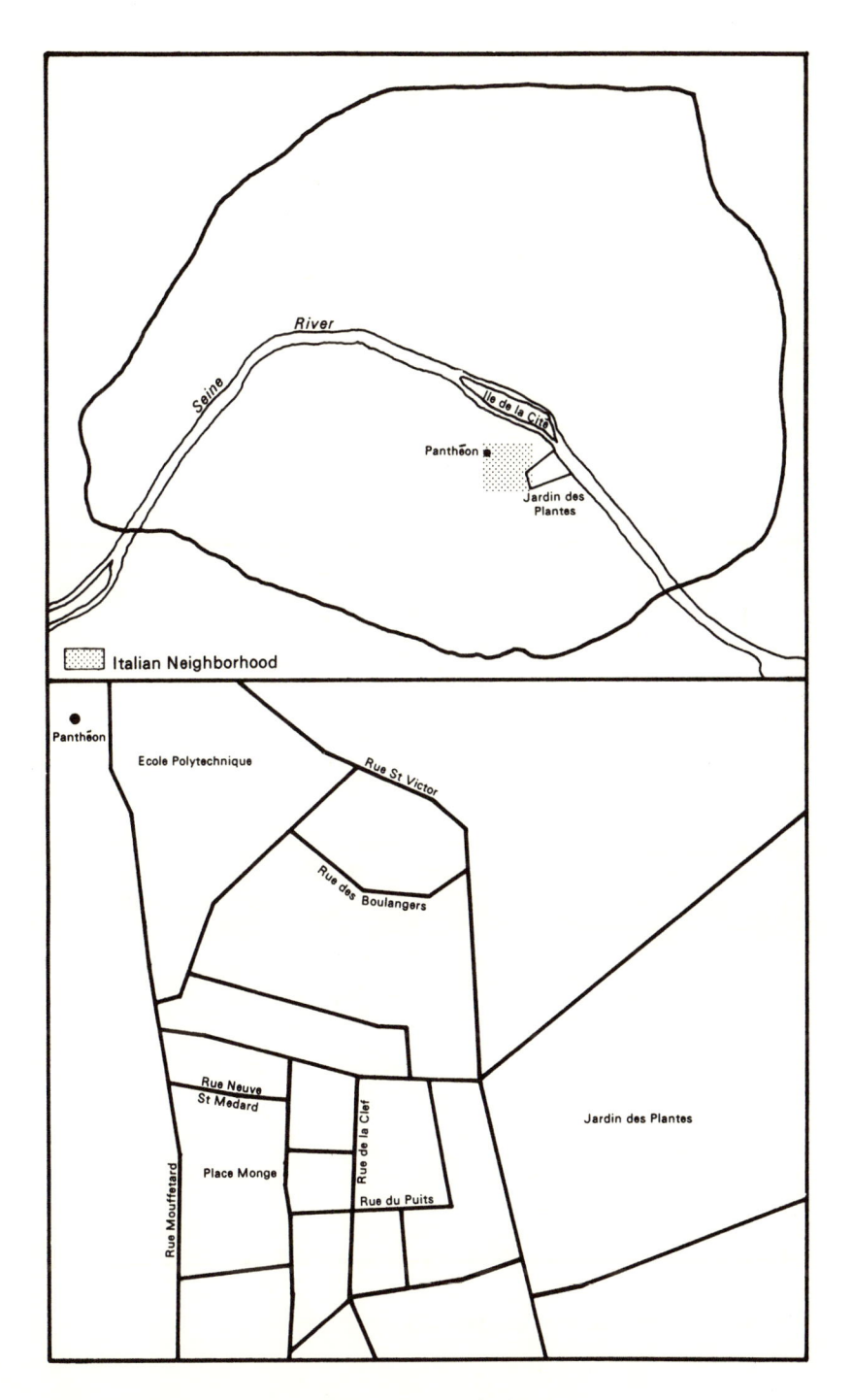

Italian immigrant quarters, Paris, 1860s and 1870s

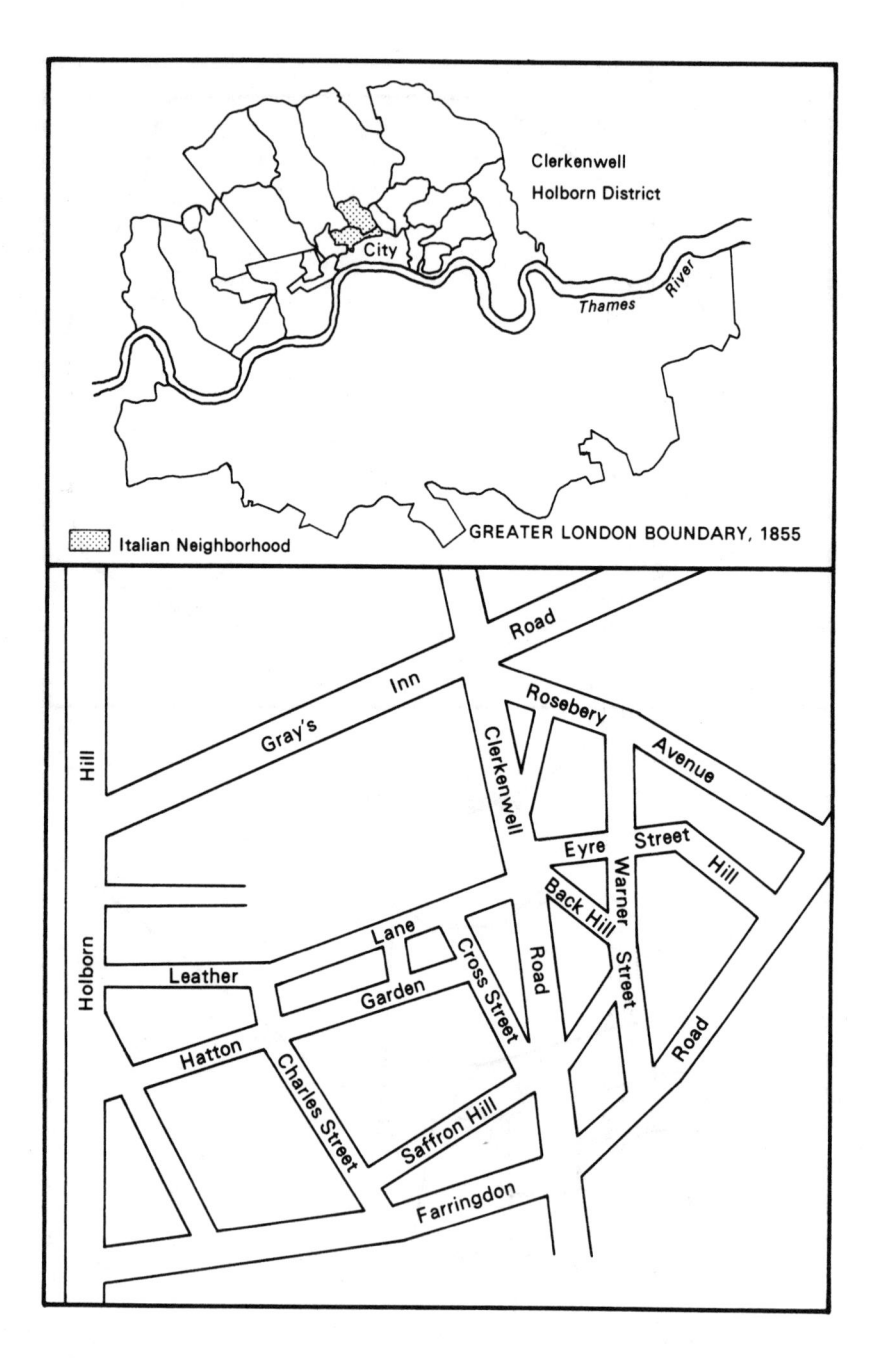

Italian immigrant quarters, London, 1860s and 1870s

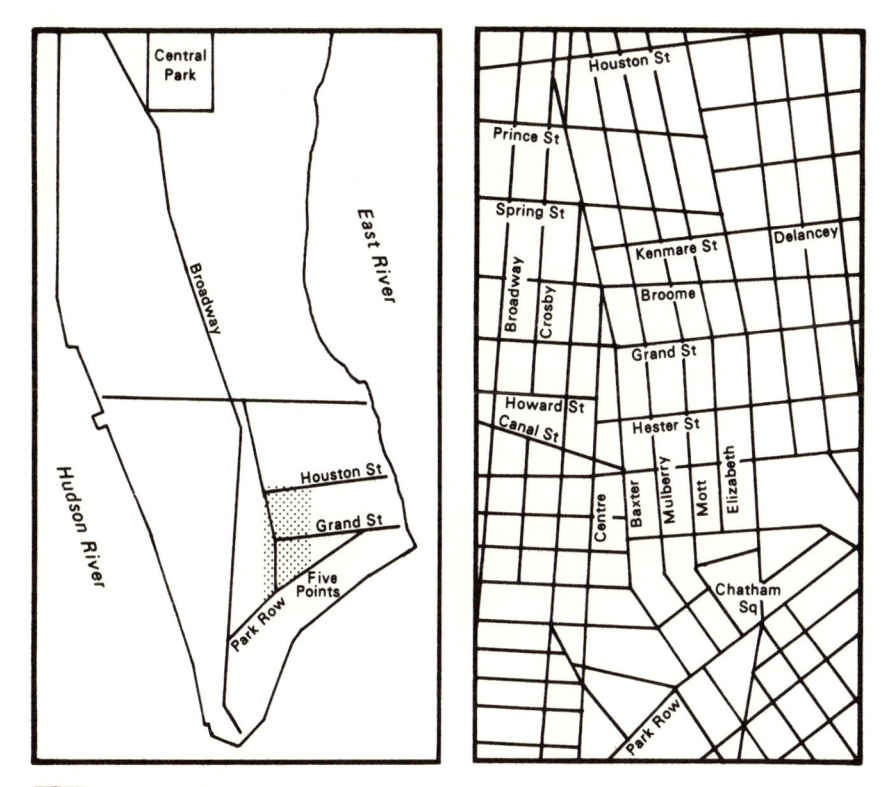

Italian Neighbourhood

Italian immigrant quarters, New York, 1860s and 1870s

The Little Slaves of the Harp

Introduction

In 1870 a nine-year-old boy named Giuseppe was awakened one night by a man who took him with eight other children from his town, Calvello, in the region of Basilicata, on a long trek to the port of Naples. Giuseppe and the boys immediately learned to call the man "padrone" and to obey his instructions. From Naples the master and his troupe set sail for New York. Their address in that burgeoning metropolis was 45 Crosby Street, which, as it turned out, was the most notorious "child den" in the city. After spending his first night with his companions sleeping on some straw, without covers, in the cellar of the building, Giuseppe (or Joseph, as he would now be called in America) was sent out the next morning to play a triangle on the streets of Manhattan and to beg for money from passers-by. That evening Joseph got his first taste of the padrone's demands and strict discipline: he was beaten because he returned home with too little money, and was sent back down to the cellar. During the following weeks Joseph was taught to play the violin, and he was instructed not to come home without at least one dollar in earnings. This meant that he had to stay out until late at night, sometimes into the early hours of the morning; often he was unable to meet his quota. This triggered the wrath of the padrone, who beat him cruelly. On one occasion his master bit him on his left ear, leaving a scar. On another he bound him hand and foot and left him in the cellar overnight.

At first Joseph did not dare to run away from his padrone. His master had a psychological hold over him, and the lad, like so many other "little slaves," was almost certain that no matter where he escaped, his padrone would always find him. However, after being beaten frequently over the course of two years, and especially after one particularly severe punishment, Joseph demanded that his master either free him or stop torturing him. In response the padrone threatened to kill the young apprentice should he ever try to run away. To add some force to his threats, he boxed Joseph about the ears and bound his wrists with a rope, leaving gashes in his flesh. When the lad could bear this treatment no longer he decided not to return home. One evening in early June 1873 he headed for Central Park and hid there for two or three days before a park-keeper discovered him, shared meals with him, and then entrusted him to the care of a woman who lived in a cottage in the park.[1]

Joseph's story was not unlike that of thousands, perhaps tens of thousands, of other children who left Italy in the nineteenth century to perform various itinerant trades. It was more dramatic than many others in that Joseph was treated very cruelly and in that his case was publicized in the press. But many other children who worked under masters as figurine-vendors, animal exhibitors, mosaic-cutters, chimney-sweeps, glassworkers, artists' models, or harpists shared similar long journeys, hard work, and in some cases, cruelty.

This book is primarily about the child street musicians who left their towns and villages in Italy for Paris, London, New York, and other cities around the world during the nineteenth century. Because they were mainly from rural areas, they worked alongside adults in their home towns, usually in agriculture, but sometimes in trades. It is difficult, then, to discuss the child performers without alluding to the adults, almost always men, who accompanied them around the world. Therefore, I will also examine more generally the spread of the street music trade from Italy through Europe and to America, and I will place the children in this context. Finally, I will evaluate the responses of the public, of philanthropic agencies, police, magistrates, politicians, lawmakers, and journalists both to the street music trade and to the child street performers and exhibitors.

Between 1840 and 1940 one of the greatest population movements in all history occurred between Europe and the Americas. Estimates of the number of people who crossed the Atlantic Ocean during that century converge at about 55 million; a number of scholars have argued that 16 million of those were Italians. Generally speaking, the strong upward surge in population from the mid-eighteenth century, the rise of industrialization, the enclosure movement, agricultural crises in the old world, improvements in transportation (especially by sea), the competition of shipping companies and agencies, and the strong, continuous demand for farmers and outdoor and factory labour in the new world led to the great migration in the hundred years before the Second World War.[2]

Among the pioneers of this movement in the early nineteenth century (and, in the case of some countries, even earlier) were artisans who detected the crisis of a population rise just as industry became less labour-intensive. These men went off in search of work in other nearby states or even farther afield. Certainly this was the experience of many journeymen in the German and Italian states and eastern Europe in the 1830s and 1840s, and of British and French tradesmen.[3] Many agricultural workers or peasants settled on new farmlands in Brazil, Argentina, and the United States, particularly Scandinavians, Italians, and Britons. Other agriculturists, especially in Italy and Germany, but elsewhere as well, sought other possibilities by training in a new trade or task that might be exportable to another region, state, or continent. This was the avenue taken by, among others, Italian and German street musicians.

Along with other tradesmen and traders – bird-vendors and horse-traders from Brunswick, sugarbakers from Hanover, and ink-vendors from Parma, to give just a few examples – the musicians and other street performers from Italy heralded the mass migration of the late nineteenth and early twentieth centuries. These migrants made a reconnaissance of economic opportunities for themselves, their family and kin, and their townspeople and regions, which led eventually to a large population movement. I do not suggest a general connection between some early trampers and a later flow of people; rather, by focusing on the street musicians who came primarily from three areas in Italy, we can see that, through their ties and communication networks, they influenced strongly the migration of artisans and peasants from their own towns and regions.[4]

The street musicians and other tradesmen and traders, whom we can categorize as the precursors of the great migration, provide an important insight into the social transition to the industrial age. In their attempts to come to grips with the consequences of the industrial revolution, social historians have usually concentrated on the "de-skilling" of craftsmen – that is, on the breakdown of tradesmen's skills into their various components, the rise of mechanization, and the employment of former tradesmen and especially migrants, either from the hinterlands or from abroad, in the new factory complex or in mining or transportation projects. Foreign labour is depicted as masses of peasants and, to a lesser extent, tradesmen who were attracted by capital and processed as unskilled labour into the industrial world. This is especially the case in North American historiography.[5]

Such a view implies that the flow of labour to capital is almost mechanistic, that all power lies with the capitalist who owns the means of production, and that nineteenth-century peasants from Europe, for example, flowed passively into the American factory, mine, or outdoor capital project. However, the story of the precursors of the great migration suggests that there was an intermediate stage in this process, that there was an element of choice on the part of the old-world peasants and tradesmen who journeyed to the European and American cities. They were not only the dispossessed of Europe; they had to come to terms with economic modernization, which they did by becoming petty entrepreneurs. When peasants and day labourers from the Val-di-Taro in the Duchy of Parma went to France or Russia as ink-sellers, organ-grinders, bear or camel exhibitors, and lacemakers, they acquired a new trade and began to test the market, following the routes of older trade diaspora. These migrants, who invariably hailed from rural towns and villages, had a sense of economic possibilities, of markets for their goods and services, because for centuries they had maintained a dialogue with urban centres. With the improvement in transportation and communications in the nineteenth century, the urban centres with which they had a rapport could be even farther removed from the migrant's home town.[6]

The relationship that the migrants developed with urban centres has an important bearing on one other topic that has attracted social historians in recent years – mendicancy, poverty, and begging. Recent studies have shown how, in eighteenth- and nineteenth-century Europe, the state usurped the role of the private charitable agencies, most of which had been the preserve of the Church. Since the Middle Ages, in times of economic distress or war, urban charitable institutions had been overwhelmed by the large numbers of rural poor who flooded the cities as migrants, wanderers, and beggars. With the economic dislocation of the eighteenth century and the Napoleonic Wars, the problem of vagrancy become even more serious. The state and even the private charitable agencies took a scientific approach to alleviating the condition of the poor. Private agencies realized their inability to confront the problems of mendicancy and continually restricted their definition of the "deserving poor."[7]

Itinerant performers and especially child street musicians proved to be a difficult case for philanthropists and charitable agencies, as well as for lawmakers, police, and magistrates. They formed part of that frightening mass of rural poor who seemed to invade the cities and threaten the social order. They were not technically beggars, wanderers, or vagrants, but their "useless" occupations, rural manners, and strange speech and dress made them a threat to the urban order. Although it could be argued that they earned their keep, they none the less requested money from people in a manner that resembled begging: they did not demand specific amounts of cash. They did not have a scale of charges or established prices for their services. The line between mendicancy and work was not clear.

In the public mind, the street musicians were "other". They were among the many outsiders who had no claim to the urban community or its charitable institutions and who had to be watched with suspicion. Although street musicians were conspicuous, no one seemed to know much about them. They lived in the dangerous neighbourhoods near the place Maubert in Paris, on a tiny street off the Clerkenwell Road or in Hatton Gardens in Saffron Hill, London, on a short stretch of Crosby Street in Manhattan. Only on rare occasions did outsiders venture into the dwellings of these musicians, and invariably they were investigators from the *New York Times*, the *Lancet*, the Society for the Prevention of Cruelty to Children, or the Charity Organisation Society in search of the pathological: rundown housing, filth, vermin, strange foods, and exotic animals such as monkeys.

The prime evidence of the pathological that the newspapers cited was the presence of the child performers. The children were outside the familial context even though they were part of the family economy. They begged for alms or requested coins in return for a lowly service: exhibiting white mice or playing a violin or a harp, even in the late evening when they should have been in bed. Like their masters they wore strange clothes – navy blue corduroy trousers and dark woollen jackets. Their "swarthy" looks gave them a delinquent air. Joseph's story, uncovered by a *New York Times* reporter, led to a long series of articles in the summer of 1873 that took the public into the neighbourhoods and "dens" of these waifs and their masters, or padroni. The reports were sensational in the purest sense of the word. On the one hand, we come away from these articles with precious little information on the masters and children; on the other, we find many details of the small rooms, the stale air, and the smell of garlic and sweat. One caricature in *Harper's Weekly* depicted one of the child "dens" complete with a macaroni case, a drawing of Garibaldi on the wall, and a number of children witnessing the whipping of one of their companions by a sinister-looking padrone.[8]

There were many similarities in the reports of newspapers, bureaucracies, and philanthropic agencies in all three major cities, including the emphasis on the pathological. One notable omission is a description of the children themselves. Almost all reports on the children gave an account of the general problem of child minstrels, or alluded to reports published elsewhere, or described their work routine, their living conditions, and especially the cruelties suffered by some of them; but very rarely did they actually describe the children except to comment on their swarthiness or filth. Perhaps a dozen sources of the hundreds I examined informed us of what the children ate. Only a handful gave us an inkling of the clothes they wore. The children were seldom quoted directly. Their stories seemed so similar that one suspects that reporters took note only of those aspects that fit their preconceptions.

Although stories about the children in London, Paris, and New York had much in common, reports in each city stressed different aspects of "the problem." This merely reflected the approach of each metropolis, which in turn was strongly influenced by social and political factors. For Parisians, the children were a "law and order" matter. The préfecture was concerned with controlling elements that might cause political instability or social disorder, especially in years of economic crisis. Effective laws backed the police, and had only to be applied stringently in difficult years and ignored in more tranquil times. Philanthropic agencies in France were not concerned with the problem, except for the Société Italienne de Bienfaisance, which was run by the Italian consul and well-off Italian immigrants. Newspapers showed just as much interest. *Le Temps* published an article on the children about once a year. The ban on street organs in 1901 created a much greater stir in the press.[9]

In London two overriding themes persisted almost throughout the century. One had to do with street noise and with the development of an effective law to keep street organists and brass bands away from middle class residential areas. The other was the problem of mendicancy. The question whether the children were beggars came up explicitly only on occasion, but most articles written about the children, especially in the 1860s and 1870s, reported on the child's or master's day in court and on the magistrate's decision as to the status of the child. More effective legislation was developed in Britain in the 1880s to protect the "little slaves." In New York the problem was placed in the realm of "child reform", which actually meant channelling the child into a "useful" occupation. Reformers did not find themselves in the same quandary as their British counterparts. The Italian children could be dealt with by quick and effective legislation and by vigilance on the part of reform agencies. The issue of the child street musicians was also important to the political parties, and especially to their Italian-American representatives.

In Italy the parliamentary deputies and bureaucrats in the Ministry of External Affairs also reacted to the problem. In the late 1860s and early 1870s they attempted to find a legislative solution from the "sending" side. It took five years for the Italian Parliament to complete an investigation into children in itinerant trades and to pass a major law protecting those children. There were many reasons for the long delay, but important questions had to be addressed concerning the right of the state to interfere in the family and the freedom to migrate and to perform trades.

Legislation emerged in the 1870s and 1880s – more than a generation after Britain, France, and New England had introduced factory legislation for children. With the industrial revolution women and children were hired as cheap factory labour. This led to abuse and to the family's dependence on the income of those members. The state responded with legislation, beginning with the English Factory Acts of 1833. France followed with legislation in 1841. While public attention was focused on child labourers, street children normally came under the aegis of vagrancy laws, usually from the eighteenth and nineteenth centuries.[10]

In each city and country politicians, bureaucrats, police, Italian diplomats, and charitable agencies considered the problem of street musicians, and more specifically child minstrels, within their own socio-political context. Unfortunately, these same individuals and groups have left us virtually all the extent documentation; the musicians were for the most part illiterate, and left virtually no written records for posterity. *Wandering Minstrel*, the autobiography of a street violinist in Britain who used the name of Cagliardo Coraggioso, is the great exception.[11] Otherwise, our information comes from the records of governmental or philanthropic agencies and commissions and from newspapers. The single best source of information on the child street musicians was the collection of documents in Rome used by a commission of the Italian Senate between 1868 and 1873 to draft legislation. This collection included hundreds of letters from Italian consular representatives abroad, senators, parliamentarians, district attorneys, prefects, ambassadors, and legislators, who reported on the children in their sending towns and at their destinations and suggested legislative solutions. In addition, the Italian consular records from various cities proved fruitful.

In New York, the *New York Times*, the published records of the Society for the Prevention of Cruelty to Children (SPCC), and the Children's Aid Society were important sources. In London, the *Times* and an 1876 report by the Charity Organisation Society, as well as published reports of the London Mendicity Society, were extremely valuable. In Paris, the records of the préfecture and a special 1868 report on the children by the Société Italienne de Bienfaisance were indispensable. In addition, there were scores of articles, short stories, novels, and passing references regarding the children.

What is most obvious in this list of sources is the middle-class provenance of the writers, though the sources represent a number of points of view. Generally, the authors of the various articles and reports were looking for the pathological, but to serve various purposes. The liberals who spearheaded the Italian campaign against the children were attempting to improve young Italy's image abroad, but they couched this goal in terms of the more apparently humane program of curbing child exploitation. The debates in the Italian Chamber of Deputies reveal the confusion over the objective of legislative action. *New York Times* reporters were affirming the investigative powers of the press and its capacity to serve as a catalyst for social reform. Writers who lamented the street organ nuisance in London were grappling with the problem of effective residential segregation. Parisian police and préfecture reports had the antiseptic tone of the forces of order merely taking instructions from superiors, and applying the law quickly and effectively to ward off social disturbances. Liberals in Italy, London, and New York loved to blame unfairly the "slave trade" in child musicians on the Catholic church or on "Bourbon misrule" in the Kingdom of Naples.

It is from these sources and in the context of their perspectives that we must reconstruct the history of nineteenth century Italian adult and (especially) child street musicians in their host societies. To understand the significance of the children's place in the street music trade we must first have a sense of the place of childhood in nineteenth-century western society. According to many historians, this was the age in which adults "discovered" childhood. Although some would disagree, there is a tendency among specialists to attach an increasing importance to childhood from the seventeenth century. Parents are portrayed as becoming kinder to their children by the nineteenth century – the same time that the state introduced legislation to protect children from abuse.[12]

The assertion that adults actually "discovered" childhood between the seventeenth and nineteenth centuries, or that parents were kinder in that era than in preceding eras, can be and has been called into question.[13] The main focus of this book is not child cruelty per se; however, it is clear that the physical abuse of the young Italian minstrels was ostensibly one of the important issues in the formulation of legislation concerning street music in a number of countries. In my research I came upon a number of cases in which the masters beat, whipped, underfed, or neglected the children entrusted to them by their parents. That those cases were well publicized in the press or in the reports of philanthropic agencies lends credence to the hypothesis that they were exceptional. The press presented the extreme cases as the norm. In other words, from reading the *New York Times* or the *Times* of London, one would think that all young street musicians were constantly abused.

Many exaggerations can be discounted on historical evidence or on intuition. Articles and reports grossly overestimated the number of child performers in the various cities. Indeed, they did not estimate, but cited incorrect figures published elsewhere. They also generalized unfairly from the specific to maintain the veneer of the pathological. The dozen or so true cases of cruelty involving child harpists and violinists were blown up in the press and in institutional and bureaucratic reports to the point where they seemed to represented the norm. In fact, a careful reading of individual cases in the *Times* of London, for example, or the SPCC reports, confirms that many of the young musicians were travelling with their fathers, or with someone known to the family – a relative, kinsman, or townsman.

In most of the contemporary literature on the child street musicians, the parents are not always portrayed as wicked and irresponsible for having indentured their children. To be sure, one comes across the cruel stepfather or stepmother who wishes to exploit the child economically, but one also encounters the poor widow who has no choice but to send her son off with a padrone for two or three years. It is difficult to draw much hard evidence from the child musicians themselves because their stories have been filtered through the perspective of middle-class writers. However, it appears that Linda Pollock's contention that parents in the nineteenth century were not indifferent nor unusually cruel to their children merits serious consideration.[14] These children lived in a pre-industrial society in their home towns and villages, in which they were expected either to participate in agricultural tasks or to apprentice with a master. Even before the 1800s, migration was a way of life for many inhabitants of these towns. The children, who were as young as five or six and as old as eighteen, were part of that tradition. It was no more cruel for their parents to send them off with a padrone than it is for today's parents to send their high-school-aged children off to plant trees in the summer.

What the press portrayed as a "virtual slave trade" was in fact a form of apprenticeship like any other, except that the child did not become skilled in a trade; few children were able to perform well on the harp or violin. As we shall see the padroni signed apprenticeship contracts. The contracts stipulated that the children were to be cared for, fed, and clothed by the padroni. The clothes they wore and the food they ate would have seemed strange to New Yorkers or Londoners. One *New York Times* reporter described a group of children "hobbling about in shoes a world too wide for their lithe small feet," wearing "scanty jackets." Perhaps it was the same reporter who, a year later, interviewed three boys aged six, eight, and twelve. Pietrocito and Rocco-Terzo were from Laurenzana, one of the important sending towns in Basilicata. Franceschito was from a nearby town. All lived in the same building on Crosby Street; all had been "sold" to a master by their parents; all claimed to have been beaten into silence by their respective padroni. The three young boys told the reporters about their living conditions. They washed once a month and never changed their clothes during that period. At the end of the month their shirts were burned and they were given clean clothes. They slept on straw beds on the floor. They woke up early in the morning and went to bed late at night. For breakfast they ate bread and macaroni.[15]

Advertisements by padroni in New York papers asking for the return of their lost or runaway children give us some idea of their appearance. One boy by the name of Joseph wore a corduroy jacket, a black outside cape, a white vest, and grey trousers. Frank Briglia, age seven, wore a black jacket, black vest and grey trousers. John Matist, aged ten, wore a black jacket, a black and white vest, and a white cap. A reporter noted that he had a scar on his upper lip and surmised that a padrone had caused the scar in order to identify the child. The children probably dressed not very differently from the way they had in their home towns. At least to New York reporters, however, their dress seemed strange, and was associated with the pathological. Girls were always described or portrayed in caricatures as dressed in colourful peasant costumes and earrings, and playing a tambourine. Boys were described as having "dirt caked upon them ... all skin and bones." New Yorkers associated Italian immigrants' clothes with poor hygiene: "The immigrants wear the costumes of their native localities, which agree well with the general filth of their surroundings. They all look romantic but very dirty." In his autobiography Coraggioso says that he wondered why a crowd of children in a Welsh mining village had gathered around him laughing and describes what he saw in the mirror:

I looked into a mirror in a shop window. I took a good look at myself ... There was a boy of about ten and a half years of age, wearing a man's bowler hat, about three sizes too large and almost covering my ears. My hair was very long. My suit was one which fit a big man; the sleeves of the jacket and the legs of the trousers had been cut; the vest was as large as the jacket. My boots had been picked out of a bucket. They were large navvy's boots, full of huge nails; there was a large cut on the top of the toes, and [they] must have been too small for the man who wore them; they were at least size elevens. I wore pieces of toe rags round my feet and a pair of thick stockings, full of holes, to keep them in shape. A big greasy muffler was wound round my neck, tied in a knot, and to complete the disaster, I wore in my ears a pair of ear-rings with three tiny balls hanging [to] each ... Every shop window I came to I had a look at myself and was ashamed of what I saw.[16]

Although a number of newspaper articles said that the children ate macaroni, other articles usually reported that "gruel" or "common black bread" was their only sustenance. The reporter who encountered the three young boys mentioned above found them eating food out of a garbage-box on Fifth Avenue. "Why do you eat such stuff?" he asked them. "Because I am hungry," one of them answered. Again, reporters took a few extreme examples to portray a general picture of emaciated children whose inadequate diet consisted of strange foods and starchy staples. One writer, Adolphus Smith, in his commentary on a photograph of Italian child harpists in London in 1877, doubted that the children starved. "Their pockets full of pence, what system of control can prevent them from buying food in the streets when they play? ... The receipts made by the boys vary from 1s. 8d. to 4s. per day, and their healthy, hearty appearance and merry faces, testify that a portion of this is spent in food. I know of at least one *padroni*, living at Saffron Hill, who has the reputation of giving his boys plenty of food. Maccaroni is of course the chief dish, but it would be fortunate if our English poor knew how to enjoy so simple, nutritious, and wholesome a dinner." Cagliardo Coraggioso recalled that "the food that we got from our boss was not fit to be eaten. He never bought tea, sugar, bread, or butter. We ate if we had been successful during the day ... He carried in his pocket a tin with sugar in it, and he put a pinch in each cup and put the tin into his pocket again ... Milk was the only thing he bought. All other things we begged from grocers ... Sometimes he gathered big turnips from the fields, boiled and mashed them, and mixed them with a spoonful of grease and onions ... On the Saturday night he bought a whole head of cow, or six sheep heads, and made a large pot of soup, into which he put a handful of rice. He collected all the old pieces of bread lying about the house and mixed them with the soup, and this was our great Sunday dinner."[17]

We can know little else about the the children's daily routine. A police superintendent in London in 1852 reported that the children "leave home between 7 and 9 in the morning and return between 8 and 12 at night ...Their diet is bread and cheese but they often get food given them in the streets. Sunday is a day of rest, they attend Mass and get a meat dinner."[18] Coraggioso's autobiography confirms this schedule.

We can assume that the children spoke little English. Susannah Strickland (Moodie), in *The Keepsake Guineas*, published in London in 1841, noted that one of the Italian "fierce looking foreigners" with eight dancing dogs and a monkey who appeared in her story "spoke English very well." Adolphus Smith commented that one of the harpists he met spoke fluently though he had been in London only two years. Smith, like so many others, also observed that the very young children were poor performers, but youth and adults were well trained in their virtù (craft). Indeed, he felt that they rendered a great service in entertaining artisans and the poorer classes. "They have repeated to the uncouth English labourer the warm melodies of the Italian opera, they have helped to spread among the poor the love for the most humanizing and innocent of enjoyments, and have nurtured in our courts and alleys echoes of purer music than could otherwise have reached those dismal bodies."[19]

Children and youths seem to have played a great variety of music on all the instruments, although the greatest selection probably came from the hand organs. The viggianesi played their own folk music as well as selections from opera, especially the music of Rossini, Jommelli, and Cimarosa. One Italian organ grinder irritated many residents in London with his repetition of the Hundredth Psalm. Themes from *Tannhäuser* and *Lohengrin* played by an Italian street organist "startled inhabitants of our crowded thoroughfares in London." Arias from *La Sonnambula* and *Il Trovatore*, *La Traviata*, *Ernani*, and other Verdi operas were not uncommon. Nor were English folk songs or Strauss waltzes and mazurkas. The Parmesan grinder of the flute harmonicum organ interviewed by Henry Mayhew in the 1850s had eight tunes on his organ: "Two are from opera, one is a song, one a waltz, one is hornpipe, one is polka, and the other two is dancing tunes. One is from Il Lombardi of Verdi." Coraggioso played contemporary tunes such as "A Bicycle Built for Two," but the most popular tune in a mining village in Durham in which he performed around 1880 was "Two Lovely Black Eyes."[20]

The street musicians, adult and child, give us a glimpse of the meeting of two worlds – the Italian village and the large European or American metropolis. The rural peasants and artisans made use of the opportunities offered by the cities to improve or maintain their traditional way of life. The urban authorities, unsure of the meaning of the growing numbers of strange people performing strange trades in their midst, sought to have them conform to acceptable standards or, at worst, to leave the city. From this meeting of cultures there developed residential and occupational niches, patterns, prejudices, and stereotypes that persisted well into the twentieth century.

CHAPTER ONE

Emigration and the Street Music Trade

Italian child street musicians appeared in London and Paris after the Congress of Vienna in 1815. The Napoleonic Wars had ended and the tenuous peace created by the new balance of power assured travellers a degree of safe passage on the roads of Europe just as the post-war economic depression gave them the incentive to leave their homes. The children were not sent to their destinations by boat, wagon, or train, at least not until later in the century. Rather, their masters led them on foot from small towns and villages in the Duchy of Parma and from the district of Liguria in the province of Genoa to London, Paris, and beyond. At first these young entertainers were not organ-grinders or musicians like their masters, but exhibitors of small animals – squirrels, monkeys, dancing dogs, porcupines, and especially white mice. By the mid-nineteenth century the peripatetic lifestyle of the children and their masters and their unusual occupations ensured their recognition in most large towns and cities in Europe and the Americas. So did the coverage of the press, especially in London and New York.

The working conditions of the children did not change much over the course of the nineteenth century. The boys and girls were indentured to a labour agent or master, later known in the English-speaking world by his Italian name, padrone, for a period of fifteen to thirty-six months. They were to display animals on the streets or play an instrument – a street organ or harp, or even a violin, fife, or bagpipes, depending on the size of the child and on his or her region of origin. The passers-by dropped their coins out of pity rather than in appreciation of the music. A report in

Paris in 1868 observed that "les plus petits sont les meilleurs instruments de travail, car ils attirent mieux la pitié des passants; aussi sont-ils plus recherchés par [les] trafiquants."[1] The children were required to bring home a certain amount of money every night or risk punishment from the padrone in the form of a scolding, a beating, or the loss of a meal.

The young minstrels went by different names in each country, and the nomenclature often suggested that they were to be pitied. In Paris they were known as "les Savoyards," a term derived from the young chimney-sweeps from Savoy who had travelled through France and England from the sixteenth to the nineteenth centuries. These young predecessors of the Italian performers not only swept chimneys but also wandered the streets of London and Paris with their hurdy-gurdies, their marmottes (a type of groundhog found in the mountains of Savoy), and boîtes-à-curiosité (magic-lantern shows). The Savoyards were well known for their soot-ridden bodies and for the jealousy they inspired in French sweeps because they had the king's approval to remain in the country as competitors. In fact, the new Savoyards were not from the Duchy of Savoy but from the Duchy of Parma; later they came from the Kingdom of Naples, from towns in the province of Potenza, in the region of Basilicata, and from what was then the province of Caserta or Terra di Lavoro (now part of the province of Frosinone in the area called the Ciociaria in the region of Lazio or Latium).[2] After a report on the children was published in Paris in 1868, they became known as "les petits italiens", "les Lazzaroni," "les néapolitains," or sometimes, mistakenly, as "les petits calabrais."

In London the children were usually called the "Italian organ boys" or simply "the Italian children." During the 1840s and 1850s New Yorkers referred to them as Savoyards or as Italian organ boys. In the 1870s, when the *New York Times* and other newspapers popularized the notorious trade, the "organ boys" became the "Italian slave children," the "Italian harpers," or the "little slaves of the harp."[3]

To understand the development of the trade, we must examine the children's regions of origin. They did not casually pick up and leave for European and American cities. They came from some of the more remote and impoverished villages of northern and southern Italy. The street organists and animal exhibitors were mostly from the mountain districts of the Duchy of Parma, especially the villages and towns between Bardi and Borgotaro: Grezzo (population in 1803, 738), Bedonia and its environs (2,090), Compiano (426), and Bardi itself (1,250). A significant number also came from the contiguous hills in the hinterland of Chiavari in the province of Genoa: especially Mezzanego, but also Santo Stefano d'Aveto, Nè, and Zoagli on the shore, among other locales. In the south of Italy the violinists and harpists were from the Appenine towns just to the south of Potenza. These were agricultural towns in isolated Appenine peaks situated at altitudes of 700 to 1,100 metres. Their populations were generally in the range of 5,000 to 8,000, and included peasants, day-labourers, artisans, and a middle class of professionals and commercial agents. The fifers, or pifferari, and pipists, or zampognari, were from the lower Appenines in the Ciociaria, especially Picinisco and surrounding hamlets near the town of Sora.[4]

These districts were among the most impoverished in the peninsula. Not only did they produce Italy's earliest significant modern migration, they were also an important source of many of central Italy's rural and urban beggars and vagrants. The migration of the street musicians should be studied in the context of the economic and social dislocation of eighteenth-century Italy. The population of the peninsula rose from 13 million to 17 million over those hundred years. To keep pace with the rise in demand for food both at home and abroad, new systems of land management were introduced; generally, they brought down the Italian peasant's standard of living. Small landholders joined the ranks of the braccianti, or agricultural day-labourers. Others faced rising taxes and were forced to increase their small landholdings; still others joined the growing numbers of mendicants and vagabonds who by the late eighteenth century were visible throughout the peninsula. The mendicants were mostly in the lowlands, although some descended from the mountainous regions of Parma and Basilicata.[5]

The peasants who lived in the Appenines of Parma were generally small landholders. In the Ciociaria and the Basilicata, they were often tenants on the latifundia, the vast properties of absentee landlords. Peasants in those areas often fell victim to the rapacious middlemen who stood between landlord and tenant, and whose extortionate systems of loans placed tenants in perpetual debt. Deforestation and the redistribution of demesnial lands also upset the peasant economy, as did the rapid increase in population.

It is difficult to generalize for all three areas of the Appenines from which the musicians came. By focusing on one of these – Parma and its adjacent Appenine towns in Liguria – we can gain an understanding of some of the general factors that motivated the street musicians and other peasants to leave their homes.

The earliest child and adult street entertainers came from the villages near Parma in a section of high ground known as Monte Pelpi. According to one source the child organ-grinders in London, when asked which part of the world they were from, would usually answer, "son da Parma per servirla" ("I'm from Parma and here to serve you"). However, the young musician probably "never saw the town or set foot on its lovely plain." He was more likely to have come from the Val-di-Taro, from one of the hill or mountain villages along the Taro, Trebbia, Magra, and Serchio rivers between Genoa and Parma. The town of Bedonia was in the middle of a high plain known as the Tavoliere dei Pelpi, located between the towns of Compiano and Bardi.[6]

Owning very little land, the peasants of these and other towns of the parmense lived by subsistence farming; however, by the late eighteenth century, that was not enough to sustain the family economy. Agricultural techniques in the Duchy of Parma had fallen behind those in other northern and central Italian states. In any case, the land at high altitudes was not hospitable. In 1804 an army officer, Captain Antonio Boccia, toured the mountain towns of Parma; he wrote that the area surrounding Bardi seemed "pleasant and fertile," and that its inhabitants "were not lacking in industry and spent extraordinary sums to render the land more fertile." He thought that the many oak trees on the hills to the northwest of Bardi should have been replaced with chestnuts, which would have yielded an important cash crop. Bedonia was one of the best cultivated areas Boccia had come across, and, as in most of the parmense, the people were hard workers. By contrast, Monte Satta to the west, in Liguria, had very poor land, and produced enough only for two months' subsistence. Boccia's observations suggest a marginal land worked to its limit by industrious peasants.[7]

Hard work might sometimes place enough food on the table, although in Monte Satta and in other towns the land could not provide even that minimum. Food was not the only problem for the peasant, however; there were cash obligations as well. First among these, though not always burdensome, was the emphyteusis, the annual payment made by small landholders for the land, much like a perpetual lease. In 1770 taxes on doors, windows, and chimneys was imposed; they were not abolished until 1816. Another onerous penalty, the much resented grist-mill tax paid each time grain was brought to be ground at the miller's establishment, remained in force. As well, in 1815 taxes and duties were reimposed on a number of foods and other items, the most important of which were salt, tobacco, and gunpowder. The peasants had also to consider extraordinary events such as marriage, which necessitated the purchase of land or dowry.[8]

To maintain a minimum level of subsistence and to pay their taxes, the Appenine peasants were forced to look elsewhere for ways to supplement their meagre incomes. Some of these could be found close to home. The townspeople of Albereto, for example, picked mushrooms and chestnuts and crafted baskets, pots, barrels, and cribs to sell at the nearby fair in Borgotaro. Others journeyed to Liguria to buy olive oil and resold it in nearby villages. The most notorious trade of the val-taresi, as the inhabitants of the Val-di-Taro were known, was that of smuggling. After the reimposition of taxes in 1815 many items could be found nearby, in liberal Tuscany, for one-half the going rate in Parma. The val-taresi became expert smugglers. One Italian writer described them as "virtually at war against all governments; and gendarmes, gougers or excisemen, seldom venture with impunity within the stronghold of the mountain fortresses ... every highlander of that district is at least a smuggler. Naturally a people of the most peaceful disposition ... they are only induced to take arms for the vindication of what they consider their inalienable right of free trade ... [To] establish a kind of Zollverein throughout the country, is the main occupation, the dearest object, the pride of the val-tarese."[9]

These activities complemented land cultivation, but they did not satisfy the peasant family's cash requirements. Because lands were marginal and holdings were small, it was not essential that all members of the family be at home throughout the year. In many cases everyone's presence might be required only at seeding and harvest times. Thus, at least from the eighteenth century, the immigrants from the Appenines of Parma and Liguria emigrated from their home towns for short or more extended sojourns. The roads in these mountains were tortuous and continuously interrupted by torrents; yet the peasants, accustomed as they were to backroads smuggling, had no problem walking to their destinations.

In 1803 Captain Boccia had been struck by the absence of so many inhabitants from their home towns. North of Bardi, in the valley of Leca, women emigrated for two seasons or more to work in the spinning-mills in Lombardy, across the Po River. Strepeto, in Liguria, was "abandoned by almost all its inhabitants, including women and girls, many of whom begged on the plains." The people of Monte Satta were "all polyglots, since they cross all of Europe, and some have even been to Turkey, and Russia with the fairs, others with ink, oil, trinkets, and similar things." Women from that town, and from the rest of the Compiano area, would descend on the towns of Parma and Piacenza to beg for alms.[10]

From early on, emigration offered the best possibilities to meet the cash needs of the peasant. An old maxim expressed this truth well: "Loda il monte e tienti al piano" ("Praise the mountain and keep to the plains"). In the peasant's world there was a clear relationship between the two levels; he may not have loved the mountains, inasmuch as they represented a world of poverty and frustration, but they were also home. What was done on the plain had a distinct bearing on the family and home on the mountain. In 1833 an English writer described that rapport between the itinerant and his home town: "The most interesting trait in the character of these inoffensive wanderers is their never-failing attachment to their mountain homes. Go where they will, let them be as fortunate as they may be, they rarely or never think of a permanent settlement, but look back to Italy and the Appenines as the place of their rest. The object of their toils and travels, their great and sole ambition, is to become the owners of a house and a little bit of land, if not on the precise spot, at least in the immediate neighbourhood of the villages in the mountains where they were born."[11]

What did these emigrants do abroad? Some men travelled to large estates on the plains for the harvest. Farther south, along the ridge of the Appenines, between the town of Berceto and the western border of Modena, some travelled to Corsica to work as agricultural labourers and woodcutters. To the south, men worked in the malarial swamps of Tuscany, the maremma, and in the corn fields. On their way to Tuscany they smuggled out rags for the manufacture of paper, because the Parmesan government had imposed heavy duties on that export in order to encourage domestic industry. Upon their seasonal return, the migrants smuggled salt and gunpowder into Parma.[12]

Although many migrants worked as agricultural labourers in other Italian states, many others worked in the spinning-mills of Lombard towns. Still others, who had learned to weave locally from the small cottage industry in the Appenines, worked in textile mills in Lombardy or elsewhere. Among the early immigrants from Bardi in Paris were lacemakers, all of them men. Perhaps because of their expertise at smuggling, the Appenine migrants from the eighteenth century became specialized in small commerce. All kinds of trinkets, smallwares, and especially ink were peddled by the val-taresi and others across Europe. Giovanni Gandi, for example, who came from the hamlet of Porcigatone in the comune (township) of Borgotaro, went to Lille and other towns in northern France with an ink-barrel in search of new markets just after the French Revolution. He journeyed for years between Lille and his home town, always selling different wares; it was said that he carried 120 kilograms of merchandise on the twenty-five-day walk to Lille.[13]

We do not have figures on the number of migrants who might have left on short or extended migrations to Europe, but we do have a good idea of their trades and destinations. The immigrants from the Parmesan Appenines were, among other things, cooks, waiters, servants, ink-sellers (inchiostrai), storekeepers, organ-grinders, hurdy-gurdy men, animal exhibitors, hatters, singers, reciters, criers, saddlers, pedlars, lacemakers, labourers, and wax figurine-makers. Their travels took them to virtually every major town and city in Europe, and to many smaller ones as well – from London, Paris, Lyon, and Marseilles through Bremen, Lübeck, and Vienna, to Istanbul, Smyrna, Salonica, and Moscow.[14] They could also be found in Beirut, Alexandria, New York, Buenos Aires, Boston, Toronto, and a host of other towns and cities.

The Appenines of the parmense was only one of many districts in Italy in which peasants sought to augment their incomes by cultivating migrant occupations. Natives of many mountain villages and towns specialized in a number of trades and crafts and developed migration routes to particular destinations. Because of the scarcity of population and resources, a trader or tradesman would be forced to go abroad; if he was successful – that is, able to return home with an impressive amount of cash – then it was likely, given the close-knit ties of the village, that others would follow him. Although many villages sent their peasants to nearby fertile lowlands to work in the harvest, skilled emigrants, for obvious reasons, moved to the cities. They often journeyed to urban areas in the Italian states or in other parts of Europe and the Americas. A review of some of these towns and their emigration will show that the exodus from the Appenine parmense was part of a larger movement in the Italian peninsula.

From at least the early nineteenth century many other districts in Italy, primarily in the north, cultivated particular occupations for export. The emigrants from the Appenines surrounding Lake Como were known in cities around Europe and in the United States as barometer-makers and fabricators of optical instruments such as telescopes and binoculars. In London the firm of Negretti and Zambra, with its five locations, was probably the city's most important optical instruments maker. In New York in 1817, Peter Bello sold telescopes, opera-glasses, spectacles, mathematical instruments, watches, jewellery, tea-trays, and snuff-boxes; and he even "blew glasses for chemical and philosophical experiments."[15]

Almost all the inhabitants of the Val d'Intelvi, between Lake Como and Lake Lugano, worked in the building professions throughout Italy, and in Germany and Switzerland. By the mid-nineteenth century the mosaic-workers from the plains of southern Friuli, and especially from the towns of Fanna and Sequals, set mosaics in public buildings and palaces in France, Austria, and Russia. Their countrymen from the town of Gemona, in the Alps, were famed salami-pedlars in the German and Austro-Hungarian states. Sbianchini or whitewashers and house-painters, were the most important group of workers to emigrate from the towns at the head of Lake Maggiore near Locarno, and from the towns farther west at the foot of Mount Simplon, just above Domodossola.[16]

Between these two areas lie the towns of Craveggia, Malesco, and Villette. Emigrants from these towns, like the Savoyards, had been spazzacamini, or chimney-sweeps, in France since the sixteenth century. They hired young boys as apprentices under a five-year contact. Farther south, around Lake Orta, most migrants worked as servants, waiters, or small hotel-keepers. Some of these men established prestigious hotels in Seville, Cadiz, and Montreal, among other cities. The towns of Sambuco, Demonte, Bersezio, and Pietraporzio in the province of Cuneo had sent their people to Paris as street-sweepers since the mid-eighteenth century. Emigrants from towns near Ivrea (Ruglio, Vistorio, Lessolo, Cuorgnè, and Cinzano) worked as miners and stonecutters in mines and on railways in France. The seventeen villages in the Val Rendena, near Trento, sent knife-grinders with their apprentice boys and barrows (argagn) across Europe and to the Americas from the mid-nineteenth century. The book pedlars from Pentremolo in the Tuscan Appenines were famous for selling cheap editions.[17]

Until the late nineteenth century, northern Italians comprised the vast majority of the country's emigrants. The most notable migrants in the south in the early part of the century were probably the shepherds from the Basilicatan Appenines who directed the annual transhumance to the mild Adriatic coast. However, some tradesmen and peasants with small holdings began migrating from the same region late in the eighteenth century, most notably the street musicians. From at least the mid-1800s emigrants from Laurenzana, a town of about 8,000 located thirty kilometres south of Potenza, travelled to Barcelona and Marseilles to work as shoemakers and jewellers. Coppersmiths travelled from other towns in the area, primarily from Lagonegro, to Spain and the Americas, peddling their pots, pans, and other copper goods. By the late 1860s people in one of these towns, Maratea, were predicting a shortage of agricultural labourers. Peasant families from the Ciociaria ventured to Paris, where they were prized as models by French artists.[18]

Among the most popular of the itinerant tradesmen were the statuette-makers and vendors from the towns and villages of the Luccan Appenines, especially from Bagni di Lucca. The figurinai had plied their trade to Paris and London from at least the mid-eighteenth century. One of these craftsmen told the Italian consul in Paris in 1860 that he had first come to the city in 1824 with his father, but that his father had travelled to Paris at least forty years previous to that. These men (and sometimes, but rarely, women) and boys travelled from Lucca in groups of eight or ten under the direction of an impresario or capo (contractor or boss), who would later be known as a padrone. The apprentices and vendors were bound to the impresario under a two- to three-year contract – usually thirty months – under which they received a fixed monthly income, a room, and laundry services. The impresario or capo set the minimum price the vendors could charge for the statuettes. Any profit above that level was called the musina, and was shared equally with the impresario.

In each town or city visited by the band, the impresario kept a supply of plaster and other goods necessary to his trade. The workers brought their tools and plaster models, so that the statues could be produced in each city rather than carried from one destination to another. The boys and young men displayed the statues of animals, human figures, or famous personalities on a board, often laid on their head, and walked through the cities peddling their wares. They were highly visible on the streets of Europe. In 1821 twenty-three of the figurine-makers were recorded as residents of Paris. Drawings of itinerant traders in early nineteenth-century London included sketches of the figurinai, and an English poet praised a young figurinaio who carried on his head "his board of celebrated Greeks" which "proclaim[ed] his trade and nation."[19] At the same time the poet lamented the fact that the child's knowledge of Homer, Milton, Locke, and Byron, whose busts he sold, was only superficial:

Poor vagrant child of want and toil!
The sun that warms thy native soil
   Has ripen'd not thy knowledge;
'Tis obvious from that vacant air,
Though Padua gave thee birth, thou ne'er
   Didst graduate in her College.

To end the poem, the poet addressed Byron:

Were I to arbitrate betwixt
His terra cotta, plain or mix'd,
   And thy earth-gender'd sonnet;
Small cause has he th'award to dread: —
Thy Images are in the head,
   And his, poor boy are on it!

Almost all of the trades shared some common elements. Most of the tradesmen were from Appenine towns situated at high altitudes, and most of them were small landowners or tenants who supplemented their family incomes with the annual migration. The majority of the towns cultivated a particular trade, a particular destination, or both for their migrations. The towns gained access in one or more cities to unskilled trades – chimney-sweeps or street-sweepers in Paris, for example – or their inhabitants were trained in a particular occupation.

Almost all of the trades were practised under an apprenticeship system. One or more padroni skilled in given trades usually directed the emigration from a town. Those who travelled with him went as apprentices bound under written or oral contracts. The padroni were obligated to clothe, feed and house their workers, sometimes to provide moral guidance, and sometimes to provide tools at the end of the apprenticeship.

In virtually all of the trades, boys, and sometimes girls, worked as helpers or apprentices on the journeys. In Friuli, boys as young as nine or ten travelled with the mosaicisti to cut the stone pieces used by the craftsmen. Chimney-sweeps left Malesco and Craveggia with their padroni for Paris. The boys from Lucca, who travelled in bands with a padrone, were a familiar sight in cities from Moscow to London.

It is important to have a sense of the greater Italian emigration of the period from the time of the French Revolution to the Italian Unification. The movement of street musicians was not an isolated story, but part of a larger one. To us, the street entertainers might appear exotic and colourful, but in reality the difference between them and other migrants was only one of degree. The organists, violinists, harpists, and pifferari, and the animal trainers and exhibitors, were also small landholders in search of opportunity and cash. Apprentices in this trade travelled through Europe with their masters. The children in the street music trade were probably the most notorious child labourers in all of Europe. For reasons we shall examine in chapter 5, the children, who were often compared to slaves, were seen as worse off than young coal-miners in Scotland, glassworkers in Lyon, flower-sellers in New York, or sulphur-miners in Sicily, even though that was not always the case, and often far from it.

The origins of the street entertainment trade in the nineteenth century are uncertain. Mariotti, an Italian writer living in London, asserted in 1846 that the idea of street entertaining came to the parmigiani from the Savoyards:

Soon after the peace of 1814, a few poor Swiss and Savoyard vagrants spread over the rich plains of Lombardy, exhibiting dancing bears, dogs, and monkeys, or playing on their bagpipes and tambourines for the amusement of an idle populace. Some of the mountaineers of the Appenines either joined them or followed their example. Beggars of this sort increased to such a degree that the Italian towns could no longer afford them subsistence. A few of the most venturous sought their fortunes beyond the Alps. Throughout France and Germany, up to the deserts of Russia, and beyond the seas to England and America, they almost miraculously piped and drummed their way.[20]

This may have been true, although the young Appenine immigrants were not known as pipers and drummers, except for the few who might have accompanied animal exhibitors before 1815.[20]

There may also be some truth in Mariotti's statement that the Savoyards gave the parmigiani the idea of street performing. The hurdy-gurdy (which, contrary to popular belief, is not a street organ but a mechanical violin) was the chief musical instrument used by the Savoyards. Many of the early musicians from Parma were hurdy-gurdy players, not organ-grinders, and may have learned about the instrument from the Savoyards. The consular representative of Parma in St Petersburg in the 1850s referred to many viellards, or hurdy-gurdy men, in that city.[21]

Neither do we know how the sister trade of organ-grinding, animal exhibition, began in the Appenines. According to one authority, the performing bear was introduced to Italy and Germany in the early sixteenth century by the Russian minstrels known as skomorokhi. Ironically, a few centuries later, Italian minstrels and exhibitors were displaying the bears in towns and cities throughout eastern Europe and Russia.[22]

The migrants from the Val-di-Taro exhibited bears, monkeys, camels, elephants, dancing dogs, wolves, white mice, squirrels, hyenas, and dancing cocks. Most of the animals were trained by the migrants: in 1857, a number of val-taresi living abroad were officially listed as monkey-trainers. The exhibitors obtained the monkeys in Spain and took them home to train. Camels and other animals were also trained by people in the Appenines before being sent abroad.[23]

Although some of the animal exhibitors were from Grezzo, a frazione (hamlet) of Bardi, most were from the compianese, especially the villages surrounding Bedonia. They had no money to purchase their own animals. They obtained capital from a provveditore, or provider, who himself was or had been an animal exhibitor. He obtained the animals from other middlemen abroad, and then resold or leased the animals to the exhibitors. One man by the name of Rossi from the town of Compiano made a fortune as a middleman; he was "the greatest speculator in his line." In fact, until the mid-1820s almost all the Italian animal exhibitors on the continent obtained their animals from Rossi, who imported them directly from Africa. Others who did not wish to go through Rossi, but could not afford to buy a bear or an elephant, bought "una zampa per uno" ("a paw each"). In other words, four men put up the capital for four equal shares in the animal: two of the partners took the animal across Europe in campagna (literally on the campaign). The profits were split four ways, and the two conductors received extra compensation for their duties.[24]

The hamlet of Cavignaga, near Bedonia, was one of the important home villages of the conduttori di animali. Most of the residents were small landholders; women, some of the men and children, and the elderly cultivated the plots, while most of the men went abroad with the beasts. Normally, they left on All Saints' Day and returned just after Easter. An animal exhibitor, if he was not a master, emigrated every second year, so that about three out of every five men would go abroad during the winter for the road show.

As opportunities came up, the men of Cavignaga expanded their activities. In the middle and late nineteenth century the town operated three circuses in Europe. Antonio Bernabò, who owned an eighty-four-animal circus, also operated a lucrative side venture: he imported camels. In the 1880s he led fifty-seven of them from the Crimea to Odessa and then to Germany, where he sold most of them to other exhibitors from Bedonia. A fellow villager travelled to Finland to purchase polar bears for resale.[25]

The animal exhibitors followed a number of established trade routes in their annual trek. One route went through Naples, Bari,

Brindisi, Salonika, and Smyrna, and on to Russia. Another went through Palermo, Tripoli, Carthage, and Alexandria, another through France and Spain, a fourth to Germany and Austria, and a fifth route through Trieste to the Balkans.[26] The animal exhibitors and circus masters ended their activities with the First World War. Indeed, some found themselves in enemy territory at the outbreak of the war, and lost all their earnings.

The street organ trade was similar to that of animal exhibition. Capital was required to purchase a mechanical organ, and one needed to know the sources of supply. A group of middlemen emerged who purchased organs from manufacturers and resold or leased them to people from Parma. The organs probably could be obtained with relative ease. Some of the best known barrel-organ manufacturers of the eighteenth and early nineteenth centuries came from the Duchy of Modena, near Parma. One of these was Barberi, who popularized the street organs throughout Europe in the middle and late eighteenth century, and may in fact have been responsible for one of its names, the Barbary organ (l'orgue de Barbarie). The other was Ludovico Gavioli, who in 1845 moved to Paris, where he produced barrel-organs and became the father of the fairground organ.[27]

Although many organists went off on their own, much like the pedlars from their villages, most of them, when young, had probably travelled in campagna together, under the direction of a master or middleman. Children or youths were among the surplus hands in the family who could emigrate, work abroad under an apprenticeship contract with a padrone, and return home with money. "Padrone" was a term of notoriety in Britain, France, and North America; later in the century, the term would also be applied in the United States to the labour agents who served as the middlemen between Italian immigrant peasants and artisans and mining, railway, construction, and canal companies.[28]

The padroni played a pivotal role in the street music trade. They were among the more influential residents of the villages; they had access to jobs, tools, and instruments, knowledge of markets, and experience with border patrols and municipal police. Apart from conscription, the padroni offered the only chance for some young people to leave the villages and seek work abroad. The padrone, then, must not be seen only as a rapacious speculator (which indeed he was at times) or as a great exploiter. He was not an outsider, but a man of the village or district. Although he profited from leading young emigrants from his village, both financially and in prestige, he also provided an important service to peasant families in search of economic opportunity. The padrone was an intermediary between the prospective peasant migrant and the foreign city.

With the peace of 1815 the number of minstrels from Parma grew steadily until the 1850s. The figures are incomplete, but the increase is evident from the reports of child and adult musicians reproduced in books and articles at home and abroad. In 1820, for example, the *Times* of London published a reference to a master and two children from Parma who displayed white mice in the streets. By the 1830s complaints regarding street organs were commonplace. In 1863 one Londoner looked back wistfully on the period between 1805 and 1820, when "there were no German bands ... and the organs were 'few and far between.'"[29] The city of Paris passed ordinances aimed at prohibiting street organs as early as 1816, and against street performers in 1790. London, Paris, and New York were only the three most important destinations of the suonatori d'organetto; their travels took them throughout Europe, North Africa, and the Americas.

It is difficult to calculate the number or the percentage of migrants from Parma who entered the street music trade in midcentury. There are good records extant for 1857 of a number of Parmesan consulates in Europe with names and details of Parmesans who registered with their representative abroad that year. No children appear in the records, because two severe laws passed in 1844 and 1852 forbade their participation in this trade (see chapter 5). Unfortunately, about one-half of the migrants were listed by their profession in their home town rather than abroad – that is, as day-labourer, landowner, or cultivator. Of the others who listed their trade abroad, the two most prominent categories were those of street entertainers and service trades. Of fifty-four persons registered in Barcelona in 1857, ten were street musicians, two were singers, and three were animal exhibitors; there were also two cooks, two waiters, and two servants. Nice was an important town of transit for those migrants on their way to France. Of fifty-six individuals who registered there in 1857, five were animal exhibitors or trainers, two were saddlers, one was a cook, five were waiters, and two were pedlars. Just over one-half of St Petersburg's Parmesans were viellards, either hurdy-gurdy men or street organists, and one was an exhibitor of wolves.[30]

Some towns directed their emigrants to a few destinations, and some were especially prominent in particular trades. Grezzo, a small frazione of Bardi, sent many suonatori ambulanti and a few conduttori di animali to a number of cities, but primarily to London. The villages around Morfasso, especially Pedina, were the home district of most of St Petersburg's street organists and hurdy-gurdy men. (Indeed, the sounds of a street organ are described in Dostoyevsky's *Crime and Punishment*.) Most of the animal exhibitors came from the hamlets surrounding Bedonia.

We do not know a great deal about the personal backgrounds of the Parmesan musicians. We can assume that they were generally from the small landholding or landless families, and that some were artisans. Those musicians who were not children were likely to be in their twenties and thirties, although at least one of them was over seventy. Virtually all of them were illiterate. Of thirty-one street organists from Parma or Chiavari listed in the Italian consular registers in Moscow during the 1860s, only four were were able to read and write.[31]

Although some street musicians came from other parts of the country, the two most important migrations began contemporaneously. The street organists from the Appenines of Parma and Chiavari probably encountered their southern counterparts, the harpists from Viggiano, in the late eighteenth century in Marseilles or Paris, or en route to those or other cities. These two groups were followed by a third in mid-century, the fifers and pipers (pifferari e zampognari) and violinists from Terra di Lavoro.

The musical emigration from Viggiano originated not with harpists but with the pipers who played the zampogna, a type of bagpipe used in rural areas in southern Italy. At Christmas the performers would stroll from town to town in the Kingdom of Naples, and by the late eighteenth century they were already a familiar figure in nativity scenes in the region. At 1,110 feet above sea level, this town of 7,000 suffered up to five months of snow annually. With the dislocation caused by, among other things, deforestation and changes in land tenure, families maximized their returns from subsistence agriculture and sent redundant members in campagna around the world. "The hoe and the harp, those are the two instruments which nature and art have contrived for this alert and industrious people," wrote one journalist about the viggianesi. Although the migrants played a number of instruments, including the clarinet, violin, and mandolin, they were primarily known as harpists.[32] The idea of playing the harp probably sprang from the woodworkers who became expert harp-makers early in the nineteenth century, although other craftsmen had earlier made simpler harps. The best known of these artisans was Vincenzo Bellizia whose work was awarded a gold medal from the Fine Arts Academy of Naples in 1845. Although his predecessors in the town had made small thirty-seven-string harps, Bellizia's was a full-size instrument, complete with pedals. During the 1840s and early 1850s Bellizia constructed 145 harps for his townsmen, but that was not enough. The viggianesi also purchased their instruments from at least one other Neapolitan manufacturer, as well as the more complicated French harps fabricated by Sébastien Erard.[33]

The viggianesi used those harps to accompany clarinets and especially violins throughout most of the world. After consulting with the mayor of the home town, to ensure that he would provide for their families in difficult times on the promise of repayment on return, the musicians went off for one or more seasons on one of a number of routes:

Oggi d'Italia mi ride il cielo,
Doman di Russia calpesto il gelo;
In ogni terra è il mio paese;
Questa è la vita del viggianese,
A cielo aperto dormir l'està,
Scaldarsi il verno per carità.

Today the Italian sky smiles down on me
Tomorrow I trample over the frost of Russia;
Every land is my home town;
This is the life of the viggianese,
Sleeping out in the open during the summer,
Begging for warmth during the winter.[34]

The world truly was a home town for the viggianesi. When a writer came on a group of them from southern Italy in 1836, he queried them about their journey: "'We're coming from Washington, Sir' ... 'Have you been to Washington?' ... He laughs! 'Do you think it's that difficult to go? It's nothing ... From Salerno you go to Calais, from Calais to London, from London to Washington – and then on the return trip you go to Cadiz; and then travelling through Spain and France you're back in the homeland.'" The town's most famous lyrics proclaim: "L'arpa al collo – son viggianese – tutto il mondo è mio paese" ("Harp on my shoulder – I'm from Viggiano – all the world is my home town").[35]

The harpists and violinists of Viggiano were a mobile population. Francesco Pennella began travelling with his harp throughout Italy and into Provence in the late 1830s playing the melodies of Cimarosa, Jommelli, Rossini, and Mercadante. His nephew left the home town a few years later, and after much travelling settled temporarily in Lima, Peru, where he gave music lessons. The viggianesi moved well beyond Europe to the Americas and even to Asia. Vincenzo Miglionico left Viggiano in 1806 and returned in 1832 after playing his harp in many cities in Europe and the Americas. On his return he gave up his music and dedicated his time to commercial pursuits. According to one writer, in the 1850s the viggianesi's harps "dispensed the treasures of their harmony throughout Italy, on the squares and in the cafés of Paris and London, among the castles of Germany, the mosques of the East, and the pagodas of China." At the same time, nearby Laurenzana, though not yet as adventurous as the town to its south, was already sending its teenage musicians to Havana and New York. Elia Pelletieri, who in the late 1840s, with two townsmen, had ventured to the Cuban capital to play the violin and the harp, came in the 1860s to Utica, New York, where he opened a saloon.[36]

The viggianesi played folk-songs and operatic arias, but they also learned the songs and ballads of other countries and brought them back to their towns. A priest travelled to Porto Santa Lucia in Naples, the normal embarkation point for viggianesi bound for Paris and London through Marseilles, and had the minstrels sing him the ballads. Padre Parzanese reworked these into poetry. The songs often dealt with romantic themes – the young woman awaiting a lover, the man abroad thinking of her – with homesickness; and with fables and stories of Spanish and Arabic origin. Many of these elements come together in "Il Ritorno del viggianese" ("The Return of the Viggianese"):

> Ti riveggo, fumoso mio tetto,
> Ti saluto tranquillo Viggiano;
> Anni ed anni ho vagato lontano,
> Ma a te sempre tornai col desir.
> Ti riveggo, terren benedetto,
> Dove appresi la bell'armonia!
> Fremer l'arpa ho sentito per via,
> Le tue torri veggendo apparir.
>
> I see you again, my smoking chimney,
> I greet you, peaceful Viggiano,
> For years and years I have wandered far away,
> But to you I have always returned with desire.
> I see you again, blessed land,
> Where I learned beautiful music!
> I heard the harp play on the streets
> As I saw your towers appear.

The poem describes the minstrel's travels through Turkey, Granada, and France. He wonders whether the young woman whom he kissed on his departure is still waiting for him. He brings back a rosary and a suit for his aging mother, sings his hundred ballads to his people, and concludes by declaring,

> Sotto il raggio del patrio mio sole,
> Appoggiato a quest'arpa morrò.
>
> Under the rays of my homeland's sun,
> supported by this harp I shall die.[37]

The viggianesi had a docile reputation; they were seen as peaceful minstrels, "dispensers" of peasant tunes and of the music of a higher Italian culture around the world. Their Parmesan cousins also had been viewed as quaint individuals earlier in the century, but the monotonous, irritating sound of the street organs had alienated many middle-class Europeans by mid-century. While Neapolitan authorities expressed concern that young harpists and copperware peddlers were leaving Potenza to evade the military draft, authorities in Piedmont, Paris, and Brazil tried unsuccessfully to keep those same youths out of their territories. By the 1870s, however, both performing groups were seen as sinister in

Europe and in North America, less because of the noise they produced than because of the appearance of the numerous children in their employment.[38]

The children of the parmigiani began crossing into France and England at least from 1815, and they were noticed immediately by the press, mendicity officers, and police in both countries. During the 1830s a number of the children were tried in French and British courts for mendicancy. By the 1870s they had been the subjects of at least three commissions of inquiry in Europe, and had made their way into the works of Dickens, Eliot, Hawthorne, Dylan Thomas, Dostoyevsky, Louisa May Alcott, Poe, Hasketh, and others. By 1880 they were the subject of at least three novels, one book-length poem, and a number of short stories.[39]

We can see the children's appearances in these works as part of the nineteenth-century sentimentalization of childhood. As working-class children toiled in the mines and mills of Britain, poets and authors wrote romantically about angelic children who were one with nature and models of virtue in a cruel world. In *The Italians, or the Lost Children of Mont St Bernard*, written by an English Catholic author, two children forgive their cruel padrone as he lies dying in a crevice in the Alps during an attempt to kidnap the children and take them to France. The children, Pippo and Nina, run to find the monks of Mont St Bernard, who give the last rites to Pietro, the padrone. Yet Blake, Wordsworth, Dickens, and others who romanticized childhood ultimately wrote about the problems of upper-class children. As John Sommerville has suggested, the children of the working classes, despite all the toil and hardship and beatings, may have been less unhappy than the children of the middle class. In nineteenth-century literature the Italian child performers usually appeared only briefly as part of the background to the main story and were not given the special attention of the child protagonists in the Romantic novel. Even Dickens, Eliot, and Alcott never ascribed to the Italian children the nobility of character, the tenderness, and the virtues of the British or American child, for the young minstrels, like their masters, were from beyond the pale.[40]

Until the early 1860s most of the Italian child musicians were street organists from Parma or the nearby hinterland of Chiavari. The child harpists and violinists were fewer in number; they came from the town of Viggiano at first, and later from Laurenzana and the other towns. In the 1860s the organists from Parma almost disappeared from the trade in the United States, Russia, France, and England. Their neighbours from Chiavari also began to take up other trades, except for the performers from the town of Mezzanego. There in late 1868 three-quarters of the town entrusted their children to padroni and animal exhibitors, of whom there were seventeen.[41]

Just as the number of parmigiani musicians was declining, the number of child musicians from the Basilicata was on the increase. The viggianesi might have been seen as a "relatively respectable class of musicians,"[42] but their neighbours in the towns of Laurenzana, Marsicovetere, Marsiconuovo, Calvello, Corleto Perticara, Brienza, and Montemurro were giving them a bad name. One official alluded to an agency in Marsicovetere that bought children and supplied them to others through contacts in Genoa and Marseilles. The Italian consul in Marseilles, who stood in the path of the immigration from the Italian south to France and England, felt that "the example of the *viggianesi* who had realized considerable rewards in Europe and in America with this profession of street musicians, had seduced the population of all nearby towns."[43] The padroni were becoming speculators in children, taking them to Paris and then returning to the home villages to round up others.

One group of officials who became concerned with the traffic in children were the Italian consuls and consular representatives. The consul in St Petersburg was an anomaly, for he was the only representative who did not see the increasing presence of child organists in the streets as a problem. When the city police passed an ordinance in 1861 requiring the masters to leave the country with their young performers, some of the padroni asked the consul to appeal to the city authorities, which he did successfully.[44] Other consular representatives worried about the prospects of the growing number of street minstrels. The consul in Paris, Luigi Cerruti, was responsible for bringing the children's plight to the attention of his superiors in Turin, Florence, and Rome (see chapter 2). He began to make representations on behalf of the children to the Ministry of External Affairs in 1862. Two years later the consul-general in Barcelona complained about the poor children who were equipped by padroni "with an organ, harp or other instrument, and [who,] for a poor and unhealthy food and board ... require them to move around the city and small towns playing their instruments." Children were to meet a daily quota or risk a beating. As a result, many children either left their padroni or sought refuge among young companions from their home town. Two such young minstrels from Viggiano could not be traced. Because of the threat to the children's health and morals, the consul asked the local police for their co-operation in stamping out the trade. The police responded that they would attempt to end the trade, and if they could not do so they would increase surveillance. Two years later the consul's successor was still complaining about the large number of Italian street musicians between the ages of ten and twelve who were "infesting" Barcelona and other Spanish cities. Not only were they suffering at the hands of their padroni, but "on the many streets of the city they were bringing a great shame on the Italian name."[45]

Across the ocean in Rio de Janeiro, the Italian consul was perturbed by the arrival of many Neapolitans of the "lower class" in 1863. They were at odds with police and were ruining the reputations of the other Italians in the city. To make matters worse, in 1864 many Neapolitan "capi squadre" (or squad chiefs, as they were known there) were to be seen all over Rio with bands of five or six boys between the ages of eight and fifteen. The children were poorly fed and cruelly beaten by their capi if they did not bring home their quotas. To make matters worse, their operations were legal: their passports were in order and their parents had signed their children over to the master under written or oral contracts.[46]

It is not clear how soon written and oral contracts were used by the street musicians or to what extent they were employed. They probably differed little between Parma and Naples. There are two examples of the written contracts, both from the town of Viggiano, one dated 1861 and the other 1865. A contract was drawn up between the padrone and the father of the child. The child's occupation was entered as "musicante," which implies that he had already been trained to some extent so that he could emigrate. The father entrusted his son to the padrone for three years, during which time the latter was to teach the son to play the harp. The padrone had to buy the instrument for the boy and give him eight ducats; if the child misbehaved he could be sent off without his instrument. The padrone was to care for the boy and feed and clothe him, and at the end of the three years was to buy him a new suit in addition to his everyday wear, according to the season. If the child tried to escape, he would be liable for the costs of the search for him; if he broke the instrument through his own fault, he would be liable for the cost of its replacement. In the event that the child fell ill, the padrone would pay any medical expenses. The father would receive forty ducats if the padrone should mistreat the child or return without him. The padrone had to pay the father 114 ducats for the child's work. The time of payment varied, and the largest instalment seems to have been due at the end of the contract period.[47] (For a translation of two of these contracts, see Appendix A).

As we shall see in later chapters, the contract proved to be a powerful tool for the padrone, and one of the ways in which the trade was stopped was the authorities' declaration that all contracts between padrone and parents were null and void. The contracts drew even more attention to the children because they were legal documents, signed by witnesses, sometimes before a notary public. In official reports and correspondence the very existence of such contracts was proof of a veritable slave trade in which parents and child speculators were implicated.

Public reports did not always exaggerate stories about individual children, but they often generalized from specific incidents. There is no evidence to show that all children were cruelly treated or that half of them died from the effects of cruel masters, as one reporter suggested. Estimates of the numbers of "little slaves" were also exaggerated. There were not 7,000 child harpers in New York in 1873, despite the claim of the *New York Times*. In 1874 the Ministry of External Affairs in Rome drew up a list of the known padroni. In all they counted 328 names – 25 from Chiavari, 11 from Piacenza, 80 from Potenza, and 212 from Caserta (Terra di Lavoro). An Italian government commission appointed to study the problem of the young girovaghi, or wanderers, estimated in the rough draft of its report in 1868 that over 1,000 child musicians were outside Italy at any one time. In 1868, according to one frequently cited source, over 1,500 Italian child minstrels were apprehended in Paris alone (see chapter 3).[48] Accurate estimates are difficult, but there were probably about 3,000 to 6,000 Italian child street musicians around the world at the height of the trade in the late 1860s and early 1870s; fewer than 1,000 were in each of London, Paris, and New York, and 25 to 100 worked in such cities as Barcelona, Rio de Janeiro, Chicago, and Moscow.

The commission appointed to examine the child itinerants problem in 1868 described the children as girovaghi, or wanderers. As we shall see in chapter 5, the term was chosen intentionally. The children were in the same occupational category as their masters and adult street musicians. They were not truly vagrants or beggars; although it seemed that their activities were nothing more than veiled mendicancy, they did in fact work for a living. The children and many of the adults were not even migrants as far as the authorities were concerned. At one time, the viggianesi probably did dispense lovely melodies with the harp, and the val-taresi probably were a truly quaint sight on the streets of London, with their animals and street organs; however, with the arrival of the children, the trade degenerated into commerce. Most of the children knew little about musical technique. As one English writer put it in 1876, "Their performances are as a rule very crude, and it certainly would be no loss to the community ... if they were sent to school."[49] The term "wanderer" was a useful description of the performers: it did not quite condemn them, nor did it give them the legitimacy of true migrants.

The term was also apposite. The minstrels, both children and adults, were wanderers, but with a sense of direction. Along with other tradesmen and traders, the suonatori ambulanti were the forerunners of Italian emigration to the Americas and to other countries in eastern and western Europe. They made a reconnaissance of opportunities around the world for themselves and for their families, kinsmen, and townsmen, and by extension for all prospective Italian emigrants. The point is best made by the 1865 report of the Italian consular agent in Paramaribo, Surinam. He noted that only two Italians had visited the town that year. One of them was Nicola Conte, a twenty-three-year-old street musician from Viggiano who had come from Boston on the fourth of October and then headed for Pernambuco in Brazil on the twenty-eighth of the same month. He obviously had not found the market lucrative enough to remain any longer. The itinerant musicians, along with other wanderers from their towns, discovered markets for services and goods in foreign towns and cities, and because of their resilience were also ready to search for new markets or even to attempt new trades.[50]

By the mid-1860s the organ-grinders from the Parmesan Appenines had begun their withdrawal from street entertainment. Consular registers and reports and newspaper articles in the major European and American cities barely mentioned them after 1870. By that time they had already established, with other emigrants from their regions, the "Little Italies" of Five Points in New York, the rue Sainte-Marguerite in Paris, and Saffron Hill in London. Once established in those areas, they looked for new venues, and their days of wandering were over. In Paris, London, and New York, the street organists from Parma were replaced by the harpists and violinists from Basilicata and by the fifers, pipers, and violinists of Terra di Lavoro. In Moscow virtually all of the street musicians after 1870 were from Terra di Lavoro, especially the towns of Picinisco and San Biagio. Many migrants from Parma entered the catering trades, mostly in Britain, working as waiters or cooks, and even opened their own restaurants and inns. The musicians from southern Italy would also leave the streets by the end of the century.

It is important that the young organists from the north of Italy and the little slaves of the harp from the south be understood in the context of the larger emigration from their home towns. Their story is only a small part of the larger story of the penetration of capitalism into the hinterlands of the larger towns – of the dialogue between city and country, centre and periphery.[51] In response to changes in agriculture, land tenure, taxation, and government, the peasants looked for new opportunities abroad. Just as the city might exploit the hinterland, so the peasants exploited the city's possibilities. Some became part of the proletariat in urban areas, as did many spinners and weavers from the Appenines in Lombard towns. Others, the street musicians among them, fought fire with fire. They went to the city as petty capitalists. Children were part of a family strategy that sought to take advantage of new opportunities. Inevitably, the padroni, perhaps because they were far from their homes and from their townsmen, succumbed to greed and caused the degeneration of a legitimate occupation into a traffic in innocents.

CHAPTER TWO

"Les Petits Italiens" in Paris

Mountebanks, charlatans, diviners, marionettists, animal exhibitors, jugglers, and musicians of all kinds had worked on the streets of Paris since the Middle Ages. In the mid-eighteenth century, public posters announced young dancers from Holland and England at the quatrième traverse, or the artificial flowers that turned into fruit at the head of the rue de la Chaudronnerie, or an "academy" of monkeys and dogs trained by a Venetian named Myoli on the rue de Paris.[1] The numbers and visibility of these entertainers are documented by the many laws that regulated them and their performances from the time of the Revolution. As the population of Paris grew rapidly in the first half of the century, so did public resentment of the outsider, and especially the foreigner. Italian tradesmen and entertainers lived in the infamous quartiers where the "dangerous elements" dwelt: Faubourg Saint-Antoine and the area around the place Maubert. They too, being poor, were identified with crime and were closely watched by the préfecture and the police.[2]

The children posed a problem for the law officers. There had always been child vagrants in Paris, but their numbers grew in the nineteenth century. There was an important traffic in children from the Massif Central, for example, into the first part of the century. As well, young Savoyards had been travelling to the city since the sixteenth century. With the arrival of the Italian child street musicians, drastic measures were considered, and were enforced in the late 1860s.[3]

The immediate predecessors in Paris of the Italian child performers were the Savoyard hurdy-gurdy players. Street entertaining was a by-product of another trade performed by these colourful peasants from the mountain towns around Chambéry. From at least the late fifteenth century, boys, often wearing tricorn hats, and girls, usually wearing loose hoods called marmottes, went on an annual treks from this region to Paris and other towns as ramoneurs, or chimney-sweeps. From about the age of eight they accompanied their parents and were even rented out to masters, like their Italian successors in the nineteenth century. When they were in their late teens they left for the cities in small groups.[4] As they reached their destinations they added their voices to the chorus of street cries. A strophe from a sixteenth-century poem describes their activity:

Puis verrez des Pigmontois
A peine saillis de l'escaille,
Criant: Ramonade haut et bas
Vos cheminées sans escale.[5]

To supplement their earnings, especially during a slow season, the Savoyards began entertaining city-dwellers. The most popular performers were those who played the vielle, or hurdy-gurdy. The hurdy-gurdy (which since the late nineteenth century has been confused with the barrel-organ) is a mechanical violin. A crank turns a wheel, which resonates the strings. The strings are forced to the wheel when the player depresses a key or keys on the face of the instrument. From the fourteenth to the mid-seventeenth century, the hurdy-gurdy was primarily an instrument of the lower classes. However, it grew more widely popular in the eighteenth century, during the arcadian revival, when the aristocracy became interested in the instrument.[6]

Besides the hurdy-gurdy, the young Savoyards were often accompanied by a groundhog known as a marmotte. This animal is a natural entertainer; it is said to dance to music without any training.[7] On the way to Paris, or London, the Savoyards played their instruments as their animals danced for the public. Many of the children also carried or wheeled along a boîte-à-curiosité, or a magic lantern show. Thus the chimney-sweeps and entertainers from the region of Savoy were easily identifiable by their youth, their hats, the strange instruments slung on their shoulders, the tools carried on their backs, and the wooden box containing the groundhog, which they carried by a handle (to this day, the nickname for the sample-box carried by travelling salesmen in France is "marmotte".[8]

The stereotype of the Savoyard as an itinerant sweeper and entertainer was misleading. From at least the early eighteenth century migrants from Savoy worked at a number of occupations in various countries. Only a small minority were ramoneurs. In the district of Faucigny, for example, between 20 and 70 per cent of the population of each village emigrated to Paris and other parts of France, to the German or the Italian states, to Switzerland and Bohemia. They worked as coppersmiths, stevedores, haberdashers, cabmen, letter-carriers, and masons.[9] And they were not the only itinerant ramoneurs, for the Italian towns of Craveggia and Malesco, near Lake Maggiore, and the Midi also supplied child and adult sweeps across France.

The Savoyards continued their migration to Paris during the nineteenth century, but they did not come primarily as sweeps or hurdy-gurdy players. During the 1700s and especially during the following century, they were joined by fellow Savoyards from Piedmont and by migrants from Lombardy, Liguria, and Parma. As was noted in chapter 1, one Italian writer suggested that the original Savoyards influenced the Parmesans to take up street performing.

The new entertainers, however, were also part of a larger Italian migration to Paris and beyond in the early nineteenth century. Because of the careful surveillance of foreigners during the Restoration there are excellent records of Italians domiciled in Paris and in other French cities between 1815 and 1830. The sojourners and permanent immigrants in these cities included men from all parts of Italy, but especially from Parma, Piedmont, and Livorno. They were students, doctors, professional musicians, jewellers, investors, noblemen, and professors. Bona Cuzzer, a Jewish woman from Verona, was travelling through France with her son in 1817 after leaving her husband, who had converted to Catholicism. Much different were the circumstances of Giuseppe Agostini, aged twenty-three, his brother Giuseppe Fontana, seventeen, and three other figurine-makers who were apprehended in the Seine in 1821 on suspicion of carrying seditious literature. Tomaso Sgricci, a magician from Florence, was under surveillance between 1824 and 1826; he was thought to be an active agent of the carbonari. In 1824 thirty-four-year-old Giuseppe Mondini, a glasswork vendor, left Spain to settle in Paris. In the same year authorities took note of the passage through France of Giorgio and Antonio Camana, two glaziers from Domodossola who were returning home after a sojourn in Spain.[10] Many soldiers who had fled Lombardy, Piedmont, and Naples after the failed insurrections of 1820 and 1821 fled to Spain to join the revolution there in 1823. Some of them were taken prisoner by the French and confined in various French centres.

The lives of most of these men and women, whether soldiers, tradesmen, adventurers, or travellers, were precarious. Because of the nature of their occupations and because of the political situation in Italy and indeed across Europe, they were constantly on the move even as they sought permanence. Most of the Italians who were resident in Paris in 1821 had arrived from other French cities or from London. A host of refugees – officers, merchants, and tradesmen – requested asylum from the French delegation in Turin and in France, Switzerland, and Spain. Most of the twenty-five Italian refugees who landed in Brussels in September 1823 were tradesmen, many of them itinerants. Two animal exhibitors from Bedonia had come from London and were heading for Antwerp. One flower-seller from Lucca was directed to Tournai. Five laundrymen and two statuette-vendors who did not state their place of origin were remaining in Brussels. In November of the same year one animal exhibitor headed from Paris to Brussels; one street organist who arrived in Brussels was coming from London and going to Ostend. A second Italian organist had come from Spain, and was on his way to Paris. Similar accounts can be found throughout the records for 1824.[11] Most of the refugees were itinerant tradesmen, and travelling was a condition of their livelihood.

Officers who had left Italy after the insurrections and been removed from Spain by the French also formed part of the Italian colonies in Paris and other cities during the 1820s. Expecting prison sentences, and in some cases death, if they should return to Italy, these soldiers looked for other countries that might accept them, or they took any occupation in France so that they could remain there. Francesco and Lorenzo Zani, for example, two Piedmontese lieutenants, were given permission in 1824 to stay in Clermont-Ferrand. Francesco found a job in a pasta factory, and Lorenzo was hired by the renowned wine merchant Nicolas. In 1824 a few Italian refugee officers in Lot-et-Garonne were given permission to embark for England. One of these, a twenty-nine-year-old sub-lieutenant, Giacomo Forneri, eventually made his way to Toronto, where he became a professor of modern languages at the university. Tomaso Vigna, a captain and surgeon from Piedmont, returned to France in 1825, and then travelled to Egypt. In 1829 he returned to Paris where he too worked in a pasta factory.[12] Although there was a clear difference between officers and itinerant tradesmen, they shared a common bond: their exile was very much a result of the economic and political conditions in the Italian peninsula during those early years of the Risorgimento.

The majority of Italian residents in Paris during the 1820s were itinerant tradesmen, mostly from towns and villages in the duchies of Parma and Lucca, especially Bardi and Bedonia in the former and Barga in the latter. Bardi's and Bedonia's emigrants in this period sent a number of street organists, animal exhibitors, and attori di prosa (street reciters) to the French capital, but the majority of the men worked as maestri di trina (lacemakers). Virtually all of the sojourners from Lucca were statuette-makers and vendors. A few shopkeepers, or negozianti, from both duchies also lived in Paris. Most of the Italians lived in boarding-houses in Faubourg Saint-Antoine, especially in the rue Ste-Marguerite. One building in this street housed nine figurinai from Lucca, all in their teens or twenties, and one day-labourer from Lucca. All the other houses contained a few men from each town, and represented a number of trades. For example, 7, rue Ste-Marguerite was the home of seven bardigiani, or men from Bardi, including three street reciters, one musician, one pedlar, and two lacemakers. Eight other men from various towns, most of them near Bardi, lived in the same house. These included a polisher, two labourers, three lacemakers, and two pedlars.[13]

The sojourners' primary links were with people from their home towns or nearby towns. In Paris, however, they broadened their contacts with other tradesmen from Italy. They shared similar backgrounds and looked for economic opportunities in the same market. They probably operated along the same commercial routes and gathered information from common sources. Four migrants lived at 29, rue Ste-Marguerite – an animal exhibitor and a house servant from Mezzanego, a ploughman from near Genova, and an organ-grinder from near Parma. Five men from three different regions lived at No 13 on the same street: they were a lacemaker, a merchant, a trinket vendor, a baker, and an organ-grinder. The variety of occupations shows the ingenuity and enterprise of the itinerants, and their ability to probe the city for economic possibilities.

The migrants also had a common bond in their mutual contempt for the Austrians who directly or indirectly controlled most of the northern Italian states and duchies. It is difficult to assess to what extent the peasants and itinerant tradesmen had been exposed to the concept of Italian nationality. Certainly during the uprisings of 1820–21 itinerant tradesmen would have had some sense of the politics of the times, but their interest in political events might have had immediate economic motives. In the regions of Isère, Loire, Seine, Rhône, and Vienne at least a dozen young figurinai from Lucca were apprehended for selling busts or plaster medallions of Napoleon or the archduchess Maria Luisa of Parma during the mid-1820s. In some cases the busts were sequestered; in other cases the tradesmen were deported. In Rouen, for example, in 1827, nineteen-year-old Pasquale Cervi was arrested along with twenty-seven-year old Giovanni Battista Francesconi and twenty-four-year-old Pietro Marchetti, for selling plaster medallions of the late emperor. The three men from Lucca and other figurinai were accompanied to the Piedmontese border and handed over to the Sardinian carabinieri.[14]

Although the French police kept a close eye on all migrants and refugees, they paid particular attention to street performers of all kinds, and the records of the Paris préfecture are a rich source of information on itinerant musicians from the Restoration to the Commune. In Paris, as in the rest of France, local laws aimed at maintaining social order emanated from the prefect of police. These laws were a response to local problems, but they also were imposed at the request of the Ministry of the Interior. The préfecture informed the various police commissaires of any new ordinances, and the latter ensured that the police enforced those laws.

The first ordinance regarding the "class" of street organists appeared soon after the return of the Bourbons. In July 1816 the préfecture of police posted an "Ordonnance Concernant les

Joueurs d'Orgues dans les Rues et Places Publiques." The ordinance expressed concern over the rising number of organ-grinders in the streets and public places of the city. It also complained of their "chansons licencieuses" and the "embarras" they caused in the streets where the musicians stopped to perform. It is clear from later correspondence and laws that the "embarras" was not only a result of lewd innuendo but also of the political overtones of the lyrics.

To control the numbers of street musicians and their influence on the public, new measures were introduced to regulate the trade. By August 1816 all musicians would need permission to perform in public places, to be renewed annually. The musician was to present a declaration of good standing and morals from two witnesses to the police commissioner or, in a rural area, to the mayor. The successful applicant would receive a permit and a licence medallion which was to be kept in a visible place. Street organists had to fasten the medallion to the organ, and the permit number had to correspond to the medallion number. Those musicians who received permits were bound to respect all laws concerning performance, and were subject to arrest if they broke those laws. To prevent the organ-grinders from singing "chansons licencieuses," the ordinance stipulated that they were to sing only songs or extracts from vaudevilles or from the standard (and therefore already censored) repertory.[15]

As the French political climate shifted to the right during the 1820s, even more stringent controls were placed on street performers. During the early years of the decade, as the régime tried to counter secret societies, including the carbonari, the prefect of police kept a close watch on street musicians and other itinerants. It was during those years that many of the plaster figurine-makers from Lucca were arrested for the "subversive activities" of selling busts or medallions of political or royal figures. In January 1822 a circular issued by the prefect of police warned police commissioners that "des *chanteurs ambulants*, et des joueurs d'orgues ou autres instruments, chantent et colportent des chansons où le respect pour le Roi, l'attachement à la légitimité, l'esprit et les institutions de gouvernement, la décence et les mœurs sont outragés plus ou moins ouvertement." He felt that some of the worst cases could "pervert the opinion of the people," and he recommended "la surveillance la plus active, et la plus rigoureuse."[16] This circular was followed a few months later by more formal instructions to the commissioners.

The new instructions of April 1822 called for greater caution in issuing permits. Only street singers and organ-grinders were covered by the measures; only forty permits for the singers were available for the entire prefecture of Paris. No words from the standard repertory or from printed collections could be changed. The singer could sell only songs that had been authorized and signed by one of two officials named by the prefect. It seems that the number of organists in Paris at that time was large and had not been restricted by legislation: the prefect stated that his office was unable to authorize all the songs for the street organists because they were too numerous. The police were to watch for performers who lent their licences or medallions to other performers, for that practice was illegal.[17]

Certain locales were particularly difficult to control because they were public, yet off the street – cafés, restaurants, and cabarets. There, singers and organ-grinders could perform without the surveillance of the police, and there too, the prefect complained in the circular, "le plus souvent des chansons où les mœurs, le Gouvernement monarchique et la Religion sont également outragés." In fact, it was a condition of obtaining a permit that the applicant could not perform in these public places, and the prefect asked the commissioners to ensure that that law was enforced.[18] In practice, the law was seldom obeyed.

It seems that legislation regarding street performances was considered important, especially during the more reactionary periods, but that it was rarely applied diligently. From 1790 to the early 1870s numerous ordinances repeat the same basic principles: the number of street musicians causes concern; therefore it is important to survey them more carefully. They must obtain permits; medallions must be visible on their instruments. They must perform only authorized music. They must not lend or lease their medallions or their instruments. They must perform only during prescribed hours and only on prescribed streets and squares. Occasionally a new ordinance was passed, but it usually changed the previous laws only slightly. Why?

Part of the answer lies in the turnover of police commissioners, prefects, and officials in the Ministry of the Interior. A new administration might choose to enforce or not to enforce certain laws.

Of greater importance, however, was the socio-political environment. Laws were reiterated or reinforced during periods of social unrest in which the state became more repressive. We have already seen that this was the case in 1822. In fact, only a month and a half after the prefect sent his circular to police commissioners, he issued another memo reminding the commissioners to keep a closer eye on street performers. Many were performing without permission, lending or leasing their instruments, and diffusing among the people "immoral and seditious" songs. Most of those songs were unauthorized. Police officers had to check the songs to make sure they had been stamped by the prefect; the matter required "la plus grande attention et une extrême sévérité." Almost four months later the prefect noted that musicians were still singing "seditious" songs and selling manuscripts, even in the courtyards of private homes. Perhaps recognizing the futility of the ordinance and the impossibility of police co-operation, the prefect proposed the ineffectual measure of a change of stamp colour so that the police might identify unauthorized music.[19]

Again, during the economic crisis, the bread riots, the growth of the population and the labouring classes, and the general turmoil that preceded the 1830 revolution, authorities became more concerned about the influence of street entertainers on the populace. In October 1829 the minister of the interior, the ultra-royalist Comte de la Bourdonnaye, sent a circular to prefects across the country, informing them of the problem of musicians who travelled through the départements entertaining the public with mechanical theatres, figurines in cabinets, and spectacles. He noted that they could not be controlled easily because no law regulated their movements or activities. Bourdonnaye reminded the prefects that the entertainers could fall within the law of 24 August 1790, which provided that entertainers must have permission to carry out their trade, must inform authorities of their residence, and must carry passports. The minister also stressed that the prefects were not to give permission indiscriminately so as to turn the procedure into a mere formality. They were to check the programs and activities of the entertainers to ensure that they were not "contrary to religion, good morals, his Royal Majesty and good taste." Entertainers who performed uncensored material were to be arrested and brought before a magistrate. The minister attached great importance to the influence of popular entertainers on public opinion. "Je n'ai pas besoin de vous faire remarquer l'intêret que se rattache à ces dispositions," he noted in his circular, "vous connaissez l'influence que ces sortes de spectacles exercent sur les populations; on ne saurait donc trop les préserver des funestes impressions qu'elle produisent et dont la vivacité s'accroit encore par les circonstances des fêtes au milieu desquelles elles viennent ordinairement la frapper."[20]

During the social unrest in the early years of Orléanist rule, the authorities turned their attention once again to the musicians. A law of October 1830 prohibited the posting, singing, or reciting of songs that might cause public disorder. In early 1832, a year of severe economic crisis compounded by a cholera epidemic, the prefect of police advised greater diligence in tracking foreign itinerant musicians, most of whom were Italian. Being "more or less in a state of vagabondage," they contravened an ordinance issued in December 1831. That law, introduced by the prefect Malleval, tried to address the problem of saltimbanques (mountebanks) who blocked free passage on the quays, bridges, streets, boulevards, and passages of the capital. It established new permits for performers, and restricted performance to certain hours of the day and certain locales in Paris. It prohibited performers from gathering crowds around loud instruments, and outlawed diviners, fortune-tellers, and dangerous animal acts.[21]

Under the new instructions of 1832, police were to encourage any migrants who did not obey the law to leave the country. A few months later the prefect was on the trail of the street singers, many of whom were singing politically suspect songs on the public roadways. According to the prefect, the songs "étaient faites dans un très mauvais esprit et de nature ... à agiter l'opinion publique, et à propager des bruits inquiétants." Once again, the prefect asked police to ensure that the singers complied with regulations. Those without permits were to be arrested and their songs were to be seized, analysed, and if necessary annexed to the evidence (procès-verbal) for their prosecution.[22]

It seems that a few years later, during the unrest of 1839, which culminated in an unsuccessful attempt at a coup, the authorities still feared the influence of itinerant entertainers. The prefect of Paris warned police that any street musician travelling without permission would have his instrument seized. He also passed an ordinance directed specifically at criers, singers, vendors, and colporteurs which required that they obtain permission to carry out their trades and that their songs, broadsides, prints, and designs be authorized. Anything that harmed "public morals, the respect due the King and the Constitutional Charter of 1830" would not be approved.[23]

As we have seen from the various ordinances, the Ministry of the Interior and the prefect of police distinguished between the various types of performers. Although they felt that some of them might come within the bounds of vagrancy or mendicancy laws, street performers had to be regulated by more specific provisions. In France, the basis of modern legislation on vagabondage was to be found in a decree of July 1808 and in the penal code of 1810. Why did the prefect not apply those laws to the street performers? He simply assumed that since the entertainers performed a service for their money, no matter how despicable their trade, they were still working for a living. Indeed, the prefect Malleval on a number of occasions referred to the musicians as "cette classe d'industriels." For Malleval, juggling, playing an instrument, reciting, or singing on the streets was not the same as begging. He asked the police commissioners to keep a close surveillance on the performers so that "l'exercice de chaucune des professions qui s'y trouvent indiquées ne dégénèrent pas en un état de mendicité sur la voie publique."[24]

The authorities had more difficulty with the Italian street organists. They were numerous; they did not follow the law regarding joueurs d'orgues; they were wanderers; and they were foreign. In 1827 the prefect of Paris expressed concern because "un grand nombre d'italiens presque tous venant des états de Parme circulent sans permission portant un instrument à cordes et à cylindre [hurdy-gurdy]." A few years later Malleval also discussed "ces individus, presque tous du duché de Parme ou du Piemont," who arrived daily from abroad, especially from England, to play their hurdy-gurdies or barrel-organs in the capital. He described them as "plus au moins en état de vagabondage." "More or less" was a deliberate expression, for although the lifestyle, dress, and type of trade performed by these men came close to vagabondage and mendicancy, technically it was difficult to classify their activities as such. These foreign street musicians offered no guarantee and did not obtain permission mainly because permits normally went to poor inhabitants of Paris. In 1826 the minister of the interior, and ultra-royalist Jacques de Corbière, had shown the same ambiguity regarding the status of the Italian musicians. He described them as itinerant performers "sans être précisement dans la classe des mendiants et vagabonds."[25]

The musicians had one other peculiarity: they tended to bring many children with them on their journeys across the country. The sight of these children performing and begging for money on the streets of Paris evidently irritated authorities from the beginning. In September 1824 Corbière authorized the deportation of children arrested on a second offence of mendicity for performing musical instruments on the street of the French capital. An ordinance from the prefect a few days later ordered all child performers to leave France within one month. Two years later the problem had not been solved, for Corbière complained to the prefects that itinerant performers were taking children from their parents rather than bringing their own children on their travels. He proposed that musicians should be required to prove the civil status of the children who travelled with them. By 1827 the prefect of Paris had investigated the problem of the child street musicians and had found that "des joueurs d'orgues louent jusqu'à cinq et six orgues, à des garçons qui sont obligés de leur payer un salaire déterminé par chaque jour." As a result, even though the number of street organists in the city was fixed (at forty, apparently) by the police, in fact the actual number of organists was four times the quota.[26]

It seems that the Ministry of the Interior and the prefect used a double standard to judge the child and the adult street musicians. The street musicians from Italy were quasi-vagabonds, only "more or less" in the state of mendicancy, whereas the children seem to have fallen definitely within that category. That was the substance of Corbière's notice to the prefects. No systematic study of court cases involving the children is available, but from the little we do know it seems that even judges considered the young minstrels beggars. For example, in June 1837 twelve-year-old Luigi Gozzolo and fifteen-year-old Vincenzo Brigi, both from the Duchy of Parma were arrested for mendicity. The judge refused to consider their work legitimate. He issued a guilty verdict, finding that "les animaux et les instruments qui sont confiés à ces enfants ne constituent point l'exercice d'une profession, et ne sont qu'un moyen de dissimuler la mendicité qu'ils exercent." The judge, the Ministry of the Interior, and the Paris prefects all regarded street music performed by children as a form of mendicity.[27]

After Corbière's actions in the mid-1820s it took more than twenty years for the French authorities to address the problem of the little Italian slaves. The law-and-order mentality of the Second Empire's prefects caused stricter legislation to be introduced and ultimately most of the child street musicians were expelled. In October 1849 the Ministry of the Interior made it illegal to employ any person under the age of sixteen to perform on the street. But the problem continued to plague the city. In 1857, the prefect, P. Carlier, reported to the commissioners that speculators had for some years been gathering children from the Savoie and also from the poorer départements in the centre of France, especially the Auvergne, promising to train them. According to this report they were taught to beg and to sweep chimneys. The prefect urged that all children found begging be arrested. A few months later, he naïvely stated that the problem had been solved. His good sense soon returned, however, for the law of 1849 was reinforced by an important ordinance of 30 November 1853 in which the old orders regarding medallions, hours of performance, and censorship of texts were reiterated once more.[28]

Despite the edicts and ordinances of the Ministry of the Interior and the local prefecture, little was known about the street musicians, child or adult, until the 1860s. Of course the police knew that they were mostly Italian; that masters came with their three, five, or ten children, whom they kept in a state that resembled slavery; that they played organs, exhibited animals, and danced; and that by mid-century they had even begun playing harps and violins. The police were aware that laws existed, but they did not bother to enforce them except for certain brief periods, especially in times of unrest. If the police had a problem with itinerant child performers, they spoke to the Italian consul, who either made arrangements for the children's return to Italy or provided some sort of interim assistance.

The Italian consul in Paris during the 1860s was Luigi Cerruti. His private and public reports to his head office, the Ministero degli Esteri (in Turin, then in Florence in 1864, and after 1870 in Rome), reveal a warm and humane individual who was deeply concerned about the plight of the Italian children in his city. He was perhaps the first Italian consul to inform his ministry of the growing problem, and he did more than any other official to promote effective legislation and to influence persons at the executive level of the ministry to recognize the child trade as a serious matter. Cerruti was also the prime mover in an investigation into the matter by the Société Italienne de Bienfaisance, which led to the publication of an important report in 1868. It is through the consul's own reports that we have some idea of the status of the children in Paris in the 1850s and early 1860s.

Cerruti's earliest published reference to the children was made in his annual report of 1862. After examining a number of occupations performed by sojourners in the city, he moved on to a survey of the suonatori ambulanti. Cerruti divided them into two categories. The first was composed of organ-grinders, harmonium players (the harmonium was a street organ whose sound was produced by air pushed from bellows through pipes), and viola (possibly hurdy-gurdy) players, all from the province of Chiavari and from the ex-Duchy of Parma. The second category included bagpipe (cornamusa) players, fifers (pifferari), and harpists from the province of Basilicata. The pipers and fifers were probably from Terra di Lavoro.

The first category of performers came from the towns near Chiavari (in the area of Liguria in the province of Genoa) and Parma that we encountered in the previous chapter: Mezzanego, Varese, Lumarzo, Santo Stefano d'Aveto, Bardi, Borgotaro, Boccolo, Bedonia, and Rivalta. In Paris they lived on the rue Ste-Marguerite and the boulevard de Charonne, in the Faubourg Saint-Antoine (as had other Italian itinerants of the 1820s). The harpists were from the towns of Viggiano and Marsicovetere. Cerruti briefly reviewed the sad plight of the children, singling out the chiavarini (the performers from Chiavari) as subject to the cruellest masters. Suggesting that his sorrow over these children might be naïve, he gave a few details of the effects of the trade on the children and teenagers – the long hours, the living conditions, the humiliating nature of the work, and the pathetic fates of some of the children: crime, serious illness, or death.[29]

Perhaps because they were new to the scene, Cerruti felt that the harpists and fifers were less cruel to their apprentices. He suggested that the former profession had a certain nobility because it "obliged the child to use his own intelligence and to develop his musical talents." However, this did not negate the fact that even the more refined musicians practised nothing other than a "veiled form of mendicity."

The consul was concerned primarily, but not solely, about the suffering of the children. Cerruti was a product of the Risorgimento, and as the representative of a country that had been recently and not yet completely united (the Papal States would join in 1870), he wished to promote the good name of his government. He contrasted a positive image of Italians with the negative image created by the children: "I know that Italy has always been the cradle of music and dance, but this does not mean that Italians have to be, outside their homeland, the laughing-stock of foreigners, playing and dancing on the streets for profit. Now that Italy has a brilliant future, now that the numerous rail line projects, both planned and already initiated, promise work for thousands of men, it will be easy for the government to end this shameful emigration." Cerruti then drew up a short list of suggestions for ending the trade.[30]

It was clear that the chiavarini fared so badly in the consul's reports because they had been in Paris longer than other itinerant Italian musicians; they were the largest regional group among the musicians in the 1850s. Cerruti had come across numerous cases in which children from Chiavari had been indentured to cruel padroni, and had never returned home. In February 1856, for example, Antonio C., of the town of Nè in the province of Chiavari, leased his thirteen-year-old son, Francesco, to Andrea D. to play the street organ in Paris. In April 1857 Francesco escaped from the padrone, who maltreated him, and headed in the direction of Breville. The mayor of Nè made inquiries about the child for the father, but as of 1862 Antonio had not been located.

Another boy, G.B.L., of Moconesi, was indentured by his widowed mother to her brother-in-law in 1859. The padrone returned home in 1860 without the boy, explaining that he had left him with Guglielmo T. in Strasbourg. The mayor of Moconesi made inquiries to the Italian consulate in Paris, but to no avail. Another child, Luigi L., from either Nè or Mezzanego, was arrested in Paris in 1855 for mendicity and vagabondage. He told the authorities that he had been abandoned by his padrone, whose name he did not know. Luigi had been found on the grounds of an estate owned by a philanthropist, Baron Hyde of Neuville, who ran a school for the sons of workers. Luigi was imprisoned at first, but then was taken into the school by Hyde. However, the baron soon expelled him because of his bad influence on the other children.

More heart-rending were the children who had forgotten their names. Stefano Francesco di Can., from a town near Chiavari, went to see the consul in October 1859. His father had indentured him at the age of eight to a padrone, whose name he did not know, to play the street organ in Paris. The padrone abandoned the boy without his papers and therefore without his name. Stefano had been working as a farm labourer for five years. When Cerruti asked him to sign his name, he said that he knew only his first names, and that his last name started with "Can." The consul tried to locate the child's parents, but was unsuccessful.

A harpist from Viggiano, in Basilicata, came to the consulate in September 1861. Giovanni M. had been indentured eight years previously by his father to a harpist called Vincenzo. Vincenzo had taken him to France, abandoned him there, and returned to Italy. The youth knew that his first name was Giovanni and that his father's name was Francesco Antonio, but he had forgotten his surname and the names of his mother and three sisters. Giovanni remembered that his father's house was in the town square and that an annual feast was held in that town, with fireworks and a procession. In this case, Cerruti was successful in tracing the town and reaching the mayor. The parents, who had been heartbroken by the disappearance of their son, were reunited with him. Cerruti maintained that there were many more such cases but that he was only presenting enough to make his point about the trade in children.[31]

Cerruti was also concerned with the moral lives of children and young adults who were hired out. The perils were numerous. Boys and girls who served under a common padrone usually slept in the same room. Since the children were out on the streets from dawn to dusk, they were exposed to bad influences. The padrone himself could not always be trusted with young women. Two short biographies reported by Cerruti give us some insight into the conditions to which the chiavarini in Paris were exposed.

The first case is that of Maria Teresa C., aged twenty-five, who had been a foundling in the hospital near Santo Stefano d'Aveto in Chiavari. She was brought to Paris by a padrone, Antonio Caff. (probably Caffarelli), to play the street organ. In Paris, Antonio tried to seduce Maria; she went to the consulate and reported the story. Caff., who had a terrible reputation, did not deny the charge.

Among the many people Caff. kept in his house was Maria M. (also née Caff.) from Mezzanego, the wife of Giovanni Battista M. and the mother of two children. When her husband and children left her and went to the United States she became her keeper's lover, and had a child by him. Later, in 1859, Andrea T., aged twenty-four, from Santo Stefano d'Aveto, was invited to live at Caff.'s house. He became Maria M.'s new lover. They had a child, whom they gave up to the foundling hospital. Andrea then became aware that Maria had other lovers, and in a fit of jealousy he threw himself from a window in 1860. He lived but he became almost completely mad. Not long after, when he began to suspect Maria of infidelity, Andrea murdered her in Antonio Caff.'s house. Andrea was arrested, tried, and found not guilty by reason of insanity. He was deported to his home town.

Another case that poignantly revealed the dangers of street life was that of Maria C., who was found in a field near the town of Tassorello in Chiavari in 1835. The child was baptized, but the administration of the sacrament was not registered. Soon the peasants who found Maria abandoned her in front of the mayor's house in the nearby town of Lumarzo. The mayor had her rebaptized and placed in the hospital in Chiavari. There she was nursed by L., who also nursed Stefano V. In 1845 a man by the name of Stefano B., an organ-grinder of disreputable character from Mezzanego, brought L. to France along with Maria C., Stefano V., and his own fourteen-year-old daughter. Stefano B. played the organ and exhibited a dancing monkey on the streets of Paris, and the two girls collected money from onlookers. One day in 1846, in the Faubourg Saint-Antoine, a carriage knocked Maria over, breaking two of her ribs. To avoid paying medical costs, the padrone, Stefano B., abandoned her on the street. He was soon expelled from France for other reasons. Maria recovered in the hospital. One of the hospital visitors took her into her home for four or five years. The benefactress promised to adopt the girl in the future, but unfortunately her husband fell in love with Maria. In distress, Maria turned to her spiritual adviser, who told her to leave the home immediately lest the husband take advantage of her. The priest placed her in the home of an old woman who lived near the city limits. This woman, who made church linens, was cruel and overworked Maria. Maria lived with her for five years, until her new confessor suggested that she seek help from the Italian consulate in Paris.

Cerruti began an investigation into the young woman's past (she was now about twenty-one). With the help of the police he traced the address of Maria's nurse, L. From information given by L. and the mayor of Lumarzo, Cerruti was able to reconstruct the details of Maria's life. He hired Maria as a lady's maid for his wife, and she remained at the consul's home until December 1860, when she married a French shoemaker. During those years Maria told the consul and his wife about the violence she had endured during her year with the padrone Stefano. In the meantime, Stefano V., who also had been nursed by L. and brought to Paris by the padrone, ran into bad company. In 1851, at the age of sixteen, he was persuaded by a companion to live in a bordello in Saint-Denis. With that same man he became an accomplice to a murder. The man was sentenced to death, while Stefano was sentenced to life at hard labour. By 1862 he was back in Chiavari.

These cases give us some sense of the marginal youth in Ligurian society who would have been most vulnerable in the trade in children and youth. The fact that the stories were preserved is a testimony to the consul's attitude. It is worthwhile to try to understand why Cerruti took a great interest in the children and fought for their cause. No other consul in Moscow, London, Paris, Barcelona, or New York, had done such a thing. Among the very few individuals to have shown any concern for the children were the patriot Giuseppe Mazzini in London, A.S. Cerqua, a Protestant teacher of Italian children with the New York Children's Aid Society, and the pastor of St Cecilia's Church in London, Father Baldacconi. These men are discussed in later chapters. Mazzini devoted himself to the cause because of a passion for educating the common man. Cerqua, in the American Protestant reform tradition, believed that the children needed schooling if they were to escape their "useless" occupations and become productive and useful to society. Mazzini, Cerqua, and Cerruti all believed in the Italian cause, and wished to stamp out the trade so as to improve the reputation of the new Italy in the eyes of foreigners.

Cerruti's letters reveal a man who was strongly influenced by the Risorgimento and by a strong sense of justice. He seemed to be less concerned with lofty solutions, such as educating the children, than in seeing that justice was done in individual cases. While he called for prefects and mayors to do their utmost to prevent the emigration of these children, Cerruti also threw himself wholeheartedly into each case that came before him. With a passion for the history of the child, he gathered all possible details. Cerruti did not portray the cruelty inflicted on the children, or the dangers to which they were exposed in moralistic terms, but rather with genuine concern for the child's well-being. He never suggested that the children would be just as cruelly treated if they worked in coal mines, glassworks, or in brick factories; he advocated reform and an end to the trade, because he understood that as long as the trade continued, the likelihood of abuse would continue.

In his 1862 annual report to his superiors, Cerruti described briefly the young musicians from Basilicata who had recently begun arriving in greater numbers in the French capital.[32] The masters who brought the children to Paris, he argued, were more humane than the rogues from Chiavari and Parma, for they were following an old and noble tradition of playing the fife, harp, and violin in the streets of Europe and the Americas. Within a couple of years, however, Cerruti's opinion and the opinion of many Italian and foreign reformers changed. The Basilicatan musicians became the primary target of all those who wished to see an end to the trade in child street performers. During the decade, the list of abuses committed by Basilicatan padroni grew longer and longer. Also, by the mid-1860s, the masters, along with the child organists and animal exhibitors from Chiavari and Parma (with the exception of those from Mezzanego), had virtually disappeared from the streets of Paris and other major cities; virtually the only offenders were the musicians from Basilicata and Terra di Lavoro.

Although a significant number of children travelled to Paris from the town of Picinisco, near Sora, most of them, until the 1870s, came from five villages in Basilicata: Marsicovetere, Corleto Perticara, Laurenzana, Viggiano, and Calvello. From these lonely, desolate agricultural towns perched on the rugged hilltops of the southern Appenines, the young fiddlers and harpists made the long trek to Paris with their padroni in groups of two to ten. Some followed the shepherds' trails and roads through the mountains and towns of Basilicata and Naples until they reached Porto Santa Lucia. From there a ship took them to Marseilles. In Giuseppe Guerzoni's novel *La tratta dei fanciulli*, two children from Calabria were brought to the port of Paola. From there a boat conveyed them to Marseilles. They reached Paris after a ten-day walk through central France. So it was with the majority of the children who landed in Marseilles: most of the children did not take the sea route, but rather were forced to walk the entire coastal route from southern Italy, through Genoa, and along the Côte d'Azur through Nice, Marseilles, and Lyon to Paris. Other children took different routes from Marseilles or Nice to other cities in France. Some children entered the country clandestinely because they had no passports. They normally went through the Val Cesena in the Alps, just west of Susa, and travelled to Briançon on the French side. In *The Little Italians, or the Lost Children of Mont St Bernard*, Pippo and Nina, two children from a town near Genoa, are kidnapped by a padrone and brought through the Alps carrying a band organ and a marmotte. They are caught in a snowstorm in the Alps, and Pietro, the padrone, falls into a crevice.[33]

According to officials, some padroni specialized in bringing children from their home towns to Paris, where they sold the children at a profit to other masters. For example, seven-year-old Luigi Larrecca from Marsico in Basilicata, who lived with his family in Marseille, was entrusted by his father in 1865 to a musician by the name of Nicolo Lasca. Twenty months later, without the father's knowledge, Lasca leased Luigi to Bernardino Vitta, a padrone in Paris, for 250 francs. Luigi's father knew that Vitta was notoriously cruel to children, and he also was aware that his son was not receiving his wages (or, more probably, the father was receiving no remuneration for leasing his son). He therefore attempted personally, by mail, and through the Italian consuls-general in Paris and Marseilles to retrieve his son. At first Vitta refused to return him, arguing that he had paid for him and that he meant to realize a return on the investment. Later Vitta left Paris, with the child, in order to avoid trouble. There is little other evidence that many padroni specialized in this aspect of the "commerce in human flesh." The Larrecca case was first published in a report in Paris in 1868; five years later, the Italian parliamentary commission's final report on legislation concerning child street performers used the same example as their only case to show that some masters specialized in recruiting children, conveying them to Paris, and leasing or selling them at a profit.[34]

Some padroni followed the practice of obtaining passports with children's names and ages inscribed, and then returning to their home towns to obtain different children. These children were subsequently brought over the French border under the other names. Sometimes the passport names were those of the padrone's own children. In 1867 Giuseppe Rossi from Marsicovetere arrived in Lyon with six children, all of whom had the same names as the six children he had brought in previously. In February 1868 Lorenzo Zuttarrelli and Antonio Briglia of Marsicovetere journeyed to France using the same scheme, as did Michele Patrone of Magliano one month later. It is not clear whether these and other men brought the children into France for their own use, or whether they recruited the children and then subleased them to other padroni.[35]

In Paris the Basilicatans moved south of the neighbourhood occupied by the organ-grinders, animal exhibitors, and lacemakers from Parma and the figurine-makers from Lucca. By the early 1860s those street traders had abandoned the Faubourg Saint-Antoine, and their successors on the harp and violin crossed over to the Left Bank where they settled near the place Maubert and the Panthéon. To prevent them from revealing any more information than necessary, the children were trained by their padroni to reveal minimum information when questioned: "Je demeure Place Maubert, – je suis di Napoli." Until the mid-1860s, most of the children lived in a single street, the rue du Bon-Puits, in the slum lodgings of Madame Tron. Tron, whom the children called "La Matrona," owned a number of buildings on the street in which she housed some 250 child street musicians, and many of the padroni. She fed the children and padroni, and provided a meeting-room for the latter. When Madame Tron retired the children were dispersed around the Latin Quarter, usually in large numbers, with different padroni, and probably in worse conditions than in the days of La Matrona.[36]

In 1867–8 the Italian consulate gathered information about 302 of the Basilicatan children and 58 padroni living in ten houses in Paris. These represented only a sample of the Italian street performers in the city; house populations ranged from seven to over one hundred. Almost all the houses contained children and padroni from a few towns in Basilicata. In some houses only one town was represented. Andrea Lamacchia, a thirty-five-year-old padrone from Viggiano, lived at 23, rue Simon-Lefranc, near Les Halles, with six children in his care. His was one of the few houses on the Right Bank. Agostino Digilia, thirty-six, from Marsicovetere, controlled seven children at 8, rue des Sept-Voies. His forty-two-year-old townsman, Domenico Antonio Varallo, at 4, rue Domat on the Left Bank, had six musicians entrusted to him. Some of the houses contained numerous children from many towns. Most notorious among these was 45, rue Saint Victor, near the place Maubert, where eighteen padroni and one hundred children lived. They came from Viggiano, Marsico, Corleto Perticara, Marsiconuovo, and Calvello, but the majority were from Marsicovetere, as were most of the Basilicatan children in Paris. Number 2, rue de la Clef, was the home of nine padroni and forty-eight children from the same town. Most of the children from Laurenzana lived at two dwellings: thirty laurenzanesi children were housed at 30, rue Traversière, just behind the Gare de Lyon, and thirty-two more boarded at two neighbouring houses on the rue Neuve-Saint-Médard, near place Monge.[37]

As the residential patterns of the Basilicatan street musicians suggest, there was much interaction between the padroni from different towns. It was economically advantageous to maintain links with other padroni, so houses were rented in common. Information about opportunities outside Paris, or France, or even Europe was picked up in stray conversations. It seems that this and other knowledge of the trade circulated informally among the Basilicatan padroni in Paris. The Italian parliamentary commission's 1873 report referred to a secret organization, a veritable *camorra* run by an invisible "Pontiff." Children were recruited, and if not delivered to London or New York, they were registered and numbered, and placed in residences around place Maubert or the Panthéon. The head of this commission, Giuseppe Guerzoni, reproduced the same information in his novel which we encountered above, *La Tratta dei Fanciulli*. However, this carefully planned, secret "corporation" (as Guerzoni coined it) was highly unlikely. The commission from the Société Italienne de Bienfaisance de Paris made no mention of it, and Cerruti never reported such a highly developed system in any of his correspondence.[38]

The parliamentary report was correct in ascribing to the padroni in Paris a key role in the spread of the trade to New York, London, and elsewhere. The trade had begun in Paris, and the French capitol was on the route to London and Liverpool, and America. Those padroni who wished to move on to Britain or the Americas could be informed in Paris by returning performers and padroni about market conditions, and about the receptivity of police and public to their trade. However, the Paris-London-New York nexus was most evident during the four or five years following mass arrests of the child musicians in Paris in 1867. According to one source, 1,544 child street musicians were arrested in the year of the famous Exposition. Hundreds of musicians and masters left the city for greener pastures, or at least for a city with less resistance to the trade.[39]

What led to the mass arrests and expulsions of the late 1860s? The international exposition of 1867 brought many visitors to Paris, and the sight of a few thousand young Italian mendicants was embarrassing not only to the Italian government but also to the French Ministry of the Interior and especially the Paris prefecture, which was responsible for the movement of people, the protection of public property, and the maintenance of peace and order. But a second reason for the restrictive measures was the political and social climate of the Second Empire. French business and political leaders, whether traditional Catholics or liberal reformers, supported legislation to ameliorate the condition of working children. The French Ministry of Commerce organized a campaign to enforce the 1841 legislation concerning child labour, and that impetus eventually led to the passage of new and more comprehensive legislation in 1874.[40]

In the late 1860s, however, the mere presence of so many street musicians prompted the authorities to take action. An 1849 law gave the prefects the power to expel the children, but freedom of movement and the right of the law-abiding foreigner to remain in the country were sensitive issues. The apprehension of hundreds of children could best be justified on the grounds that the children were abused by their masters. Reports of abuse were publicized effectively by Cerruti and by the Société Italienne de Bienfaisance. The Parisian press also had a hand in exposing the shame of the trade, but their articles tended to centre on the annoying spectacle of Italian child singers and musicians begging for coins on the streets.

As we have seen, throughout the early and middle nineteenth century, laws and police ordinances were passed to deal with the problem of street musicians. On 6 January 1863, one year after Cerruti had submitted his report to the Italian Ministry of Foreign Affairs, the French minister of the interior released a circular reminding prefects that street performers had to have special permission to carry out their trade, and that they must renew that permission every time they moved to a different département.[41] Even stronger measures were adopted by the Paris prefecture a few weeks later. A new ordinance provided that only French citizens could receive permission to perform in public. To obtain the necessary permit, the performer must have resided in the area served by the prefecture for one year. He must renew his permit every three months. He could perform only in sixty-three public places named in the ordinance, and he was required to carry a his permit medallion with him. Even more important, the performer could not employ children under the age of sixteen to perform with him; he could not lend or transfer his medallion; nor could he divine, interpret dreams, or perform services related to pedicure or dentistry. Six hundred permits would be distributed – 150 to mountebanks, 150 to organ-grinders, 150 to singers, and 150 to musicians.[42]

To ensure that the clauses regarding children had effect, the ordinance stipulated that an applicant for a permit must indicate the number of persons who normally accompanied him, and their age, sex, given name, surname, and place of birth. All personal details regarding the performer and his entourage had to be recorded in a twenty-four-page booklet, which had the validity of a passport. If a child was arrested, he or she was to be held temporarily. The Italian consul was always advised of the arrest. At some point the padrone would claim the child, who was always handed over by the police. After the third arrest, however, the child would be expelled from France, and a note advising repatriation would be sent to the consul. In practice, repatriation was useless. The child could return to France with another group of youngsters and their padrone. It was difficult to make identity checks at the border crossings, and it was unlikely that the child would be stopped.[43]

The police in Lyon were even more severe than the law required them to be. G.F. Gambarotta, the Italian consul to that city, informed his superiors on 4 September 1865 that the prefect of his département had announced that all street musicians would be expelled from Lyon within twenty-four hours. The prefect asked the consul to inform the Italian Ministry of Foreign Affairs so that would-be itinerant musicians could be forewarned not to leave home.[44]

Despite the restrictions, the number of child performers continued to grow. One report estimated that 3,000 Italian child musicians were performing on the streets of Paris in the summer of 1867: 1,200 were between the ages of eight and ten.[45] To combat the influx, the police chief of the second bureau of the Paris préfecture, Charles-Jérome Lecour, took extraordinary measures. In late 1866 or early 1867 he appointed a man named Rossi a special agent of the préfecture; Rossi was to survey the movements of street musicians. Lecour was in close touch with Cerruti, and the two worked together to wipe out the trade by sharing information and using their authority to control the musicians' movements. For example, Rossi carried information both to Lecour and to Cerruti – information about the treatment of the children and the addresses of the padroni. The Italian consul found Rossi useful, and in late January 1867 Cerruti asked the minister of external affairs in Rome to approve a subsidy of 40 lire for the agent. So zealous was Lecour in attempting to stamp out the trade that in late February 1867 Costantino Nigra, the Italian minister in Paris, asked the Italian minister of foreign affairs to give Lecour a decoration of honour.[46]

The Ministry of the Interior ordered police to interpret more strictly the expulsion measures, "which, up to the present had been interpreted with much reserve and had had little efficacy." In addition, Cerruti asked the prefecture to take a harsher stand against the padroni. As a result, the police began a campaign of mass arrests.[47]

The children's masters felt the pressure. On 10 October 1867 Cerruti received a petition from fifty-one padroni in Paris. They were disappointed with the ministry's circular, and even more so with the Italian consul:

A decision of the French government provoked by the Italian Consulate-General obliges itinerant musicians to abandon the hospitable land which was bread and shelter to them for many years. Far from opposing the decrees of the Imperial government influenced by the Italian Consulate General, before leaving they [the padroni] feel it is their strict duty to express their deepest acknowledgements of the general Parisian hospitality. At the same time they protest the Italian consular authority, which instead of providing for the interests of numerous Italian itinerant musicians, advocates such a decree in a period when the children, who account for the majority of these musicians, will suffer greatly the long crossing, the uncomfortable voyage; for we are dealing with individuals with no means, who in the most uncomfortable season of the year, due to the severity of the climate, see themselves abandoned in difficult straits by the consular authority, whose first duty it is to protect his co-nationals. We sign for all Italian street musicians.[48]

Virtually all of the signatories were from the Basilicatan towns south of Potenza, such as Laurenzana, Marsicovetere, and Viggiano.

Because records are incomplete, it is impossible to know how many padroni and children were actually deported. In fact, even the fifty-one signatories may not have been deported; they might simply have feared the possibility of expulsion. The only solid evidence of deportation is a letter from Lecour to Cerruti dated 27 December 1867, in which he says that twelve children were to be repatriated to Italy. The children ranged in age from nine to sixteen, although most of them were under twelve. Only one of them was a girl, and virtually all were from Basilicata. One was from Picinisco.[49]

The children were now highly visible, and the Italian government became even more disposed to look for ways to stamp out the trade. It was embarrassing that so many Italian mendicants should be so conspicuous during the Paris Exhibition. Nigra informed his ministry that just as the Exhibition drew poor people trying to earn a living in any way possible, "so did the competition among street musicians from Italy, and especially child musicians, grow in a particular way ... The scourge has grown so serious lately, the number of children wandering the streets of Paris is increasing so much, and the expressions of public indignation are so often directed to this office, that I find it my duty to bring to your attention a topic which I have put before your Royal Ministry a number of times, the last time on 10 August 1866." He asked that Italian officials be more selective in issuing passports to individuals who wished to take children abroad. In France (and this was a few months before the passage of the special police ordinance in Paris) the police were helpless: they were obliged to allow entry to those individuals and could not expel them until they actually broke a law.[50]

The many letters and reports sent to the Ministry of Foreign Affairs by Cerruti and Nigra were not sufficient to convince officials in Florence that the Italian government should take effective measures to end the trade. Ministry staff and directors were aware of the suffering to which the children were subjected. After all, Consul Cerruti had pleaded since the early 1860s for action on the part of the Italian government to end the shameful commerce ("commercio vergognoso"). The Italian government had not responded by April 1867, when Cerruti complained that "almost every day children arrested for mendicity and vagabondage are brought to this Consulate and their state is pitiful," and that even the forthcoming police ordinances, like other laws, might be rarely enforced.[51]

Diplomatic eyebrows were raised in August when a few of the children from Basilicata in Paris were expelled. The form of expulsion was at issue: since 1838 the two countries had followed a convention of shipping deported nationals to the French-Italian border at the expense of the deporting country. This time, however, the children were brought to the Italian consul in Paris, and he was responsible for sending the children back to Italy. Yet even this did not move the Italian government to address the problem at the source – the sending villages in Italy. Leaders of the Italian community in Paris realized that a more effective means of persuading the Italian government must be found.[52]

A strategy was devised by the directors of the Société Italienne de Bienfaisance, which was established in May 1865 by the Italian consul in Paris and a few interested professionals and businessmen from within and outside the Italian community. The main goal of the Société was to help destitute Italians in Paris. Its headquarters were located in the Italian consulate. The board of directors included a banker, a number of doctors, a French senator, a professional singer, a jeweller, a French insurance executive, an engineer, and a lawyer. At the annual meeting in early June 1868, the members of the Société knew that the young musicians were a serious problem. "Les petits italiens" were well known in Paris, not only because of their great numbers, but because of newspaper editorials and the numerous arrests. The board of directors organized a committee to investigate and report on the problem to the Italian Ministry of Foreign Affairs.[53]

The committee was composed of five members: Maurizio Bixio, Luigi Cerruti (the Italian consul), Francesco Fortina (a medical doctor), Antonio Ronna (an engineer), and Emmanuel Cavaglion, who served as chairman. Cerruti placed all his documentation at the commission's disposal. The report was completed in early 1868, and through the Italian minister in Paris, Nigra (who was also the honorary president of the Société), the report was delivered to the Italian government in mid-February.[54] The Ministry of the Interior had the report translated into Italian and delivered to the prefect in the province of Potenza, which was the worst offender. In May 1868 the Italian Parliament set up a commission of inquiry into the trade in children. The commission and the resulting legislation are examined in chapter 5.

The *Rapport sur la situation des petits italiens* was a powerful document. Many newspaper or magazine articles and reports by philanthropic agencies, and certainly every reference in the Italian Parliament that dealt with Italian street musicians, quoted extracts from the document. The report summarized the origins of the musicians in the previous decade and during the 1860s. It examined the living and working conditions of the children and the padroni. A number of appendices contained case studies of some of the maltreated children in Paris and London. Although the French government was about to bring in strong measures, the members of the commission still felt that the problem of the children had to be attacked at its roots in Italy. This was a matter of national honour, for the country had now grown up: "Il est de toute nécessité que nos compatriotes comprennent que c'est à la fois une question d'humanité et de patriotisme ... À l'Italie divisée, sans liberté, sans travail, on pouvait beaucoup pardonner. À l'Italie unie, voulant devenir industrielle, ayant besoin de développer les merveilleuses ressources de son sol et de son génie, l'Europe a le droit de dire 'Gardez vos pauvres, si vous en avez. Instruisez vos citoyens, faites-en des hommes, il vous en faut.'"[55]

The reformers in Paris objected to the trade in children on a number of grounds. The trade, by its very nature, was immoral. The children were exposed to maltreatment, to immoral characters, to bad living conditions. This could only lead to their becoming malfattori (common criminals). "Everyone knows what will become of these children," argued the authors of the report, "undernourished, clothed in rags, lodged in miserable conditions, subjected to maltreatment, continually in contact with men capable of anything, having no good example, exposed to nothing which could raise their spirit, deprived of everything ... leaving the dirt of the streets only to walk the dirt of the prison cell. The unhappy young Italians who survive so much suffering, become brigands for their own country, and criminals wherever they may be!"[56] The argument that underpinned the program of the reformers was that society itself suffered by the trade: if it did not do something with the plight of the children, today's exploited waifs would come back to haunt society tomorrow as criminals.

The image of the children as a future threat to society was juxtaposed with sentimental descriptions of those same children as helpless victims. This view reflected the ambivalent attitude of Western society to children in the nineteenth century. "Qui n'a pas rencontré," asked the authors, "en sortant du spectacle, en rentrant le soir chez lui, ces pauvres êtres chétifs chargés d'instruments plus lourds qu'eux-mêmes, trainant péniblement leurs pas à la suite du passant attardé?"[57] They painted one particularly touching picture:

Dans les journées les plus froides d'hiver que nous venons de traverser, nous avons souvent remarqué sur la place de la Concorde deux jolies petites filles de quatre à cinq ans, accroupies toutes deux sur le trottoir du ministère de la marine. Leur jeunesse, leur beauté vraiment angélique attiraient autour d'elles un cercle de personnes empressées à les questionner, mais leur curiosité n'était jamais satisfaite,– car elles ne répondaient que par de longs et tristes regards, qui faisaient pleuvoir sur leurs genoux le billon et la pièce blanche.– Ah! le maître de tels esclaves doit être bien envié par ses pareils![58]

All of the reformers made a case for ending the trade by citing specific examples of child abuse. This was true of Cerruti in his correspondence with his superiors in Florence; of the editors and reporters of *Le Temps*; of the parliamentary commission in Italy that reported on the trade in Paris and elsewhere; and, of course, of the Société Italienne de Bienfaisance. Each case cited by the reformers made a particular point about one form of abuse or another. Each case was also presented so as to shock the listener, to evoke pity for the victims, to drive home the injustice committed on the children. Reformers argued that the virtual slavery of the children – the nature of their work, their living conditions, and their relationship with their masters – was immoral in itself. They did not contend that the few extreme examples of child cruelty they presented were indicative of the experience of most of the children; even though most children were not treated cruelly, the system of leasing children to masters who took them all over the world increased the likelihood of abuse.

The Société's 1868 report quoted a Neapolitan doctor – he may have been one of the doctors on the board of directors – who stated that of every one hundred children of both sexes who left their villages with the padroni, only twenty returned home eventually. Thirty established themselves elsewhere in the world, and fifty succumbed to illness, maltreatment, and deprivations of all kinds; that is, the mortality rate for these children was 50 per cent.[59] It is impossible to prove the doctor right or wrong; however, on intuition, the figure seems exaggerated. If the newspapers did not report the deaths, Cerruti would certainly have informed his ministry.

Extreme cruelty to the children and even death were not common, but neither were they nonexistent. One celebrated master from Parma, known as "Il Cieco," made a fortune in Paris. He quit the French capital in 1865 to move to London, and he abandoned two of his young musicians. Francesco Robajatti died at the Sainte-Eugénie hospital on 8 December 1865; his companion died nine days later at the Saint-Antoine hospital. Meanwhile, Il Cieco was said to be enjoying a 200,000-franc fortune in London.

The following June, eight-year-old Domenico Damasca, son of Tomaso, from Laurenzana, was tortured by his master. Domenico had been brought to Paris by a padrone named Pellettieri. When the child was unable to meet his quota for a few days, Pellettieri tied the child to his bed with a harp-string for four days and four nights. The string cut into his wrists and swelled them. The police captain of the prefecture where the boy was discovered was so moved to pity by the sight of the child that he gave the Italian consul the equivalent of twenty Italian lire to give to the boy. Cerruti kept the lad in his home for several days. Meanwhile,

Pellettieri escaped from the city and was sentenced to four months' imprisonment in absentia.[60]

The cruelty inflicted on the children originated not only with vicious padroni but also with the structure of the occupation, which took the children away from the home environment and the controls that it provided. One tragic case occurred in May 1868. Carmine Ianora had been brought to Paris at age twelve by two padroni, Raffaele Dimaria and Agostino Digilia, from Marsicovetere, under a contract between Carmine's father and the two masters. On a Sunday in early May Carmine made his way to the bois de Vincennes to play for Parisians relaxing out in the country. At the same time a padrone from Laurenzana, Francesco Abbate, was travelling in the same direction with his nine-year-old daughter, Emilia, and two other boys. He wanted to get back to Paris, and when he encountered Carmine, whom he already knew, he asked the youth to accompany the other children to Vincennes, and to come back at night with the day's receipts.

In the late afternoon Carmine took the girl through different paths in the forest to shake off the two boys. Late that night he brought her to a secluded meadow and raped her. Emilia's screams attracted the two other young musicians, who persuaded Carmine to leave his victim lest he be punished by her father. Ianora then returned home accompanied by Emilia. They arrived at 45, rue Saint Victor (the most notorious home of child street musicians in the city) at 1 a.m. and slept in the same room that evening. The next morning, when Francesco awoke, he noticed blood on Emilia's nightshirt and realized that she must have been raped. Neither she nor Carmine would answer his questions. The other two boys, however, told the father how his daughter had been lured away by Carmine. Abbate did not report the crime for fifteen days, hoping that Carmine would agree to marry his daughter at a later date. When the youth refused, Abbate went to the police. In late June Carmine was tried for rape, found guilty, and sentenced to seven years in a house of correction.[61]

Emilia's father, Francesco Abbate, was himself accused of cruelty to another of the children entrusted to him soon after his daughter's tragic episode. Maria Micheli, aged twelve, had lost her father. Her mother lived in the village of Cianciurlo, near Calvello, in Basilicata. Abbate, who was her uncle, took her to France as a suonatore in late 1866. Maria subsequently became very ill, and her uncle had her placed in a children's convalescent home in Vaugirard. When she recovered, Abbate went to retrieve her, but she refused to join him, complaining that he beat her. When the hospital staff realized that force would be required to return her to Abbate, they informed the consul. Cerruti forbade Abbate to take the girl with him without the permission of the mother, signed and documented by the mayor of Calvello. The mother forwarded the permission, asking that the daughter remain working with her uncle and that she not be sent back home. "Your excellency must know," Cerruti informed his superior, "that work in this case means wandering the streets of Paris from morning until evening, begging with a violin under her arm, for her uncle's sake."

Abbate told the consul that he would take the girl with him to America. Cerruti responded that he could not take his niece with him, and that she could not perform in the streets. He would have her brought back to Italy as soon as a reliable person could be found to accompany her. The consul then returned to Vaugirard and interviewed Maria in front of a teacher. The child reiterated her unwillingness to join her uncle. Maria declared that her uncle had on various occasions whipped her, while she was naked in bed, for not having brought home enough money from her performances. In addition, she did not want to sleep in the same bed with him and his daughter. Finally, she wished to remain in Vaugirard until September so she could make her first Holy Communion. Cerruti realized that he might have been abusing his powers by keeping the girl at the school, but, as he informed his superior, "I could not authorize her release to Abbate without a feeling of guilt." Maria Micheli was left at the school until her First Communion in September. She was then free to be returned home if her mother wanted her back.[62]

The Italian legation in Paris kept the Ministry of External Affairs in Rome informed about cases of child abuse involving Abbate and other padroni and children, and the reports had some effect. Some of the cases were cited in government debates on the children, and appeared in the appendices to the report of the legislative committee that drafted a bill to end the trade in 1868. Many newspaper reporters and reformers also cited the stories in their writings. Cases of abuse provided an extra impetus to pass legislation to protect the children, and as we shall see in chapter 5, the Italian government, after five years of preparation, finally passed a comprehensive bill in late 1873.

This is not to say that the Italian legislation or even the work of the Parisian police brought a sudden end to the trade in the French capital. Nor did the arrests of 1867. The 1,544 arrests in that year were followed by 698 arrests in 1868 and 437 in 1869. The declining figures may indicate that fewer musicians were working in the city, but one writer suggested that in fact they probably represented laxity on the part of officials. It seems that just as the Basilicatans harpists and violinists were leaving the city, the players of wind instruments from Sora were increasing their presence there. Late in 1869 the prefect of police, Pietri, drew the attention of police commissioners to the problem of the growing number of "jeunes mendiants italiens dits pifferari." He proposed they be expelled from France according to the law of 1849. Many of them were living at 23, rue Simon le Franc, which had been an important residence for viggianesi harpists and violinists. Pietri urged police to check hotels and lodgings immediately for these children, to get their names and ascertain their civil status, their ages, and the names of their exploiters.[63]

As in the past, the prefect's instructions probably were not heeded. But as one writer suggested in the spring of 1870, "la question est plus grave qu'une question de simple police." Even if the children were arrested and expelled, they would be brought back across the border. Even if their padroni were arrested or expelled, they would be leased to another cornac (a slang term for "master"). Mass expulsions was no remedy either, for that went against humanity and in any case would probably bring reprisals.[64]

In the end it was neither policing, nor expulsions, nor press exposure that reduced the number of child street musicians. Rather, the Franco-Prussian War was probably the single greatest influence in the decline of this commerce. From 1869 to 1870 the number of Italian immigrants in France declined from 143,000 to 114,000; in addition, the number of clandestine immigrants declined by almost 50 per cent (from 15,250 to 8,350). Street musicians were in the latter category. It is virtually certain that the proportional decline in Paris was even greater.[65] Cagliardo Coraggioso recalled in his autobiography that his father and two other street musicians were arrested twice during the war on the way back home from England. Once they were mistaken for German spies, another time for French spies.

This is not to say that the trade had ended. In 1874, Charles-Jérome Lecour, the Parisian police chief who had devoted much effort in the 1860s on the street children, set up a program to work in conjunction with the 1873 Italian laws governing the young minstrels. All Italian minors performing on the streets were to be apprehended and brought to the Italian consul-general. This was very likely part of a program to deal with juvenile workers not covered by the 1874 Child Labour Law. In any case, a new law promulgated on 7 December prohibited children under sixteen years of age from engaging in street trades and performing without their parents' permission.[66]

The consul was probably carrying out his orders from Rome, according to the new law. By then, however, the trade had already declined in Paris. Although some of the young musicians probably stayed on in Paris and continued their trade in later years, most of them moved to England or the United States with their padroni, or, as we shall see in chapter 6, they entered other trades in France and elsewhere.[67]

Boy with a hurdy-gurdy in England in the early 1840s. The crank turns a wheel while keys under the child's left hand depress a string, causing it to resonate as it touches the turning wheel. The barrel organ has a similar crank, and has become known locally as a hurdy-gurdy. Albumen print, photographed by an associate of William Henry Fox Talbot. Science Museum Library, The National Museum of Science and Industry, South Kensington, London, neg. no. 1437/73

Portrait of an Italian exhibiting in London. The itinerant barrel organists were often accompanied by dancing dogs, white mice, or monkeys. This caricature first appeared in the *Penny Magazine* in London in 1833. From Charles McFarlane, *Popular Customs, Sports, and Recollections of the South of Italy*, 1846

An organ grinder, probably in France in the 1850s. Andrée-Adolphe-Eugene Disderi, *The Organ Grinder*, ca. 1853, salt print, 15.1 × 12.1 cm. The J. Paul Getty Museum

Italian pipers (pifferaro and zampognaro), probably in France in the 1850s. These instruments were played by peasants from the feast of the Immaculate Conception (8 December) throughout the Chrismas season. (André-Adolphe-Eugene Disderi, *Two Natives of Calabria*, ca. 1853, salt print, 17.6 × 12.1 cm. The J. Paul Getty Museum)

This street musician was probably an Italian piper in France in the 1850s.
Gustave Le Gray, *Portrait of a Street Musician*, 1855, albumen print, 22.2 × 16.9 cm.
The J. Paul Getty Museum

The street organ nuisance frustrated many middle-class Londoners in the 1860s and led to campaigns to control the street music trade. *Punch* published a number of caricatures in the 1860s. In this cartoon the musician has frightened the pony but cannot be arrested under the law at the time. From *Punch*, 11 June 1864

"Ballo degli orsi, Bear-Dancing at Rome." The bear exhibitors were from the same towns as many of the street organists in the Val-di-Taro in the Duchy of Parma. From Charles McFarlane, *Popular Customs, Sports, and Recollections of the South of Italy*, 1846

THE ORGAN-GRINDER.

An organ-grinder, meagre and sorrowful,
  Stops in the sun in the street below;
The ragged street children come trooping about him,
  Crowding and eager and glad, I know,
Their bright eyes peering through tangled tresses
  With childish wonder and happy trust:
Even the boys stare, quiet a moment,
  Scraping their toes through the tawny dust.

But the organ-grinder is bent and weary;
  Nothing is new to him under the sun;
The tinkling notes of the old, old music
  Mean scanty crusts when the day is done.
A waltz may come, or an Ave Maria;
  The children may listen or run away;
The organ-grinder is old and weary,
  And he turns this handle the livelong day.

What is he thinking, our tired brother?
  What do these sorrowful gray eyes see?
Vacantly gazing—at nothing about him—
  Is he looking in faces that used to be?
Is he thinking of old, old times and people,
  Of days when the sun in truth was bright,
When the sweet winds blew to him perfumed fancies,
  And sunset castles rose fair in his sight?

Does he hear, instead of the old, old music
  His brown, stiff fingers are grinding out,
The dear wife's laugh in the pleasant twilight,
  And the baby's step and tiny shout?
Does he feel the pressure of loving fingers—
  Deadly chill when he touched them last!—
Biding the troubled dream of the present
  In the gracious glow from the real past?

Our worn-out brother! He is only weary;
  No fairy dreams are kissing his eyes;
His life is sordid and narrow and sorrowful:
  The pennies fall rarely—for this he sighs.
No lovely phantoms are floating about him;
  No echoes are sounding within his breast
From the voice divine of that love supernal
  Which shall surely somewhere give him rest.

And the bruisèd spirit is mate with the body:
  He will hear with a stare that God is good.
Silently add to the store of his pennies,
  And brighten his desolate solitude.
Stifle the Pharisee pity that rises!
  Who links the merciless chain of fate?
Through what dim cycles slow gather its atoms?
  In what fine junctions—while we wait?

Poem and cartoon on the organ-grinder from *Harper's New Monthly Magazine*, 1873. Dozens of poems, novels, and short stories in the nineteenth century dealt with Italian street musicians in the United States and Britain.

CHAPTER THREE

"The Organ Boys" in London

The young boys from Parma made their first appearance in London soon after the end of the Napoleonic Wars. In March 1820 the *Times* reported that "the public have of late been exceedingly annoyed by the appearance of a number of Italian boys with monkeys and white mice wandering about the streets, exciting the compassion of the benevolent." Apparently, two Italian men brought at least twenty children from towns near Parma to London on a fifteen-month contract for the express purpose of begging in the streets. Each boy was given a monkey, mouse, or squirrel, and at the end of the period of indenture he could keep the animal and go into business on his own. The trade was lucrative; two Italian masters had returned to Italy at the end of the summer of 1819 with fifty pounds in earnings.[1]

Close on the heels of these young boys was the London Society for the Suppression of Mendicity. This agency was formed in 1818 to stamp out a problem that had lately come to the attention of many Londoners – the growing number of beggars on the streets of the city. In 1820 the Mendicity Society had supplied the *Times* with the details of the trade. The Society's 1822 annual report devoted a short paragraph to the "considerable number of boys, principally of Italy, who have infested the streets of the Metropolis, for the purpose of begging under the pretence of exhibiting different animals." The appendix to the report, which examined some of the cases handled by the society during the year, referred to "A.J.," an Italian boy, seventeen years of age, who was apprehended with two dogs and a drum. He "was one of those unfortunate beings the property of individuals who compel them to bring a certain sum home every night, under pain of being sent to bed with empty stomachs." The society brought the boy before a magistrate, who committed him for a month, not so much to punish him as to deprive the master of his services. When a passport was obtained for him, the child was returned to Italy. The managers of the society believed that with the co-operation of the magistracy, "this evil ... will eventually be entirely eradicated from the Metropolis." With the passage of time, however, Londoners resigned themselves to the fact that the Italian children were there to stay. Indeed, the society continued its campaign against the masters into the late nineteenth century.[2]

At first the children earned their keep exclusively by exhibiting dancing animals. By the 1830s they displayed not only monkeys, mice, and squirrels, but also dogs, tortoises, and even porcupines. The master rented the animals to the children at a fixed daily rate. A tortoise or a box of white mice, for example, went for 1s 6d a day, while a porcupine, more in demand because there were only two in the city, cost 2s 6d a day; for 4s a boy could also rent a barrel-organ. The dancing dogs came to 5s a day, but for that price the boy got four dogs in dresses, along with a spinning wheel, pipe, and tabor. By the 1830s the children had begun using inanimate items in their entertainments – a plain barrel-organ, or an organ with waltzing figures, or even a box of wax figures. An 1831 article in the *Times* reported that some of the boys made as much as six or seven shillings in a day, and one waif claimed that he had made fifteen shillings in one day in Brighton, with a dancing dog.[3]

Until the late 1830s the "Italian Boys" were primarily seen as displayers of white mice. In George Eliot's *Middlemarch*, set in that decade, Mrs Cadwallader, understanding that Dorothea will lose Casaubon's inheritance if she marries Will Ladislaw, believes that Dorothea "might as well marry an Italian with white mice." Soon the boys were playing musical instruments as well as exhibiting animals. In Dickens's *Little Dorrit*, Flora describes Italy, "with the grapes and figs growing everywhere and lava necklaces and bracelets too, that land of poetry with burning mountains picturesque beyond belief though if the organ boys come away from the neighbourhood not to be scorched nobody can wonder being so young and bringing their white mice with them most humane." By the 1840s the boys with white mice were becoming known as "the organ boys."[4]

The image of the Italian boys as street organists was impressed on the English public's mind by the frequent reports of children or masters being brought to the magistrates' courts for begging; the children seemed always to be equipped with street organs and white mice. The most sensational report in the early years of the trade occurred in 1845. The hearing concerning Joseph Leonardi was not a mendicancy case, but rather an inquiry into the death of the fifteen-year-old musician, "one of those unfortunate creatures who are brought over in shoals to this country to perambulate the streets with hand-organs, and to solicit charity."[5] Joseph was found in the streets "in a state of destitution"; he died in the St Giles workhouse a few days later. Although the coroner testified that the boy had died of natural causes – he described Joseph's lungs as "one mass of disease" – the judge gave the boy's master, Rabbiotti, a severe reprimand. The young Leonardi had constantly complained about his sore chest, but Rabbiotti persisted in beating him and sending him out on the streets.

A number of Italian political exiles, or fuorusciti, took great interest in the case of the young Leonardi, and they attended the inquiry with their solicitor. Adhering to their philosophy of "thought and action," to their belief that the Italian nation could be created only when the peasants were educated and made aware of the meaning of fatherland and nation, these men had founded, patronized, and taught at the Italian school for destitute boys in Hatton Garden, just off the Clerkenwell Road in Saffron Hill. The school had been established by the Italian patriot Giuseppe Mazzini. When Mazzini first came to the city of his exile in the spring of 1837, he was greatly moved by the sad sight of young Italian boys displaying animals, selling plaster statuettes, or grinding the organ: "By conversing occasionally with some of the lads who wander about the streets of the vast city playing upon the organ, I learned, with profound grief and astonishment, the history and method of a traffic carried on by a few speculators, only to be qualified as a species of white slave-trade; a disgrace to Italy, to its government, and to its clergy, who might, had they chosen to do so, have prevented it."[6]

Mazzini formed an association for the protection of neglected children, and occasionally he brought masters to court when they used violence on their apprentices (at that time there were about six padroni in the city): "When they found they were being watched, they gradually became less cruel and arbitrary in their conduct." The famous republican also opened the Italian Free School in November 1841. The children would come to the school in the evenings between nine and ten o'clock, bringing their organs with them. There at Greville Street, Hatton Garden (the building still stands), just around the corner from their residences on Saffron Hill, the boys were taught geography, arithmetic, drawing, reading, and writing. On Sunday evenings the children listened to a lecture by Mazzini on "Italian history, the lives of our great men, the outlines of natural history, any subject in short, that appeared to us calculated to elevate these unformed minds, darkened by poverty and their state of abjection to the will of others ... Nearly every Sunday evening for two years I lectured to them upon Italian history or elementary astronomy ... and upwards of a hundred discourses upon the duties of man, and various moral subjects, were declaimed by Filippo Pistrucci ... whom I had made director of the school, and who identified himself with his mission with unexampled zeal." [7]

Within a few months 160 children were attending classes subsidized by Italians and Englishmen in London. Angelo Maria Baldacconi, the pastor of Saints Anselm and Cecilia church (which had many Italian parishioners until St Peter's church was opened), had also organized classes for the young Italian boys. An Italian Catholic school had been established in London in 1817, and there is some dispute as to whether Baldacconi revived it in 1835. In any case, he took over the Italian Free School after 1848, and it remained under clerical direction until the end of the century.[8]

The attempts by Italian reformers, statesmen, and bureaucrats to improve the physical and moral conditions of the children were, until the 1880s, very much based on national pride. During the Risorgimento and in the years following, these men considered the presence of their country's children on the streets of London, Paris, New York, Moscow, and other cities not only a tragic episode in the lives of the nation's peasants, but also a national disgrace.

The children, of course, did not constitute a majority of the street musicians in the city, and until the 1860s they did not even constitute a majority of Italian street musicians. The street entertainment trade in London grew as quickly as the city. While the population of London in 1851 stood at 2.5 million, by 1871 it had increased almost to 4 million. As a number of urban historians have shown, with the development of the suburbs and the growth of the middle class, the city became more and more segregated. The classes lived apart from each other both in the centre and in the peripheries. The entertainers performed mostly in or near the city centre, but by mid-century they began bringing their acts to the suburbs; this was especially true of the Italian organ-grinders.[9]

Who were the street entertainers and what forms of entertainment did they offer? The best source of information about the street trades in mid-nineteenth-century London is the collection of interviews published by Henry Mayhew in 1861, *London Labour and the London Poor*. Mayhew was fascinated by all sorts of street entertainers, not only musicians. Unlike some of the parliamentarians and magistrates, he saw these performers not as vagrants but as citizens with a valid occupation that often involved great sacrifice. His collection includes interviews with a Punch and Judy exhibitor, a fantoccini (marionette) man, an exhibitor of mechanical figures, a telescope exhibitor, acrobats, a strongman, an owner of peep shows, a street juggler, magicians, strolling actors, clowns, stilt-vaulters, tightrope dancers, reciters, and a one-legged war veteran who performed a military drill using his crutch as a gun.

Mayhew also interviewed many street musicians and vocalists. He divided them into two classes – the blind, who depended on the pity of the public and who were therefore beggars; and the "skilful," who earned their keep by the quality of their work.[10] The most touching example of the former was "Old Sarah." In 1802, at the age of sixteen, Sarah was left blind and orphaned. A poor woman in the workhouse taught her to play the hurdy-gurdy for a living. With her seeing-eye dog and her cymbal, as she called the instrument, Sarah performed in the streets of London and for clients in the suburbs. As she was approaching old age she was struck down one day by a cab. She spent the rest of her days in hospital beds or at home, never again to play in the streets. The "skilful" musicians included English and German street bands, Ethiopian serenaders (British singers and banjoists who performed black American melodies), bagpipe-players, French hurdy-gurdy men, harpists, organists with monkeys and dancing dogs, tom-tom players, drum and pipe performers, ballad-singers, and whistlers. Mayhew estimated, from information gleaned from the performers themselves, that the street musicians in the city totalled about 1,000; in addition, there were about 250 street vocalists. Those numbers increased during the 1860s.[11]

Street entertainment was an important part of the urban definition of London. About 250 bands performed on city streets in the 1850s, along with many hurdy-gurdy men, street organists, and non-musical entertainers. English bands, which predominated, were composed primarily of string and woodwind instruments; they complained about the Germans, who were undercutting their market. The German bands consisted mainly of brass instruments. In Mayhew's time there were only five such bands in the street, but they were highly visible. Their endurance was due in no small part to their frugality. One man interviewed by Mayhew admitted sleeping three in a room with his comrades and spending as little money as possible: "We play sheaper zan ze English, and we don't spend so much. Ze English players insult us, but we don't care about that. Zey abuse us for playing sheap ... I want to save enough to take me back to Hanover."[12]

Most of the musicians interviewed by Mayhew were Italian, and virtually all were from towns near Parma. The Italians differed from the other street performers in one major way. Whereas the English, Scottish, Irish, and German performers worked on equal terms, or trained young men to learn instruments until they were ready to work on equal terms, the Italians (or, at least until the 1860s, the musicians from the towns near Parma) carried out their work in the context of a master-journeyman contract. We have already observed this arrangement in the case of the child performers; however, many of the young men also had a contractual relationship with their masters. There were two reasons for this. Most of the young men had grown up in a master-servant relationship as child musicians, and were therefore bound to the socio-economic structure of the occupation. Second, the allocation of instruments and animals perpetuated the relationship. Until the 1860s, and even afterwards, the difficulty of obtaining trained animals and especially barrel-organs forced many musicians to depend on suppliers. Those suppliers were, in essence, masters. They themselves played on the streets but they usually owned a number of organs. They either rented the organs for a fee or collected a percentage of earnings from the musicians who used the instrument.

One of the interviews recorded by Mayhew illustrates the nature of the master-journeyman relationship. As a young boy this organ-grinder had gone begging in his home district: his father had died, leaving a family of ten. His uncle offered to take him to Paris. There the boy exhibited white mice and collected money while the uncle played the organ. Soon the uncle had to return to Italy, and the boy, who did not want to return, was consigned to another master who took him to England. He worked five and a half years with the new master, under two contracts, and then went into business on his own. Rather than lease his organ, he bought it from his former master and paid for it over eighteen months. The man also spoke of his strong ties with his native village, especially in the early years. When he earned enough money, he regularly sent remittances back to his village: "When I had a little bit of money I was obliged to send it home to my broder in Italy, for to keep him, you know." To a great extent this attachment to the village distinguished the Italian street musicians from the other performers in London. The English musicians interviewed by Mayhew were committed to their occupations for life, and they spoke fatalistically about being left to die in the St Giles Workhouse. The Parmesans, however, like the Germans, were migrants. They did not intend to spend a lifetime as street performers, although in some cases they ended up doing so. But their intention was to return to the peasant farm with a nest-egg, to perpetuate the traditional peasant way of life.[13]

From the beginning of the nineteenth century, both the barrel-organ and Italian street musicians seem to have received a mixed reception from the English public. In *The Miseries of Human Life*, published in 1806, Rev. J. Beresford alluded to the organ-grinders or ballad singers "of the basest degree ... exhausting their whole stock of dissonance within two or three yards of your ill-starr'd ears. Yet you cannot drive or even fee them away as they are paid, for torturing you, by some barbarians at the next door."[14]

The objections to the noise made by the musicians grew more and more virulent throughout the nineteenth century. However, some people enjoyed the music. One of the early laudatory tracts about them was published in William Hones's *Everyday Book* for 1825. Under a drawing of three Italian musicians, Hone wrote a poetic caption:

Italian Minstrels in London at Xmas 1825
Ranged in a row with guitars slung
Before them thus they played and sung:
Their instruments and choral voice
Bid each glad guest still more rejoice;
And each guest wished again to hear
Their wild guitars and voices clear.

It did not take long for this charm to wear off. The introduction of the children, and their increasing presence during the 1830s as street musicians or as animal exhibitors, gave a bad name to the musicians, especially the masters. More important, the growing opposition of Londoners to street noise brought an end to their romance with the quaint minstrels.[15]

The public's frustration with the noise was expressed in print from the turn of the century. The campaign to bring the noise to an end emerged in full force a few decades later. In the 1840s, 1850s, and 1860s, the pages of the *Times* and other newspapers frequently featured articles, letters to the editor, and editorials complaining about the street noise. These usually referred to the musicians, or, more specifically, to "those Savoyard fiends" and "filthy Germans." The complaints can be summarized briefly: the noise from the musicians was incessant; the music was classified as noise because it was loud, tedious, repetitive, or out of tune; the law on street noise was vague, and either it should be changed or judges should be less liberal in its interpretation.[16]

One individual who wrote to the *Times* in 1843 signed himself "One who Loves Not Hurdy-Gurdies." He was annoyed not only because his street was "the most favourite haunt of perambulating organs," but also "because there are a few performers who put their pipes and wires out of tune, producing miserable dissonance, and with these same ventralgic instruments besiege my window for an indefinite time, smiling when I appear to motion them away, and persisting in their *charivari*." In 1855 "PQR" complained to the editor of the same paper about the "touters, organ grinders, street shows, and costermongers [who] combine in raising a perfect Babel of sounds and cries, which are the curse of every street in London." He also called for a change in the laws because policemen did not know what to do; some officers would tell the organ-grinders to move on, while others did not believe they had the power to do so. A few days later, "An Industrious Man" wrote to complain about the "ridiculously-dressed vagabonds known as Ethiopian serenaders" (he also mistakenly referred to them as mountebanks). He felt that judges were too liberal in their interpretation of the noise by-laws: even if only one person was disturbed, the musician should still be convicted.[17]

The word "Babel" seems to have been a favourite among the citizens frustrated by the street musicians. The *Times* could not resist the analogy in one editorial. It feared that the din created by the hawkers and itinerant musicians was "so great as not only to affect Londoners with a chronic irritation which is destructive of health as well as of pleasure, but also to convey to strangers their invariable idea of the metropolis, expressed in that name suggestive of deafening noises and meaningless clamour – Babel." In fact, the editors made a telling point. One of the characteristics of the mid-nineteenth century city was its noise, which to a great extent was thought to be caused by the itinerants, most of whom were migrants into London. Although these "nomads" might be despised by upper middle-class families, they had become part of the great city by mid-century.[18]

By the 1860s the street noise created by the musicians was being attacked on various fronts; however, the suonatori ambulanti found their nemeses in two individuals – the inventor Charles Babbage, and the member of Parliament and brewing magnate Michael Thomas Bass. In 1863 Bass attempted to introduce the issue in the House of Commons. Because he received an encouraging public response, he decided to publish some of the correspondence he had received. The collection, published in 1864 and entitled *Street Music in the Metropolis*, contained thirty-two letters from the public, only "a few" of the total received by Bass. The booklet also included newspaper editorials, magistrates' decisions, and parliamentary proceedings that dealt with the problem.

Bass's main argument was that the law had to be reformed. The laws regarding street music were at that time to be found in (1839) 2 & 3 Vict., c. 47, sections 57 and 63, and were clarified for London officers in a police order of 17 December 1859. Street musicians could not be removed by a constable "unless at the request of an inhabitant on account of illness of an inmate of the house, or for other reasonable cause." If the stated cause was other than illness, the constable had to report the cause to his sergeant, and obtain instructions from his superiors. If complaints were lodged against the constable for removing the musicians, the householder had to appear as a witness before the magistrate. If a musician continued to play after being ordered to depart by a constable, the constable had to record the musician's name and address. This law, of course, favoured the musician. Only a householder could ask the musician to leave, and the constable had to catch the musician in the act of playing. If his name was recorded, he could always give a false identity and address.[19]

The judicial treatment of the organ-grinders depended on the magistrate's reading of the law. The reported cases before 1864 indicate that the minstrels were fined as often as they were released. Bass recounted the case of Antonio Pentulai, charged with annoying Fredrick Stanford in front of Stanford's home in Langham Place by playing an organ. Antonio was fined five shillings. In late 1864 Antonio Taglioni, a native of Piacenza, was charged by Charles Babbage with playing an organ in front of his home while Babbage was sick in bed. A servant had been sent out to order Antonio away. The judge fined Antonio a hefty forty shillings. In another case, when Antonelli and Carlo Manfredi persisted in annoying the residents of Bedford Square in January 1863, one of those residents had them arrested because they were playing their instruments while he was trying to dress. The judge dismissed the case because he felt that an organ could not disturb one's dressing.[20]

Bass's book, the *Times,* and Babbage's memoirs are replete with instances of frustrated middle-class professionals or scholars lambasting the ubiquitous street musicians, sympathetic judges who dismissed charges against musicians, and MPs who would not pass more stringent laws. Babbage appealed to the Home Office and finally to the Court of Queen's Bench to overrule the judgment of one Marylebone magistrate who "possibly ... thinks that all Italian music is high art, and therefore ought to be excused." The secretary of the London Mechanics' Institute complained that the classes and the public meetings at the Chancery Lane offices were constantly disrupted by "nigger melodies and much worse music matters"; however, the officers of the institution could not call a summons (lay charges) because they were "not householders within the meaning of the Act," and therefore could not order the musicians to stop performing.[21]

The determination of the upper middle class to put an end to the street music trade was reflected in the mid-Victorian tendency to segregate the urban milieu. All of the correspondence published by Bass came from desirable London addresses – Philpot Lane, Manchester Square, Hyde Park, Highbury New Park, Grosvenor Square, Morgate Street, Little Campden House, Trevor Square, Kensington, Hampstead, and St John's Wood, among others. The very wealthy were immune from the street din: "It is true that the inhabitants of the largest dwellings in London are somewhat less incommoded from this cruel nuisance, by the fact of their houses being generally more or less inaccessible in the rear of them." The houses of merchants, professionals, and scholars became the victims of the organ-grinders and the German bands. "The brass bands and organs, the Savoyards and German vagabonds," argued Bass in the House, "are not to be found in the alleys and courts, but in the squares and handsome streets."[22]

The musicians had a good sense of the importance of class divisions to their remuneration. As competition grew in the 1850s and 1860s, the German and Italian wanderers did not rely solely on the coins of passers-by. Rather, they resorted to a form of extortion. They played their instruments relentlessly in upper middle-class neighbourhoods, repeating melodies ad nauseam, out of tune, if necessary, until the owner of the house finally bribed them to leave. "The German bands are not paid in pence but in silver and gold," lamented Bass. "The organs are more moderate in their extortions, in proportion as their power of annoyance is less, but you must pay both, and all day long." The organ-grinders were assisted by spiteful neighbours or members of the lower classes. A number of cases came to court, usually involving the mathematician and inventor Charles Babbage, who argued that the street organist was paid to play in front of his house or his neighbour's house by the neighbour himself. The frustrated Babbage described a typical scene on his street:

Some of my neighbours have derived great pleasure from inviting musicians, of various tastes and countries, to play before my windows ..., even with the accompaniment of the voice divine, from the lips of little shoeless children, urged on by their ragged parents to join in a chorus rather disrespectful to their philosophic neighbour ... and I have been obliged to find a policeman to ascertain the address of the offender. In the meantime the crowd of young children, urged on by their parents, and backed at a judicious distance by a set of vagabonds, forms quite a noisy mob, following me as I pass along shouting rather uncomplimentary epithets.

Although some politicians denied it, the organ-grinders could always find support in the poorer classes. "The fact is," stated one editorial, "that the rude majority of the inhabitants of London do like organ-grinding and kindred noises, which the more refined minority call nuisances. Even in respectable streets and squares, the servants covertly encourage those performances which drive their masters and mistresses to desperation."[23]

Street Music in the Metropolis was published just a few months after Bass had given notice that he would reintroduce a bill to control street music in London. On 3 May 1864 Bass outlined his proposed legislation to the House. It differed significantly from its predecessor in one aspect: while under the 1839 act only the householder "could require any street musician to depart from the neighbourhood of the house ... on account of the illness of any inmate of such house," Bass's act gave that power to the householder, his servant, or any police constable of the Metropolitan Police District. The ensuing debate was rowdy, jocular, and at times serious. Lord Fermoy (Marylebone) and Sir John Shelley (Westminster) were the two members most adamantly opposed to the legislation. Gladstone, the chancellor of the exchequer, also voiced his disapproval of a measure that would give veto power to the despotic desires of one individual. This led the member from Northamptonshire West to remark that the "Chancellor of the Exchequer opposed the Bill as a friend of the Italian cause, forgetting that Savoy had recently been annexed to France, and that barrel-organs were not included in the French treaty." Sir Robert Peel voiced his support for a second reading of the bill. He lived next door to a religious association which was visited every Sunday morning by an Italian organ-grinder who constantly played the Hundredth Psalm. More tolerant than Babbage, Peel did not chase the man away, but rather instructed his servant to ask whether he had any other psalm-tune; "but he said he had none other in his repertoire." [24]

On 29 June, after Bass's book was published, the discussion continued in the House. After examining the question whether Punch and his accompanying instruments would be outlawed by the proposed legislation and whether the special amendment should guarantee the protection of this national symbol, the House tabled the bill for a third reading. The bill was passed in a brief session on 7 July.[25]

One of the perplexing characteristics of this debate was the almost complete absence of the "child slavery" issue. Although probably a minority of the children played an organ (as opposed to playing another instrument, or exhibiting animals), they still formed a significant part of the street music problem. Moreover, almost all of their padroni (Bass's collection has one of the early references to this Italian word for "masters") were organ-grinders, and might have been vulnerable if the English public had also attacked them on this front. One letter to Bass indicated that the street music trade was "not a charity but a kind of slave trade. The boys imported never get through a second winter. A *certain* vice is brought from Italy, and no doubt practiced in and about Mutton Hill and Clerkenwell." There was also a reference to German boys being inveigled from their home towns to perform in the brass bands. Otherwise, the "child slavery" problem did not arise even as a minor issue. The street noise, the class tensions, and, occasionally, the filth of Italian and German foreigners were the significant questions.[26]

This did not mean that the children were totally ignored by English society or by its charitable organizations, although they were placed in a different category from their masters or adult colleagues. While the organ-grinder was perceived as a nuisance and was continually brought before the courts for creating street noise, the organ-boy was from the very beginning viewed as a beggar. Of course, reformers often alluded to the serious injustices of the padrone-child relationship, but there was no law to prohibit this form of indenture. Thus, when the child was brought before the magistrate, the hearing always focused on whether he or she was guilty of begging. Perhaps this was a result of the children's early association with the London Society for the Suppression of

Mendicity. The society, which was the first British organization to take an interest in the boys, viewed their work as begging, and officers of the society apprehended the children on those grounds. We have already mentioned the case of seventeen-year old A.J., who was taken into custody by society officers in 1821 for "begging" with two dogs and a drum. Five years later, fourteen-year old P.G. was found "exhibiting a monkey, with which he was importuning every lady that passed, who, in order to get rid of him, generally gave money."[27] At the time of his arrest, the lad was carrying £21 7s 6d in earnings. The boys continued to be surveyed by the society, but as time went by the charge of mendicancy was questioned by a number of judges. Some of those cases will be examined presently.

During the 1850s the British authorities did not seem particularly concerned with the problem of Italian street children in their cities, despite requests from the Sardinian government for help in controlling the growing problem. The Sardinian minister, V.E. d'Azeglio, wrote to Lord Malmesbury at the British Foreign Office in 1852 "au sujet des [sic] nombreux enfans [sic] italiens joueurs d'orgues de barbarie, qui sont éspandus dans les rues de Londres pour exploiter la charité publique au profit de leur maître." D'Azeglio hoped that the Foreign Office might encourage the Home Office to co-operate in a scheme whereby precise information on children brought before the courts might be gathered "avant de rendre un jugement qui est dans l'intérêt de l'humanité." The children could then be given passage to France and from there back to Italy.

Malmesbury agreed that the immigration of Italian mendicant children should be prevented, and he promised that the Home Office would co-operate with the Italian government as long as the latter bore the cost of returning the children to their homes. However, he also warned the Italian minister that the solution was not straightforward, because the boys, "while in England, are under the same protection of the Law as British Subjects." D'Azeglio accepted his suggestion that the onus should be on the Sardinian government to prevent the emigration of the children.[28]

As in Paris and New York, the cause of the Italian child street musicians did not really become an important issue in London until the middle to late 1860s. The impetus for reformers in the city to take an interest in the children seems to have come as a result of two developments. One was the growing number of children. During the 1860s, as was mentioned in chapter 1, the main source of the migration shifted from the countryside of Parma in the north of Italy to the towns south of Rome, near Sora. The more visible presence of these children and, perhaps even more disturbing for Londoners, their swarthy looks and foreign dress drew the attention of reformers. Just as important as the arrival of this new contingent was the foundation of the Italian Benevolent Society in London in 1861.

The Italian Benevolent Society was conceived and instituted by the Italian minister in London, Emanuele d'Azeglio. D'Azeglio had been so moved at the sight of Italian organ boys begging from him that he was determined to put an end to the trade. The charter of the institution gives us a good indication of the rationale behind the society, and perhaps even of some of its influential sources. The association was committed to providing for Italians in need of food, lodgings, or heating ("pane, alloggio e fuoco in comune") by means of tickets ("per mezzo di appositi biglietti"; that is, begging letters); to help them find employment; to help them repatriate; to provide the services of a physician or surgeon, or to provide for burial costs in needy cases; and "to provide nocturnal refuge, especially for boys found wandering the streets late at night." The annual report for 1863 contained an addendum to the original charter. It noted that in earlier days children of Italians who had been in England for many years were to be seen wandering the streets of London, but that recently this begging had ended. Now the Italian beggars in the city were "imposters, or were sent to beg professionally by their masters." Italian mendicancy in London, stated the report, would cease when Italians in London stopped giving alms to Italian beggars, and instead directed them to the Italian Benevolent Society.[29]

This approach, of course, was identical to that of the London Society for the Suppression of Mendicity, founded in 1818. That society had called for an end to indiscriminate alms-giving and for the introduction of a begging-letter system by which the public would direct beggars to the society rather than give alms directly. The two most important assumptions of the Italian Benevolent Society are suggested in the charter itself, but are even more apparent in the correspondence of the agency in the ensuing years. The first of these was that the children and adults who played music or exhibited animals on the streets were beggars, in that they produced nothing of value. The second was that begging dealt a blow to Italian national pride. A country about to attain the status of a great power could not embarrass itself by allowing its citizens to beg on the streets of foreign capitals. Thus in July 1861 the secretary of the society paid for the young Domenico Bellagamba's repatriation as far as Boulogne, "because I thought that here with his vile trade of street organist he was shaming the fatherland." By exposing the trade to reform agencies, government, and the press, the Italian Benevolent Society helped impress on the English public, and especially on the authorities, the idea that street musicians, and especially child street musicians, were essentially beggars.[30]

The police were indeed convinced by this viewpoint, and they co-operated with the Italian Benevolent Society in a program to stamp out the trade. On 7 December 1861, just a few months after the founding of the agency, a police order was distributed to London officers: "Should any Italian boy be given into custody on a charge of vagrancy, or be found begging in the public streets by the Police during any hour of the night, he is to be taken into custody and the magistrate before whom the charge is heard is to be acquainted that the Marquis d'Azeglio, the Italian minister 23 Park Lane is prepared (on application being made to him) to send any such boy to his own country."

Many children were repatriated through this program: 43 in 1864, 14 in 1865, 24 in 1866, 11 in 1867, and 10 in 1868. The number of Italians apprehended for begging by the Society for the Suppression of Mendicity was 5 in 1864, 43 in 1865, 45 in 1866, 80 in 1867, and 38 in 1868. This suggests that although the two agencies were running similar programs, they nevertheless were independent of one another.[31]

Although by the 1860s Londoners had become used to the sight of the Italian children entertaining in the streets, they became especially concerned with their growing presence from the beginning of that decade. In the early 1860s the children from Parma reached the peak of their migration to London and to all of England. By the late 1860s they were surpassed by the waifs from Terra di Lavoro. Throughout those years and into the 1870s the sole concern of magistrates and reformers with regard to the young migrants was their vagrancy.

As with many other social problems, the public became aware of the children through some of the more sensational cases that came before the courts. The many children who were repatriated during the 1860s by the Italian Benevolent Society all had a hearing before a magistrate, so that some of the cases would have caught the public eye. Perhaps the most important case following Joseph Leonardi's death in the St Giles Workhouse in 1845 was that of Giuseppe Bassini, heard by Magistrate d'Eyncourt in September 1865. In fact, the charge of begging was not brought against Bassini but against his padrone, Antonio Viasani. Viasani was charged under the old Vagrant Act of 1824 (5 Geo. IV, c. 83, section 3) which stated that "every person wandering abroad, or placing himself or herself in any public place, street, highway, court, or passage, to beg or gather alms, or causing, or procuring, or encouraging any child so to do, shall be deemed an idle and disorderly person within the true intent and meaning of the act." Viasani was convicted on 30 September of that year, but he appealed the conviction on the grounds that the child, Bassini, was not proved to be a child.

Giuseppe had been brought to London the previous April by Lorenzo Segadelli, and had been handed over to Viasani at 11 Saffron Hill, Hatton Garden, where the padrone kept other boys. Giuseppe's father was dead, and his mother lived in Italy. He had no other relations in England. In the witness-box, Bassini claimed that he was sixteen years of age, although he could not prove it. He appeared to be about twelve. Within the meaning of the act, a child was anyone under the age of fourteen; however, it was up to the panel of eight judges to decide whether or not Giuseppe was a child, and they concurred that he was under the age of fourteen. Viasani's lawyer contended that the court could not accept part of a witness's evidence – in this case, Bassini's – and reject the rest. The justices stated that they were allowed to do so, and the conviction was affirmed.[32] The Viasani case was significant in that it set a precedent for other charges involving padroni. Viasani was the first padrone to be charged, not with kidnapping or inveigling children, but with causing them to beg. It is puzzling that the ruling was rarely invoked until 1877, when new developments led to a higher conviction rate.

At the root of the problem was the lack of stringent laws that would curb the activities of the padrone by regulating his relationship to the children. Consider the tragic story of Anna Bacigalupo, from the town of Nè, near Chiavari. In 1864, when Anna was thirteen, her father leased her to Giovanni Tiscornia, a thirty-nine-year-old townsman, to play music on the streets of London for eight lire a month in the first year and ten lire a month in the second year. On 1 June 1867, at age sixteen, Anna died in the Royal Free Hospital of pneumonia brought on by typhoid fever and venereal disease. Tiscornia was never charged with an offence. What is particularly shocking is that he had the audacity to keep a list of all of Anna's medical and lodging expenses during her sickness, and to submit it, after her death, to the Italian consul, Baron Heath, for reimbursement.

Equally tragic was the story of Carminello Ada. The five-year-old boy was brought from his home town to London in about 1869. Soon after his arrival his padrone began to get upset with the child because he did not meet his daily earnings quota. In a rage, the padrone one day suspended the child by his hands and legs from the ceiling with a rope. Upon seeing the boy begin to bleed, the master went into a fit and began biting the boy in the forearms and ribs. He left the child in that condition and fled from the city. Carminello was brought to the St Pancras Workhouse by officials of the Italian Benevolent Society, where he died a few days later.[33]

The Italian Benevolent Society, of course, did not restrict itself to the exceptional cases. From its inception in 1861 the society interested itself in every case involving Italian child street musicians, and indeed extended its help to all needy Italians in London. One of the first programs organized by the directors was the formulation of a set of criteria for giving passage assistance to destitute Italians who wished to return to Italy. Consideration was given only to applicants who had been in Britain for at least six months (those stopping off in London on the way back from the Americas or elsewhere were ineligible), and who had a legitimate trade. An exception was made for street musicians. They would be invited into the workhouse, and would receive a free trip only as far as the French shore, "so as not to have the expenses of the Society aggravated by undeserving souls; yet, all in all, it is worth our while to send them off towards Italy, because here they are a dishonour to their fatherland."[34] With this decision, the committee of directors regulated what the society had actually been doing for some months.

As we saw earlier, the society's officials worked in conjunction with the police from 1861. They also sought to advise magistrates on the best course of action for dealing with the Italian children. In January 1862 three children were placed by one police magistrate in the Kensington Workhouse while he decided what to do about their case. Only one of the three boys agreed to be sent back to Italy. Sebastiano S. Faenza, a priest and an official of the society, told officials that the boy would probably go only as far as France. He also wrote letters to the other police magistrates, asking that in the future they postpone these cases for a day so that they could get in touch with him for advice.[35] In fact, officers of the Italian Benevolent Society began attending all the vagrancy trials of the Italian children.

When Pio Melia, another Italian priest and an official of the society, attended the next hearing of the same three boys, he even interested the magistrate in proceeding with charges against their padrone, who was in Italy at the time recruiting more children. Nothing came of that. The padrone, Giovanni Battista Massa, apparently heard of the threat, and sent his wife and twenty-three-year-old Domenico Rivara to accompany "a caravan of children" between the ages of eight and fifteen from their home town near Chiavari to 2 Eyre Place, Eyre Street Hill, just off Leather Lane in Holborn. Pio Melia, who had been keeping track of them, tried to find a way to charge the padrone or to stifle the trade; he was unsuccessful.[36]

In its early years, the society devoted much attention to the children. Officials stopped them on the streets, attended their hearings, questioned them, tried to gather all possible information about their backgrounds and about their padroni, attempted to prosecute the padroni, advised police officers and magistrates, and gave money, clothing, medical care, lodgings, and a free trip as far as Paris to the children whenever the need was justified. When the directors found that even these approaches were not effective, they considered opening an office in the West End where they could bring in the children. That plan was replaced by a more practical decision to credit 2s 6d to police in the West End or to officials of the society for the Suppression of Mendicity for each child brought before a magistrate on a charge of begging.

The Italian community in London was not very large in the 1860s – of about 2,000 people, 400 were carpenters and joiners, picture-framers, looking-glass manufacturers, glaziers, and makers of optical instruments and barometers all from the towns near Como. Some 200 Swiss Italians from Ticino worked in the city's confectionaries and ice-cream shops. Lucca's plaster figurine-makers and vendors totalled about 250, many of them children; many of the men lived with their wives and families in the city. Six hundred Italian organ-grinders walked the London streets in the early 1860s, many of them children or youths, managed by about 10 padroni. In the late 1860s the immigrants from towns near Parma and Piacenza were joined by children from towns near Sora, in the province of Caserta. Very few immigrants from Potenza came to Britain in those years. The colony also included about 250 "professional adventurers and miserable travellers, and others waiting for any sort of employment." The population had not changed much over the previous ten years. One irritated reader of the *Times* noted in 1853 that "if we take the Italian residents in London, including all the image-makers [from Lucca] and image-adorers, Signor Mazzini and his exiled friends, for whom of course the 'Holy Father' is anxious to provide, shall we have 2,000?" However, the Italian colony mushroomed over the ensuing twenty-five years. In 1879 the Italian Anglican missionary in the city estimated its population at about 10,000, "engaged chiefly in sculptors' studios, in image-making, picture-frame moulding, and stone-cutting. About 2,000, it is believed, earn a living by organ-playing."[37]

From the 1820s until the 1890s, Italians resided chiefly in Holborn, on Great Saffron Hill, Little Saffron Hill, Hatton Garden, Leather Lane, and Eyre Street Hill, all off the Clerkenwell Road. That area, along with St Giles, which was adjacent to it, had been the residence of the destitute Irish from the eighteenth century. It was in the 1860s, as the "organ-grinders' colony" (a term used by the city press) grew, that Saffron Hill became better known among Londoners as the Italian quarter rather than as an Irish slum or "old Fagin's stomping-grounds." Until the 1870s the police reports on child vagrants and noisy organ-grinders almost always showed their addresses on Saffron Hill, or especially on Eyre Street Hill. An article in the city press in August 1864 briefly discussed some of the problems discovered by sanitary officers of the Holborn district. The great offenders were to be found on the two hills, and they were organ-grinders charged with overcrowding. In Eyre

Place the health officer, Dr Gibbon, found fourteen organ-grinders in one room, "and not content with that, beds were made up on the staircases." Gibbon found the stench unbearable, and he came down with a fever one week later.[38] The tenant of Nos 1 and 2 Eyre Place, Angelo Collarossa, was summoned to Clerkenwell Police Court, but the summons was postponed for a month when it was found that many of the occupants had returned to Italy. (This was the location where Massa, the padrone pursued by Father Melia, kept his children.)

Eyre Street Hill remained the most notorious of the Italian quarters for many years. It was from there, in 1845, that the young Joseph Leonardi was taken before his death in the St Giles Workhouse; it was from there that Anna Bacigalupo was taken to die in the London Free Hospital in 1867, and there that Carminello Ada was tortured. And it was there that health inspectors located the city's worst overcrowding. In 1870, one doctor reported sixteen persons in the kitchen of one Italian lodging-house; he was told that fifty persons slept at Nos 1 and 2 Eyre Place, the infamous house formerly owned by Collarossa. Lucio Sponza has traced the residences and activities of a number of Italian dwellers in the neighbourhood. One of these was Luigi Rabbiotti, a shopkeeper and former padrone, and most certainly the master of Joseph Leonardi. Between 1841 and 1871 Rabbiotti lived on Laystall Street, just off Leather Lane. In 1841 he was listed on the census returns as married, thirty-one years of age, with no children. His eighteen-year old brother Antonio was listed separately even though he lived in the same house. Under his name were twenty-five young musicians.[39]

Although the *Holborn Journal* and the medical officer of health had been investigating these neighbourhoods for years, the best-known report was filed in October 1879 by the medical journal, *The Lancet*. The report of the Lancet Special Commission on the Sanitary Condition of the Italian Quarters was remarkably balanced for its time. It dismissed protests about the organ noise, arguing that the noise had "helped considerably to spread some knowledge and taste for good music among the poorer classes whose opportunities of hearing any sort of music was very limited." *Lancet* had already inspected penny-ices made by Italians and found them, contrary to popular opinion, safe for consumption. And as for the child musicians, "the plump cheeks and bright smiles of the Italian boys we meet in the streets may lead us to infer that the cases of cruelty are at least somewhat exaggerated." The investigators even gave honourable mention to the property owners for being so courteous as to allow them easy access to the houses. Although no children were reported in the houses visited by this commission, the Eyre Street Hill neighbourhood was still the prime residential quarter for the "little slaves," even though some had moved out to Hammersmith by then.[40]

The *Lancet* investigators first visited Luigi Rabbiotti's house on Laystall Street. His house was "tolerably clean" because he had "had the good fortune to secure an English wife." His basement and the house in the back, however, were a different matter. These were sublet to organ-grinders. The basement "was formed into a sort of kitchen, with shelves along the walls where the barrel-organs might be deposited, a long table for the rolling out of macaroni ... The floor, ceilings, and walls were black with smoke and dirt." The house in the back was leased to a padrone. Technically, Luigi did not charge rent to his workers, but he obviously received the equivalent from leasing the organ or taking his share of the daily proceeds. He taught his men to deny to authorities that they paid rent, because that would bring him within the Common Lodging-House Act. Dirt and overcrowding were the two main problems in this house. The floors had not been swept in two years. The windows were so dusty that one could not see through them. The house had no furniture, only double beds wherever they could be fitted. Two or even three men slept in each bed. In another house on Eyre Street Hill the inspectors found one bedroom with three double beds, in which slept a woman and child, a padrone by himself, and a married couple. The padrone admitted squeezing twenty-seven persons into this one house. Each room had three double beds and some also had a crib.[41]

As the *Lancet* commission's report and other reports suggest, these were the normal conditions in which most Italian street musicians, children or adults, lived. From what we know about the earnings of the organ-grinders, they could have afforded better living quarters. But as Charles McFarlane indicated in the 1830s, these men and women lived within very narrow bounds; their prime concern was to earn enough money to return home and perpetuate the traditional values of the home town – owning a plot of land, supporting a family, purchasing dowries. These musicians lived in London, as did their counterparts in Paris, New York, and Moscow, in suspension, and any living conditions, no matter how undignified or degrading, were acceptable as long as they were cheap and efficacious in meeting long-term goals.[42]

This was the case not only for street musicians but also for other Italian tradesmen, many of whom lived in the same neighbourhood. The figurine-makers and vendors from Lucca and the penny-ice men also lived their lives with the same sojourner's mentality. If the returns of the particular trade were not sufficient to meet long-term goals, the migrant might switch trades temporarily or permanently. In bad seasons the ice-cream man turned to organ-grinding, or vice-versa. If there were no alternatives, the migrant would go elsewhere with his trade, or return home. In its report, the *Lancet* noted that "the cold, wet summer [of 1879] has proved more disastrous in its effects on the penny-ice trade, and an enormous amount of Italians have returned to their native country to await a more propitious season."[43]

The Holborn neighbourhoods remained important districts for itinerant Italian tradesmen throughout most of the century. Even though the provenance of the street musicians changed over the years, the residences were passed on from group to group. The parmigiani of the 1820s sold or leased their houses to the next generation of parmigiani in the 1840s and 1850s. In the 1870s Eyre Street Hill was largely occupied by street musicians from towns near Sora – Val Rotondo or Picinisco. This had much to do with the fact that an Italian itinerant tradesman, on his arrival in London, sought out Italian boarding-houses in the city, which in the mid-nineteenth century were to be found on Saffron Hill. Mayhew's Italian "gun exerciser," or the hurdy-gurdy player from the area near Dijon, and others remarked that they had stayed in Italian lodgings on Saffron Hill when they had first come to London. As the old performers retired to their home towns in Italy, the newcomers took over the houses where they had previously been lodgers.[44] Saffron Hill and Eyre Street Hill also formed the nucleus of an information system for Italian padroni and street musicians across London, and indeed throughout the British Isles. Bass and Babbage both complained that whenever a street organist was sought for giving a false address, or for making a nuisance, his padrone would send him off "in campagna," on a travelling stint through some of the smaller towns. One London boy interviewed by the *Times* in 1831 told of performing with his dancing dog in Brighton. In fact, many organ-grinders and animal-exhibitors from London were to be seen in that resort town; it remained one of the lucrative sites in the country for street entertainers into the twentieth century.[45]

Because the Paris-London route was the road most travelled by Italian street musicians, the English capital provided vital information to the trade. Most musicians went through London to Liverpool on their way to New York, Chicago, Rio de Janeiro, or Montreal for one or more seasons. Those coming back from America brought news about the trade in the major cities there. Those coming through London on their way to America brought news about economic conditions or police and immigration surveillance in Paris, Marseilles, and other European cities. The French hurdy-gurdy man interviewed by Mayhew performed in Paris at first, and then moved on to the channel towns of Calais and Boulogne: "It is there that I had the idea to come to England. Many persons counselled us, told us that in England we should gain a great deal of money."[46]

The importance of London to the street music trade was reinforced by the establishment of barrel-organ manufacturers in the city. Until the mid-1860s, street organists depended on their padroni to supply them with instruments. Those organs were acquired by the padrone or an agent in other European cities. We have already discussed, for example, the Gaviolis, originally from Modena, who opened an organ firm in Paris in 1845. The exhibitor of mechanical figures interviewed by Mayhew bought his first music box in Paris. At the time of his interview (in the 1850s) he was operating a music box which he had had sent from Germany.[47] The oldest London manufacturer of barrel-organs was Longman & Broderip, founded around the turn of the eighteenth century. One of the partners in this firm was the famed keyboard composer and performer, Muzio Clementi. When the partnership dissolved, he set up his own business in 1802 at Cheapside, and in 1820 he took in another partner.

The most important name in the barrel-organ industry in England was that of a former apprentice of Gavioli, Giuseppe Chiappa. Chiappa started his business in London in 1864, in the midst of an organ-grinders' colony at 5 Little Saffron Hill. After moving to

New York to open a fairground organ company, he returned to London in 1877 and began to produce various types of mechanical instruments. The new firm was still located in the Italian quarter, this time at 6 Little Bath Street (now 31 Eyre Street Hill), just down the street from the most notorious boarding-houses of the padroni. Among the many instruments the company manufactured and repaired were the barrel-organs and, later, barrel pianos used by the local street musicians. Other companies followed in Britain, such as Chiaro Fratis's at 5 Farringdon Road, in 1876. Peter Varetto opened an organ factory at Manchester in about 1885.[48] Chiappa & Company, however, remained the most important firm; the business closed in 1983.

The men and boys who went out in campagna, then, usually received information and even instructions from London or, more specifically, from Holborn. They could return to that neighbourhood for new instruments or to repair old organs. Being in campagna meant being on the road, or in a small town, or perhaps even in a large town temporarily. Although at first the term referred to a "campaign" outside the home town, it eventually came to include trips outside a major nucleus of the trade, such as London, but within its orbit – that is, in the "countryside."

During the 1860s and 1870s the child street musicians were reported in many towns in England. The Charity Organisation Society in 1877 published a special report on "The Employment of Italian Children for Mendicant and Immoral Purposes." In compiling the report, the authors received information on Italian child street musicians in 108 cities, towns and villages in thirty-four counties (shires) in England; in nine counties in Wales; and in sixteen counties in Scotland and the Isle of Man. The head-constable of the last district reported that at least three parties of Italian child musicians had been in Douglas the previous summer (1876). The first group consisted of a middle-aged man and three boys aged twelve to fifteen. The second party included a man of about thirty years, and two boys and two girls between twelve and sixteen years. The third party was a fifteen-year-old girl and her twelve-year-old brother. According to the constable, the siblings, whose parents lived in Liverpool, earned more money than the other two groups combined. The men in the first two bands stayed at home and cooked for the children. The children returned home with their earnings daily, and "if not considered enough, these men used to get very angry and sometimes slapped them."[49]

The children, of course, did not stay for any great length of time in most of these towns and villages, except in the larger cities. Most of the reports indicated that the child musicians came through a given area a few times a year. The chief constable of Nottingham instructed his force to apprehend Italian children for begging. On the day he gave the orders fifteen children came into town with their padroni, followed by five more children the next day. The magistrate did not punish the children, for "they hardly came under the heading of 'begging,' as they play an instrument." In Forfar (Forfarshire, Scotland), the wife of a lodging-house keeper told the superintendent of police that four Italians had lodged at her place: a man between the ages of twenty and thirty, a girl of about sixteen, and two boys aged ten and twelve. "The girl and the two boys appeared to stand in great dread of the man in charge. The girl was very angry with me when I would not allow her to sleep in the same bedroom with the man and the two boys." The troupe remained in the town for four days. The superintendent of the Dublin Metropolitan Police reported that no Italian children could be found in the streets of his city, that in fact very few Italian organ-grinders and no German bands were to be seen in Dublin. "It is presumed that the strong prejudice which exists in the humbler classes in this country against Italians on account of the occupation of Rome, and against Germans from the time of the Franco-Prussian war, has the effect of keeping those itinerant musicians away."[50]

Although the children were young and on the road, they were nevertheless always aware of information important to their trade. Those children who escaped from their padroni knew enough to head for London to inquire about returning home, and some even went directly to the Italian Benevolent Society for help. On 30 June 1864, for example, Domenico Montana, aged sixteen, and Domenico Casagrande, aged twenty, both of whom seemed much younger than they claimed to be, walked into the society's offices. The boys were from San Colombano, Chiavari, and had been brought to England twenty-six months previously by a townsman based in Manchester, Andrea Monteverde. They were to receive ten and eleven Genoese lire a month respectively, provided that they completed a thirty-month contract. As the indenture period drew to a close, however, the padrone began to beat the boys severely. His plan was to force the boys to leave so that he would not have to complete his part of the bargain. The boys did leave, and they walked, begging, all the way from Manchester to London. Because they were illiterate, an acquaintance wrote a letter on their behalf to the padrone, demanding their wages; however, Monteverde refused to pay them, stating that the boys had left before the contract period was over. The Italian Benevolent Society paid for the youths' passages to London and looked into the possibility of prosecuting Monteverde lest he should treat other children in the same manner.[51]

London, then, remained the centre of the street music trade until the end of the century. Many of the organ-grinders and padroni moved their headquarters from Holborn to Hammersmith during the 1870s, although Holborn remained an important residential centre for the entertainers. It is not known exactly why Hammersmith was chosen as a new area of residence. Even though *Lancet* noted in 1879 that Italian street musicians "will return in the evening to Saffron-Hill, and huddle together with their fellow-countrymen, rather than live near their 'beats,' and be compelled to mingle with the English," many padroni and children had by that time already moved to Hammersmith, a residential suburb west of London, in the midst of many of the upper middle-class suburban "beats" of the street entertainers. One author suggested that the padroni moved there to avoid the truancy officers of the London School Board, who would force their children back to classes and thus hurt their trade. The reformer Charles Ribton-Turner also pointed out to Home Secretary Richard Cross in 1877 that "it is utterly impossible, when you go outside the sphere of the London School Board, to deal with the Italian children under the Elementary Education Act of 1876. It must be remembered that these children are wandering about in the higher-class streets, and the School Board officers are, as a matter of duty, more concerned in looking for children in low-class neighbourhoods, and thus there is a great difficulty in getting at these children."[52] By living in the comfortable suburb of Hammersmith, the padroni could almost certainly avoid the truancy officers and keep the children under their control.

The Hammersmith contingent, however, found it difficult to maintain anonymity. Although fewer arrests for begging were made in Hammersmith than in another suburb, Wandsworth, the case of Nicholas Corio gave the Hammersmith "organ-grinders' colony" notoriety. Corio was a seventeen-year-old organ-grinder in that suburb who had been convicted of disturbing the peace with his organ in November 1878. In January 1879 he was once again brought before the courts with his girlfriend, Alice Tomes – she for stealing a gold scarf-pin, he for accepting it with the knowledge that it was a stolen good. At trial the prosecutor described the Italian colony of Hammersmith: "There were a number of English girls there, ranging from fourteen to eighteen years of age, who had once been in service, but had been decoyed away by these Italian organ-grinders. They dressed them as *contadini* [peasants] and sent them out with the organs. If the girls brought home less than £1 per day, they were deprived of food for the night." The judge believed Tomes had been victimized by Corio. He dismissed the charges against the girl on the condition that she return home. He sentenced Corio to four months' hard labour.[53]

Over the following years some writers expressed their concern that innocent English girls were being seduced or influenced by the organ-grinders. The *Lancet* report of 1879, for example, voiced this fear. One reader of the *Times*, signing himself "A TAXPAYER," complained that "not only do the Italian organ-grinders distress the sick, studious, and really musical, but we know that they have introduced a new species of demoralization in our midst. It is high time our philanthropists bestirred themselves in behalf of the poor English girls whom these vagabonds lead to destruction." Another writer observed that the "Italians *never* bring their countrywomen to dance" at a pub on Saffron Hill frequented by organ-grinders. They preferred to dance with English and Irish girls who were working in the neighbourhood as polishers of looking-glass frames.[54]

The Corio incident (and the subsequent exposure of the Hammersmith colony), however, was only one of a number of developments that over the previous two decades had brought the public's attention to the "Italian children," or, as they became known in the 1870s, the "Italian white slaves": Besides seeing hundreds of these children on the streets, Londoners also heard about their plight either through Bass's campaign against the organ-grinding noise, or through the reports of the Society for the Suppression of Mendicity, or through the occasional article or court report in the *Times* or *Evening Standard*. Beginning in the late 1860s, after Bass's street noise measures had been passed by the House of Commons, more reports concerning the child musicians appeared in newspapers and journals. At first the articles dealt mainly with the vagrancy problem, but eventually they also became concerned with the conditions of quasi-slavery in which the children lived. Giuseppe Prato, writing in 1900 on Italians in London, suggested that the attention paid by reformers to the children's living conditions was a new tactic to rid the city of street musicians, once public clamour had subsided following the passage of Bass's bill. It is difficult to prove that the new approach was calculated, but Prato was correct in stating that the street music problem reached a new plateau in 1867 as more and more reports of the children's suffering emerged.[55]

One of the first reports of this "second wave," presented by James Greenwood in the magazine *London Society*, dealt with "The Private Life of a Public Nuisance." Greenwood visited the adult musicians at an organ-repair shop on Saffron Hill, and then followed them to the Golden Anchor, a local pub popular among the Italian street performers. Greenwood's curiosity about the minstrels probably reflected that of the London public:

Has he a wife and children? How do they employ themselves? Are the white-mice boys and the guinea-pig boys, the monkey-boys and the boys with the hurdy-gurdies the organ-grinder's children? Are those his daughters that go about with a silk handkerchief about their heads, singing and playing on a tambourine? Where is his wife? Is she still to be found working in the vineyard of the sunny South or does she reside with her "old man" on Saffron Hill, occupying a snug little room, ironing the grinder's shirt and mending his stockings and preparing something comforting and savoury for the poor fellow's supper, when at midnight he stomps in from Sydenham and Brentford?...Do the little grinders go to school?[56]

In the months following the publication of Greenwood's article, public attention focused more and more on the children rather than on the adult performers. The first important document to draw the public's attention to the children was the report of the Société Italienne de Bienfaisance in Paris, discussed in the previous chapter. On 9 April 1868, not long after the report appeared, the *Times* published an extensive summary, and could not help adding its own comments about the cause of the trade: it referred to the "policy of that Lazzarone government [presumably, the Bourbon monarchy in Naples] to encourage ignorance and discourage increase of population," as well as the "slothful, lawless, and wretched population of Basilicata" (the area most responsible for sending musicians to Paris at that time).

The Italian press in London also kept the city's Italian immigrants informed of the activities of the padroni during this period. *La Gazzetta Italiana di Londra* was published by two monarchists. Even though they admitted that the "child slavery" problem began in the happy days ("tempi felicissimi") of the Bourbons, the new statesmen were none the less to be blamed because they did not teach today's youth, as did their predecessors, about love and defence of the fatherland. In fact, Charles Vivaldi's and Giuseppe Profumo's greatest concern seemed to be that 2,000 street organists in London were not fulfilling their military duties. The editors praised the work of the Italian Benevolent Society, and urged Italians not to give indiscriminately to the children but to help liberate them by withholding alms.[57]

Amid all this publicity, the Society for the Suppression of Mendicity, which had been following the children for almost fifty years, stepped up its campaign to get them out of the city. Between 1866 and 1873 the society apprehended between thirty-four and eighty Italians annually for begging, and it can be assumed that most of these were children. In 1834, for example, when thirty-four Italians were recorded as having been assisted by the society, the annual report noted that "thirty-four Italian children have been apprehended, and though this is a less number than the corresponding return of the previous years, it is enough to show that the iniquitous trade of the *padroni* who import them ... still continues with its evil consequences." Two years previously, all of the fifty-four Italians apprehended were children.[58]

While all these reports were being published and the apprehensions were being publicized, the increasingly visible presence of the children on the streets of London drew the attention of British citizens. The turmoil of the years leading up to the Paris

Commune caused many foreigners to leave the French capital. Many of these, as well as native Frenchmen, migrated to England at that point. Among the foreigners were many street musicians, especially children, most of whom probably went through London on their way to Liverpool and on to New York and Chicago.

The British condemnation of the trade did not subside once the Italian laws of 1873 were enacted. On the contrary, the trade received even more coverage in the ensuing years. In 1874, for example, *Chambers's Journal* briefly discussed the organ boys in an article on street musicians entitled "German and Italian Vagrants." Three years later the same magazine published a second article on "Italian Vagrant Children," which discussed the plight of the children and legislation in Italy and England. In the dailies, court reports frequently appeared, discussing case after case of child street musicians tried for begging. Letters to the editor complained about the children and more often about the noise of the street organs. Thomas Barnardo, the famous director of the home for destitute and neglected children, felt compelled to contribute to the discussion. He noted that three abused Italian children had been taken into his institution at different periods. Barnardo did not call for a new law to end the trade: he simply believed that "the law relating to vagrants should be vigorously applied to adults and children."[59]

In 1876 the *Times* ran an important editorial in which it defended the Italian government against charges that it was doing nothing to stop the "Italian kidnappers." The editorial cited the Italian 1873 law and asserted that the British public was to blame for the condition of these children: "It is mainly to their ill-judged charity that the traffic is due. The English public can do more than the Government to put a stop to the trade by one simple measure. Let them never give a farthing more to one of these children."[60]

In 1877 the special committee of the Charity Organisation Society released its report. The document, along with a visit by Sir Charles Trevelyan and other members of the Charity Organisation Society and the Italian Benevolent Society to the home secretary inspired a new wave of interest in the children. All the national newspapers discussed the document and the visit. Naturally, so did the *Charity Organisation Reporter*.

In Parliament, one member demanded that the House be informed about whether the Foreign Office had had any correspondence with the Italian government regarding the importation of Italian children. Sir Henry Drummond Wolff, the British ambassador to Madrid, was genuinely concerned with the problem of child vagabondage. He asked that if any correspondence on the topic did exist, it be presented to Parliament. A few days later a blue book was produced on "Correspondence Respecting the Introduction Into and Employment in this Country of Italian Children." The collection included seven letters exchanged between the Foreign Office and the Italian legation in London in 1874. The letters revealed that the Italian minister, Carlo Cadorna, had informed the Foreign Office of the law of December 1873, which was intended to eliminate the traffic in children. He had noted that the laws would be ineffective without the help of other countries in ending the trade within their own boundaries. Cadorna and his successor, General Luigi Menabrea, therefore had requested that the padroni be included in a list of criminals who were liable to extradition under the extradition treaty of February 1873, between Italy and Great Britain. The Foreign Office had refused the request.[61]

The publication of this correspondence, along with the Charity Organisation Society's report and numerous articles in newspapers, magazines, and journals, focused public attention on the children. The publicity proved very effective. Once the delegation from the Charity Organisation Society visited the home secretary to discuss the problem in July 1877, Richard Cross issued instructions immediately to the police to use all available means to suppress the traffic. As a result, between July and late December 1877, "478 apprehensions were made throughout the country, 33 padroni were convicted and sentenced to terms from 14 to 60 days, and 83 children were handed over to the Italian consular authorities and sent back to Italy." [62]

This campaign was interesting for its pragmatic nature. Here was a problem which Sir Charles Trevelyan, in speaking to the home secretary, had described as "a case of slave trade and slavery in the midst of our English Christian civilisation." Yet Cross felt that no special law was required to protect the children. Instead, on 29 August 1877, he issued a special police order to all metropolitan London police stations. Officers were to arrest and charge children and padroni under the Vagrant Act. The children, as beggars, or as minors without proper guardians, were to come under the provisions of the Industrial Schools Act and were to be placed in such schools. Cross ordered that a report on each case be sent to the home secretary. Between 15 August and 18 December 1877, Cross received eighty-seven letters from police clerks across England requesting instructions regarding the Italian children or communicating information on what had been done with them once they were apprehended. In most cases the children were sent to the Italian consular representative.[63]

The Home Office also summoned the aid of the Education Department in tracing the Italian children and arresting them for truancy. The secretary of the Education Department urged the more stringent application of the 1876 Education Act by which working children were required to attend school. However, this tactic proved useless. If the Italians were merely passing through, they could not be apprehended. "Many of the Italians wander about the country during some portion of the year leaving tools or goods in some place where they have dwelt before and whither they intend to return. How does a School Board prove residence however?"[64]

An examination of some of the cases that came before the courts shows us what the lawmakers and the courts perceived as the unjust nature of the trade. In mid-August 1877, a few weeks after Cross conferred with the Charity Organisation Society officials, but a few days before he issued his special police orders, one magistrate and a detective anticipated the home secretary. An itinerant street musician by the name of Caimonini, from Eyre Street Hill, was sent from the Clerkenwell Police Court to the House of Correction for one month, "for causing his two children, a boy and a girl, aged five and three, to beg of foot passengers."[65] The children were placed in the St Pancras Workhouse. Cross, who was consulted on the case, suggested that the children be handed over to representatives of the Italian consul (the Italian Benevolent Society) and that they be returned to their mother in Italy rather than to their father in England. The magistrate agreed, and he handed the children over to the consul.

In early September, just a few weeks after the Caimonini case and a few days after Cross's special orders were issued, five Italians, including two adults, one youth, and two children, were brought before the Maidstone magistrates. The two men were charged with causing the children to beg, and the youth was charged with begging. The three of them were carrying twenty-five pounds at the time of their arrest. The magistrates, however, "decided that it was extremely doubtful whether a conviction could be supported under the Vagrancy Act, as the circular of the Home Secretary had suggested, as it was possible that people gave their money to the children in return for the amusement which the singing and dancing might afford." The court dismissed the case, but warned the prisoners "to be careful." The implications of the case were important. The issue of what constituted begging was once again brought into question. If it could be shown that the children were not begging – that they were not vagrants – then Cross's approach to solving the problem would be undermined.[66]

From trial reports it is apparent that the "slave trade" was to be controlled by two approaches: charging the children with begging, and charging the padroni with inciting the children to beg. In late September 1877, for example, Nicolata Creola, a female musician aged fifteen, of 18 Eyre Street, Saffron Hill, was charged at Marylebone Police Court with begging of foot passengers in the Bayswater Road. The magistrate questioned her "parent." The father claimed he did not speak English. The judge did not press charges against the parents (or padroni, if they were not her parents). Although he remanded the case, he predicted that the girl would be sent home to Italy.[67]

A few weeks later, two girls were arrested for begging, which led to the arrest of their father for causing his children to beg. He was charged after his daughters' trial had begun. Giuseppina and Anna Tortolani, aged fourteen and twelve respectively, were apprehended at Greenwich by a Charity Organisation Society official, who found them begging "in Italian costumes and wearing earrings and necklaces of beads." The girls were sent to an industrial school for Catholic children at Eltham, where they would be interned until their parents returned to Italy. The girls' father, Antonio, denied knowing that his children had been out begging on the day referred to. There was no evidence to the contrary, and the case was dismissed.[68]

In Wimbledon, Louis Zanetti's father made the error of playing an organ and allowing his son, who was standing nearby, to collect money from the public. The magistrate's judgment was perhaps tempered by the fact that the ten-year-old's father had four other children and an English wife. He imprisoned the father for one day and sent Louis to the workhouse, from which he would be placed in an industrial school. At Marylebone Police Court, Giovanni Lanni received a stiffer seven-day sentence. He and his eleven-year-old daughter Maria were arrested in Paddington, he for playing the accordion and she for soliciting money in the nearby homes. This was at least the third time that they had been charged with begging.[69]

Sir Richard Cross's special orders, the nature of the the charges against padroni and children, and the reasons for the convictions or exonerations were all concerned with a specific issue – vagrancy, or begging. Although by the 1870s philanthropic societies, journals, and newspapers had exposed the nefarious traffic in Italian children, the government and the courts seemed to show less interest in the possibility that a slave system existed in their "liberal Christian" country than in the possibility that vagrants and beggars should overrun Britain's major cities and towns. It may be that Cross and the Home Office were aware of the problem, but felt that the quickest and most efficient approach was to enforce existing laws – in this case, the old Vagrant Act. That might have been the case; however, that would also mean that no guiding principle was enshrined in the law to inform the public of its true purpose. Taking Cross's special order of August 1877 at face value, we surmise that its main intent was to rid the streets of all child beggars. What is also puzzling about the new order and the judges' decisions is the lack of concern for the children as maltreated victims of a society that allowed youngsters to work on the streets all hours of the night. The problem of child labour barely was mentioned in the reports of societies, journals, newspapers, or in the laws and special orders of the state. Although, as George K. Behlmer has noted, the events of 1877 for the first time drew the English public's attention to the problem of child labour in the streets, it was not until the late 1880s that British lawmakers would draft effective legislation to remedy that problem.[70]

Very Fine Very Cheap. A child vendor of plaster statues. The boys from Lucca who worked for the figurinai (figurine-makers) carried their wares on boards over their heads. This caricature was drawn in 1815 by John Thomas Smith. From John Thomas Smith, *Etchings of Remarkable Beggars* (London 1815). Reproduced by permission of the British Library, London

"I viggianesi." A mid-nineteenth-century caricature of street musicians from the town that sent scores of harpists around the world.

Italian child street musicians in London in 1877. The presence of the harp suggests that they are from Viggiano or a nearby town in Basilicata. From John Thomson, *Street Life in London*, 1877–78

"The Italian boys in New York – tortures of the training room," by A. Gault. New York newspapers and magazines launched a campaign in 1873 against the abuse of Italian musicians by their padrone. From *Harper's Weekly*, 13 September 1873

Italian children rescued from the padrone Ancarola. Ancarola was the first master to be convicted, in 1879, under the "Padrone Act" of 1874. From New York Society for the Prevention of Cruelty to Children, *Fifth Annual Report*, 1880

"The Wandering Italians." This frontispiece to a book by Susannah Strickland (Moodie) shows street musicians in London with dancing dogs ca. 1840. From *The Keepsake Guineas; or, the Best Use of Money,* 1841

Maria Antonia Tardogna and Maria Gargano, aged 11 and 9, in New York. Their padrone was Antonio Briglia. From New York Society for the Prevention of Cruelty to Children, *Fourth Annual Report*, 1879

Italian Minstrels in London,
AT CHRISTMAS, 1825.

Ranged in a row, with guitars slung
Before them thus, they played and sung:
Their instruments and choral voice
Bid each glad guest still more rejoice;
And each guest wish'd again to hear
Their wild guitars and voices clear.

"Italian Minstrels in London, 1825." A caricature and poem on the subject. From *Hone's Everyday Book*

CHAPTER FOUR

"The Little Slaves" in New York

Child street musicians had been travelling to New York well before young Joseph, whom we met in the introduction to this volume, was discovered in Central Park. Some may have lived in the city in the early part of the nineteenth century, but not much was made of their presence until the 1840s. New York began to emerge as the centre of commerce and trade in the United States in the late eighteenth century; when the Italian organ-grinders reached North America, it was only natural that the city should also become the centre of the child musician trade. As in Paris and London, the earliest performers were the adult street organists from Parma and Liguria and the children they brought with them. And again, as in Paris and London, performing was one of a number of trades for which Italian children and adults were hired, including bootblacking, statuette-selling, and flower-making. But it was as street performers that the young Italians appeared most conspicuous. Nevertheless, the social reformer Charles Loring Brace observed some years later, "So degraded was their type, and probably so mingled in North Italy with ancient Celtic blood, that their faces could hardly be distinguished from those of Irish poor children – an occasional dark eye only betraying their nationality."[1] Their occupations, however, helped to distinguish them.

Even though the child musicians were prominent in the city streets in the 1850s, the New York newspapers and magazines did not devote much attention to them. Nor did they take much interest in street trades and traders, and performers, as did their London counterparts. The best source of information on the performing waifs in New York during this period are the reports of A.E. Cerqua, a teacher employed by the New York Children's Aid Society, but even these are of limited value. Cerqua taught at the Italian School, which was opened under the auspices of the society in 1856. The school was located in Five Points, the Italian residential area that had been inherited from other poor immigrant groups. Cerqua, an Italian exile and a Protestant, was the first teacher at the school. He conducted evening classes in the neighbourhood for two decades. In its quest to improve the lot of the lower classes and to instil new values in foreign waifs, the school directed its activities to street children, especially those engaged in "useless" occupations. Only through education could these children be made useful citizens who learned a trade, helped themselves, and kept off the streets where, at best, they would be of no use to society and, at worst, might pose a threat to others. "The Little Italian organ-grinders and statuette sellers, who traverse our streets" became the prime target of the Italian School. Although in the first year almost all of the fifty children who attended the school were street musicians, during the next few years only fifteen to twenty followed "the organ-grinding vocation." Others sold statuettes or fruit, or were bound in trade apprenticeships. A few adults also attended the classes.[2]

It is difficult to estimate the number of organ-grinders in New York in the 1850s, for they were always on the move. New York, Boston, and Philadelphia housed a number of barrel-organ owners, so many of the street musicians in these cities were in town only for a few weeks, or even a few days – long enough to buy an organ. They then moved on to California, Louisiana, or some other state. Those who had already bought or leased an organ could not "be numbered because they go and come continually." Even the children were constantly on the move; if they were unsuccessful in New York, they would "take the railway, and walk alone to Boston, Philadelphia, &c., with their little organs."[3]

By the 1840s going to New York was not an unusual adventure for the organ-grinder; just as he had previously travelled to the French or English capitals, so he now moved on to another major city that could serve as the headquarters for a new market. The migration of the organ-grinders to New York was closely linked to their migration to Paris and London, and even to Moscow. Organ-grinders in all four cities came from the same towns and villages, and decisions were made in the home town as to who would travel to which city. And even later, in Paris or London, new decisions were made as to which townsmen might move on to New York and beyond. The living conditions and life-styles of the organists were similar on both continents. Cerqua observed that the minstrels in Five Points lived "like beasts! as many as ten besides monkeys, live in one room about ten feet by twelve," although "some of them seem to improve in this respect, for they are moving uptown, and in 17th street, near First avenue, there is a little colony of them." So the organ-grinder did not arrive in New York or Boston or Philadelphia on a whim. If he was not a pioneer, there was already a townsman or someone from a nearby town to whom he had been recommended. Usually this master (who could also provide a barrel-organ if the new arrival came without one) covered the travel expenses of the new organist, and was repaid within six months or a year. If the new immigrant had problems he could turn to a townsman in the same trade, or to his master: "No one of them has ever been an inmate of the almshouse, for they help each other."[4]

In February 1860 Cerqua was able to report "a considerable reduction of organs and monkeys in [the street musicians'] apartments, usually filled with such instruments and beasts. The vile traffic of hireling children is also almost extinct ... while in former years a boy was invariably attached to an organ-grinder, now never, or very seldom, is one seen in that trade. A girl may be seen now and then, but generally, the grinder travels alone. Of the boys, many are learning trades, the most favourite of which with them is the jewellers." Most of the children, however, blacked boots at the city hall, peddled soap and matches, and rolled barrels of flour to and from ships at dockside.[5]

Most of these trades could be classified as street occupations, with the possible exception of the flour-carriers. In that sense they all had a stigma attached to them, but reformers attacked the conditions in which the children worked rather than the occupations themselves. The reason behind this was the usefulness of the work: the children were from poor families, and their wages were not squandered but were used to support parents and siblings. A job helped to educate a child, and introduced him or her to the value of being a useful citizen. "Every evil has its bright side, at least, comparatively," wrote Cerqua, "and it is safe to say that the street vocations these children follow, confer upon them some advantage." Their parents confined "their social intercourse to their own townsmen, without knowing anything more about the country" and formed "their own colony at Five Points." Children who did nothing for a living followed the example of their parents and remained "the most ignorant of their countrymen," whereas the children in street trades expanded their horizons, practised thrift, and helped their parents financially. However, there were no kind words for child street organists: even though their occupation might be remunerative, the profits went to greedy padroni; and in any case the profits were reaped from a trade that was of no value to society.[6]

By the mid-1860s the Italian School officials could boast that no more child organists were attending classes, that through the work of the school the trade had been stamped out. In a sense they were right. The children had almost disappeared from the streets, along with many of the Parmesan street organists. Organ-grinding was to a great extent confined to the new immigrants; the children who had arrived earlier had changed trades. Thus, the children would be returned to Italy as "useful and intelligent mechanics instead of ignorant beggars and organ-grinders." However, they were being replaced gradually by a similar group of boys, also from mountain towns, but from the south of Italy. Cerqua reported that in 1864, 136 children were enrolled in his school. Of these about 40 attended day-schools, 30 worked in artificial flower-making, shoemaking, printing, and confectionery, 10 worked as bootblacks, and 20 were fiddlers. Cerqua did not seem particularly concerned with these children, and in fact did not even mention them in his reports until three years later. By that time the *New York Times* also had begun to take an interest in them.[7]

At first the young violinists were regarded not as a serious problem but as merely an irritating presence. By 1868, however, the "black-eyed varlets" were becoming more numerous, and New Yorkers were being made uncomfortable. Over 1,500 children had been expelled from Paris during the exposition of 1867, and over 400 were deported the following year. Many of them travelled to London and especially to New York, or at least were brought there by their padroni. In early 1869 Charles Loring Brace, the founder of the Children's Aid Society, brought the issue to the public's attention in a letter to the *New York Times*.[8] He noted that during the previous winter there had been many reports of half-frozen young harpists and violinists wandering the streets late at night. Unlike the organists, these children could not be drawn to other trades. At least the street organists were attracted to the Italian School on Centre Street, but the harpists and violinists shied away from the building. Unlike the organists, these children were short and dark; they wore more colourful clothes and thus were more conspicuous.

Most of the children were from towns south of Potenza: Laurenzana, Viggiano, Corleto Perticara, and Marsiconuovo. Many travelled to Philadelphia, Chicago, Cincinnati, Baltimore, and San Francisco. Others went to Charleston, Providence, Buffalo, New Orleans, Louisville, and Troy. Over half of the street musicians, however, settled in New York City. In 1868 a man from Viggiano informed the Italian consul that 72 padroni operated from that city; 153 adults and 198 children and teenagers worked under them.[9]

It is difficult to estimate the population of padroni and children. The newspapers tended to exaggerate the numbers of child street musicians in the city. They glanced carelessly at Italian government reports, and took the estimated total population of Italian child musicians in the world or in the United States and applied it to New York City alone. The *New York Times* on a number of occasions asserted that 7,000 to 8,000 such children wandered the city streets. By the autumn of 1873 G.F. Secchi de Casali, the level-headed editor of New York's Italian-language newspaper, the *Eco d'Italia*, challenged the overestimates; he stated that there were only a few hundred Italian child street musicians in New York, and that the number was diminishing. They did not cost the padrone 100 to 500 lire, as the English-language dailies reported, but only about 50 to 60 lire. Nor was there a premium on females, as one writer had suggested – both the boys and the girls could be had for about the same price.[10]

The course of the trade in New York was to a great extent determined by three factors: the goals and initiative of the padroni, the investigations and reports of reform groups (primarily the Children's Aid Society and the Society for the Prevention of Cruelty to Children), and the propaganda campaign of the newspapers, especially the *New York Times*. Until the early 1870s the padroni had a free hand; their only hindrance might be the activity of the

Children's Aid Society in trying to direct the children into other careers, and the attempts of some reformers to persuade pedestrians not to give alms to the children. The newspaper campaign made the general public and the politicians aware of the plight of the "little slaves of the harp." Laws were passed in 1874 and 1876 by the state and federal governements, and the activities of the padroni were greatly curtailed. Those laws are discussed in more detail below.

Until the early 1870s, the New York newspapers had little to say on the topic of street musicians, child or adult. The reader would come across the occasional article on child beggars or child stage performers. Charles Loring Brace submitted letters about the Italian children to the *New York Times* in 1867 and 1869, as did the Italian consul and an Italian voluntary association in the city. Cerqua, the director of the Italian School, lamented the problem in his 1869 report. In July of that year the *Evening Post* published a short commentary on the organ-grinders and harpists of New York, describing these men and boys as unfit for useful pursuits in life. The editor of the *Eco d'Italia*, though no great lover of the street performers, retorted that these men were actually good farmers, and that they desired better work but could get none: they "prefer[red] street work to the Almshouse."[11]

The issue of the child performers came to the fore in the city in 1872. In July of that year a reporter from the *New York Times* was sent out to investigate the living conditions of Italian children performing in New York streets. The newspaper already knew – probably from the reports of the Société Italienne in Paris – that the dealings with the children amounted to a slave trade – in fact, according to the *Times*, "as absolute a slave-trade as ever existed down South, and ... in its details infinitely more repulsive"; that the children were from Basilicata and had come to New York by way of Genoa and Marseilles; that they were provided with musical instruments by their masters, and indentured to them under a contract. And so the reporter went in search of the headquarters of the trade, which he found on Crosby Street, two blocks south of Broome Street (just west of the present-day Little Italy). Here, from the "horrible back tenements ... boys were continually issuing, fiddle in hand, with their dingy harps slung across their backs."[12]

The reporter was shown around Crosby Street by Cerqua who also served as translator. Cerqua told the investigator the story of a young fiddler who escaped from his padrone and took the ferry across to New Jersey, where a farmer took him into custody and adopted him. When a group of padroni came to reclaim the child, they were chased out of the village. He also told the story of a young fiddler who died of consumption in his friend's arms, remembering his mother as he died.[13]

The New York press became more interested in the "child slave" issue in mid-June 1873. The interest was sparked by an Italian soldier of fortune, formerly a parliamentarian, Celso Caesar Moreno. Moreno had gone to the United States in 1868 to negotiate for that country the acquisition of a small island in the Malayan Archipelago just north of Sumatra. He had tried to do the same in Italy in the previous year, claiming to have married several local princesses. He was a man of grandiose yet inconclusive plans, a detractor of the Italian colony, and usually dishonest in his claims and accusations. In May 1873 Moreno published a letter in San Francisco's Italian newspaper, *La Voce del Popolo*, in which he accused the Italian consul in New York, Ferdinando De Luca, of responsibility for the child slave trade. The communication was reprinted in the *New York Times*. A debate erupted immediately between the consul's supporters and opponents. A.E. Cerqua came to De Luca's defence, declaring that for years the consul had been urging the Italian government to bring an end to the cruel system.[14]

Rather than publishing claims and counter-claims, the *New York Times* decided to investigate the problem on its own in the hope that some padrone might be arrested and tried. It was this initiative that led to the interview with Joseph, whom we encountered at the beginning of this volume. A reporter went in search of the children as they played their instruments in midtown. He realized that the harpers were instructed by their masters not to talk to strangers, or at best to give prescribed answers to certain questions. Nevertheless, he spoke to three youngsters who had laid down their instruments temporarily as they ate a "semi-petrified beef bone" from a garbage-box along upper Fifth Avenue. One of the boys, a six-year old triangle-player, claimed that he had been sold by his mother for sixty ducats (he had forgotten his father's and his own name), and that he was required to bring home eighty cents a day. He had arrived in the country with his master and four other children and was threatened with a beating if he did not meet his daily quota. The other two, aged eight and twelve, were both from Laurenzana. They also asserted that they had been sold by their mothers for sixty ducats, which led the reporters to believe that the boys had been ordered by their master to give this answer whenever questioned. One of the two had been away for six months; the other had arrived in New York only six days previously via Naples and Marseilles with ten other boys and a padrone.[15] The three musicians smelled bad, and were infested with vermin; they explained that they washed once a month and that between baths they never removed their clothes. They were awakened at daybreak, given a piece of bread and some macaroni, made to practise their instruments for an hour, and then sent into the streets.

The editors bemoaned the cruelties suffered by Joseph and by all the Italian child musicians: "It seemed impossible that the world had given up stealing men from the African coast, only to kidnap children from Italy, and that the auction-block for negroes had been overturned in the Southern States only to be set up again for white infants in New York." They felt that none of the black slaves had "ever narrated cruelties more brutal than has this wretched boy [Joseph]." Like Moreno, the editors blamed the consul for inaction in the face of suffering. Fingers were also pointed at clergymen: "These boys all reside in a neighbourhood where churches abound, but no minister of religion has ever visited them, and as far as Christian precept or example is concerned, they might as well live in the centre of Africa."[16]

The 1873 campaign against the street children in New York can be seen as part of the reform movement's program to seal the defeat of Tammany Hall. Boss Tweed's machine was dealt a severe blow in 1871, and the process would be completed with the election of a new slate of minor city officials in the autumn of 1873. In the aftermath of the major defeat of 1871 there arose a nostalgia among reformers in the city for the good old days of the Republic when a meritocracy ruled, a world in which dirty politics could not triumph with the support of alien and uneducated masses. The return of nativism in 1871 certainly made New Yorkers sensitive to the growing numbers of Italian street children, especially when leading anti-Tweed publications such as the *New York Times* and *Harper's Weekly* printed sensational reports and caricatures of these odd immigrants. The *Times*, for example, reported that almost three hundred fiddlers and harpists had arrived in the city between mid-April and mid-June. In this climate the political élite in the Italian community had no wish to be shoved aside. The Italian political associations that formed part of the vast array of groups supporting the city's reform forces promoted themselves as controllers of the "alien masses."[17]

Charles Loring Brace, the head of the Children's Aid Society, felt that the onus of ending the trade and reforming the children was on the Americans. The Italian laws prohibiting the emigration of children for street professions were of limited value: "The Italian officials are fully awake to the evil, and are anxious to reform it, and indeed, they would be very glad to stop all the emigration from the Italian Kingdom to the United States. But the difficulty lies in the fact that these rogues of padroni can manage to elude any law which may be passed on the subject."[18] Brace realized that it was extremely difficult to separate children from padroni in New York, but the problem could only be solved from within the city. One method of solving it was education. After all, by attending the Italian School on Franklin Street a "large band of ... organ-grinders and harpists ... have become first class mechanics." A second method was a truancy by-law. Brace advocated an act similar to an ordinance passed recently by the Boston Common Council. Students working in the streets, if questioned by an officer, were to present a certificate proving that they had been attending a half-day school.

Ferdinando De Luca defended his position by citing the 1873 Italian law and by publicizing his role in the drafting of that law: his reports to his superiors regarding the trade were among the principal documents printed by the committee responsible for the law. The consul vowed to place himself at the disposal of the *Times* to stamp out the evil. He too envisioned the problem's being solved from outside Italy, for his home country had "done her duty in this matter; henceforth let all countries imitate her, and this infamous traffic will soon disappear from the world."[19] The federal, state, and city governments, however, had no laws on their books governing child street performers or the immigration of indentured children.

The *New York Times* stepped up its campaign by sending a reporter and a plainclothes police officer to the "children's dens" on Crosby Street one evening. The investigation began in one of the principal saloons on that street, where the owner, an immigrant named Luigi, gave the names of the padroni, and revealed that over one hundred children lived in the house over his saloon. After visiting a number of these establishments and watching the children trudge in with their harps and violins late at night, the two men decided to visit the lodgings of the children in one of the back alley-ways. After climbing the rickety stairs of a damp building, they gained access to a room whose stench "was almost suffocating." Four men, one a hunchback, were sleeping in three straw beds on the floor. The adjacent room, measuring five feet by seven feet, contained a platform covered with mouldy straw and filthy rags. Seven boys, all under the age of twelve, slept in that "bed." Two men, three women, and a little girl were found in a back room. In all, seventeen people lived in an apartment designed for two. Moreover, all the windows were sealed.[20]

A few nights later, the team went out for a second visit to Crosby Street. Another building was selected. On his way up the stairs, one of the investigators tripped over a ten-year-old boy who had fallen asleep clinging to his harp. The boy had been locked out of the house for having arrived home too late at night. At the top of the stairs they entered a room, ten feet by twelve, in which four men were sleeping, perspiring, since they were wearing their daytime clothes and no windows were open on a late June evening in New York. After some resistance the team entered the small back room where ten boys slept on a bed of straw, surrounded by their harps and violins. "Their arms were twined about each other as though they were seeking companionship in their misery." An eight-year-old had lash scars on his back and rope scars on his wrists, as did some of the other boys. The padrone explained that the boys had misbehaved. The children were filthy; the dirt "was caked on them." Other rooms in the same building were examined that evening, each of them revealing similar scenes.[21]

The two "midnight visits" proved sensational, so much so that one might question the truth of some of the details. Rumours spread that a steamer was due to arrive any day with about fifty children who were to be sold in the city and then sent to other states. The *Times* asserted that plans to suppress the traffic in children were being completed and that some action could be expected within a few days. In the meantime, to keep readers interested, reporters returned to the case of young Joseph, noting that the padroni had posted a reward for his return. Authorities were keeping a close eye on him because he could be used as a witness against his master in the near future. The padrone, Luigi Careli, lived at 45 Crosby Street, the most notorious children's den in the city; over one hundred "little slaves" lived at that address. Careli was among the first of a new type of middleman rising in the Italian immigrant community (and in a number of other ethnic groups) in North America. He kept a saloon and provided a mailing address for newcomers to the neighbourhood. He was also a labour agent, and found employment for many immigrants in the emerging Little Italy.

An uneventful month passed. There were occasional reports from Italian associations and prominent persons in the Italian community who were taking action to end the trade, but no sensational stories were printed until late July. Italians in New York City, seeing that their own officials were ineffective, urged officials in other cities to take action to prevent the spread of the problem in their own neighbourhoods. New Haven was the first city to respond. That city's first case involved Giovanni Glionna, one of the padroni from Laurenzana, who lived at 45 Crosby Street in New York. In November 1871 Glionna had brought four children with him to New York as street musicians. The boys were bound by four-year contracts for which their parents received twenty dollars annually. In early June of 1873 he sent the children to New Haven to play instruments and shine boots on the street. Reporters alleged that Glionna was young Joseph's master, and that he had left the city to avoid arrest. Nothing came of that charge. Glionna went to Boston, and when he failed to find a lucrative market there, he moved to New Haven. The district attorney and police chief in that city had Glionna arrested at his "den" on Oak Street for holding the four children as slaves. The arrest was made under the Personal Liberty Bill of 1854, which had been passed to nullify the Fugitive Slave Act but had never been used for that purpose.

At the first hearing the boys described their experiences under Glionna. Two of them were bootblacks; the other two were brothers, one a harpist, the other a violinist. They ranged in age from fourteen to eighteen years. One of the bootblacks described how he had been beaten by Glionna for not bringing home his daily quota of sixty cents, even though on some days he had accumulated over a dollar. The youngest boy, a bootblack, once ran away from his padrone because he had been threatened with death should he return without the money. Glionna had allegedly told him to steal if he could not meet his quota. This harpist had left home for Buenos Aires at the age of twelve, and had come to New York four years later.[22]

The hearing was held to establish whether or not the children were slaves. If they were bound to their padrone by a contract that specified mutual obligations over a certain period of time, the children might qualify as apprentices. The judge rejected defence claims that the children were apprentices and should therefore be returned to their master; under Connecticut law, the apprentices had to be able to sign their names to the contract, and they had to be taught a trade by their masters. These children had not been instructed in a trade; they were illiterate and had been treated cruelly. Therefore, Glionna should be tried. The judge remanded the case for trial in October. Glionna was placed under $4,000 bail. He could not furnish the bond, and he was jailed. In the meantime the children were placed in the State Reform School until the trial. However, in early September, friends of Glionna were able to get his bail reduced to $1,000, which they immediately paid. After his release, Glionna's name no longer appeared in the press. However, within a few months he had established himself in Toronto, where he began a significant migration chain of laurenzanesi from New York and directly from Italy.[23]

The Glionna case caused a great sensation in New York because it was the first time that a padrone had ever been arrested for holding a child in slavery. Previously some padroni had been fined for causing children to perform in public, but never for holding children against their will. The public was as fascinated with Glionna as it had been a few months earlier with the boy Joseph. Although the child musicians and the padroni were a common sight on the streets of New York, they lived in an underground world. Now, either through persuasion, as in Joseph's case, or through legal means, as in Glionna's case, the public was able to penetrate that world. Of course, the press realized this and often resorted to sensationalism to whet the appetites of readers; thus the recourse to connecting Joseph with Glionna, to reporting in detail the bruises and scars on the children and assuming that these were the vestiges of beatings.

The reporters also understood the reader's desire to hear the details of the lives of the masters and children. In their late-night visits to the "child dens," reporters described the living quarters and personal habits of the inhabitants: the odours in the rooms, the dampness of the floors, the strange food they called "macaroni" (which they usually spelled "maccaroni"), the instruments lying about the floor, the straw strewn on platforms that served as beds, the frequency with which the children bathed and changed clothes. *Harper's Weekly* published a full-page caricature in the summer of 1873 which tried to capture all possible details of the Italian stereotype of the period: a monkey lying on an organ looked on as a number of children in a tiny room, holding their various instruments, watched a padrone whip one of the youngsters. A portrait of Garibaldi hung on the wall above a case of macaroni from Naples.

There was a positive side to the newspaper reports: as more light was shed on the living conditions of the children, so the calls for justice towards these children increased. Laws had to be developed, laws that were directed specifically at the problem of "child slaves." It was not enough to rely on old statutes such as the Personal Liberty Bill, which had, after all, been drawn up for other purposes.

In the meantime, new stories of cruelty emerged. Two lads sought protection from the Italian consul in New York about one week after Glionna's arrest. They alleged that their own padrone, Michael Carcano of Crosby Street, had been cruel to them. They had been leased from their parents for forty dollars a year on five-year contracts, and had been promised music lessons. Upon arriving in New York, however, they were sent out on the streets as bootblacks, given quotas to meet, and punished in the same way as the street musicians. A warrant was issued for Carcano's arrest, but he had escaped to Philadelphia. The children were released from his custody and placed temporarily in the care of the Children's Aid Society.[24]

Two weeks later another padrone from the infamous den at 45 Crosby Street made his way into the newspapers. Two of his "slaves," aged thirteen and eighteen, decided to escape from their master, and set off with a harp and a fiddle. By the time they reached a small village in Rockland County called Spring Valley, a resident of that town had noticed an advertisement in the newspaper offering a fifty-dollar reward for their capture. He therefore arrested the children; however, other villagers, upon learning of the children's plight, appealed to the squire, who had them released. When the padrone, Joseph Macino, showed up to claim the children, he was advised by the villagers to leave immediately for his own safety.[25]

The *New York Times* continued to pursue the padroni. They hired a lawyer, John N. Lewis, who explained the difficulties of proceeding without legislative authority. The Italians from the various community associations urged him on none the less, and Lewis decided to have the young Joseph file a complaint against his master under the Civil Rights Bill of 1866. At this point a second problem arose: how to arrest the padrone? No United States marshal could speak Italian, "and consequently could not expect to find him in the Italy of Crosby Street." Therefore, a *Times* reporter (probably of Italian descent), H.D. Monachesi, who had been among the movers in the investigation of the trade, was sworn in as a marshal.

The padrone under warrant of arrest was Vincenzo Motto, also an inhabitant of 45 Crosby Street. Knowledge of Motto's address did not make the search any easier. Forty-five Crosby Street included front and rear buildings, each of which was five storeys high. The arresting officers persuaded an Italian boy to enter the house and to find Motto on the pretext of wanting to purchase a monkey. The officers followed him into the house, and a chase ensued when Motto was discovered near the top floor of the rear building. Motto climbed a ladder to the roof, and in total darkness leaped to the roof of the next building, fifteen feet below. The officers followed him but lost his trail. The following evening, carrying lanterns, they went back with Joseph, who led them to the top floor of the rear building and pointed to his former "prison." Joseph knocked at the door and expressed his desire to return to his master. The door was opened to reveal a six-by-eight-foot room that housed seven men and two boys. Joseph identified Motto, who denied that he was a master, and protested that he had been in the country only three days. In fact, Motto was probably right. He was honourably discharged after the first hearing when the judge was satisfied that the case was one of mistaken identity.[26]

New York was not the only American city in which the Italian child street musicians had become an important issue. Through the Glionna case, of course, the issue came to prominence in New Haven. Following the lead of the *Times*, the *Chicago Tribune* began reporting the problem in that city. In fact, the town of Laurenzana had sent a considerable number of harpists and violinists to South Clark Street. The Italian consular representative in Chicago believed that the reports were exaggerated; he estimated that there were not more than 150 Italian child street musicians in the city. Philadelphia also had a problem. There, the city police indiscriminately arrested hundreds of Italians in September 1873 on vagrancy charges. Ostensibly they were apprehending street musicians, but they ended up taking into custody craftsmen, artisans, and fruit-vendors. The vice-consul and other prominent Italians complained to the mayor, and most of the prisoners were released. Only 8 padroni and musicians were actually detained. The next day, with the aid of the vice-consul, new arrests were made as the police chief, forty officers, and several captains descended on Carpenter Street, the centre of the Italian street music colony. One house with three eight-foot by ten-foot rooms contained 46 residents. In all, 159 men, women, and children were arrested. One master had 32 children under his care.[27]

In response to sensational press stories, arrests, and public outcries, one New York state senator began formulating a law to prohibit street performers under the age of sixteen from performing in public. Over the winter of 1873–4 George Scherman consulted a number of people, including Ferdinando De Luca, and in early February 1874 he introduced a bill in the New York legislature. The bill provided for a thirty-day to one-year sentence and a $200 maximum fine for receiving children under the age of sixteen years to perform on the street. The legislature passed the bill on 3 April, and it became effective 23 April.[28] Alonzo M. Viti, the Italian vice-consul in Philadelphia (whose jurisdiction included the entire state of Pennsylvania), also promoted the passage of a bill in his state's legislature; and by May 1874 Pennsylvania also had a law, modelled on the New York act, which prohibited the use of children in street performances.

New York newspapers took little note of the new law, but Ferdinando De Luca did not wish to see it remain merely an ineffective symbol. Fed up with general ideas and good intentions, the consul took a practical approach to ensuring that the law would be enforced. He decided that it would be best to have the authorities send the children to him for repatriation to Italy. He reminded the city police about the law so that they would actively pursue the children and padroni.

De Luca and the Children Aid Society's counsel, Charles Whitehead, visited the mayor of New York on 24 April – the day that the New York statute became effective – to ensure that the city would enforce the provisions of the statute and take even more stringent measures. The mayor endorsed the consul's recommendations, and he wrote a letter of introduction to the president of the Police Commission, Hugh Gardner. The following day De Luca delivered a proposal to the police commissioners; it recommended (1) that the police arrest Italian street performers under the age of sixteen; (2) that they be brought before the Italian consul, who would question them; (3) that they be detained in custody for a few days at the expense of the consulate so that people could come to claim them; (4) that the child's master be prosecuted for a misdemeanour under the statute that prohibited children from performing in public; and (5) that the children be returned to Italy by the consul if they were not claimed. In the meantime the police commissioners proceeded with their own plans to arrest any children found performing in the streets. Gardner and the Police Commission endorsed the plan.[29]

For one week, De Luca spent two to three hours a day helping with investigations. On 2 June the police began apprehending individuals. The arrests caused much distress among Italian immigrants, who travelled to the police headquarters to inquire about what might happen to their children. On the first day eleven minors and a mother of two were arrested. The consul asked that the women and her children be arrested. He then asked the police chief to release children only on the condition that their parents took an oath not to allow their children to work in the streets again. The police chief could not comply with this request, since it was not within his jurisdiction. He agreed, however, to hold the children a few more days so that De Luca could consult his lawyer. The following day five children and two adults were apprehended. (The *Times*, exaggerating as usual, claimed that thirty boys and several girls had been apprehended.) Over the next three days thirteen children and five adults were arrested. In all, thirty-seven arrests were carried out in a week, including twenty-nine children. Of these, sixteen were young harpists and violinists; eight were accompanying organ-grinders; five were arrested for begging for bread and leftovers.

The padroni were found guilty at a hearing on 6 June. Although Charles Whitehead asked that the judge impose the maximum sentence so that they might serve as an example, because this was their first offence they received the minimum penalty – fifty dollars or thirty days. As for the children, three were held, either to be sent back to Italy or placed in a state school; another fifteen-year-old was sent to his uncle in Chicago; and two from New Jersey were placed with the Children's Aid Society. The *New York Times* reported that De Luca had spoken vaguely about a scheme developed with the Children's Aid Society to send the children out west, "to be placed in families, and reared in comfort and usefulness."[30]

Some parents came to claim their children at the police headquarters, and the children were returned with a warning that they might be handed over to the Children's Aid Society if they were found begging or playing musical instruments on the street. Twenty-three children were returned to their parents, who were their employers; only six of the children apprehended were hired by padroni. On the whole, the placement plan was difficult to implement. The police had to contend with the children's parents or guardians, the Children's Aid Society, the Italian consul, and reporters, and with their own sympathies for the children who might not want to be sent to an unknown family. The Italian consul and the editor Secchi di Casali blamed this on the New York law: unlike the Italian law, it did not prohibit parents from hiring out their children.[31]

The law was not implemented solely within New York City. In late June three men in Saratoga asked De Luca about arresting a padrone who had gone to that town from New York to sell five children. The padrone was arrested and sentenced to thirty days' imprisonment. Three of the children were taken into custody and sent to the Children's Aid Society in New York. Two of the children claimed that their mothers lived at 45 Crosby Street. No further arrests under the New York law of 1874 were reported.

The law seems to have been effective in the short run. The Italian chargé d'affaires in Washington informed the British Foreign Office a few weeks later that "the streets of New York had been cleared of this scandal; that [De Luca] had sent a considerable number of boys back to Italy ... and that [De Luca] believed that a large proportion of the 'padroni' and their victims, who had been dislodged and deprived of their means of livelihood ... had betaken themselves to England." In early July and in early September the editor of the *Eco d'Italia* noted that street musicians under the age of sixteen were no longer to be seen in New York.[32] In the long run, however, the law of 1874 was inadequate. It could never extirpate the trade because it did not punish parents either for consigning their children to a padrone or for using their own children in street performances. This was not remedied until 1876, mainly through the work of the Society for the Prevention of Cruelty to Children, founded in 1875. An Act to Prevent and Punish Wrongs to Children provided that

any person having the care, custody, or control of any child under the age of sixteen years, who shall exhibit, use, or employ, or who shall in any manner, or under any pretense, sell, apprentice, give away, let out, or otherwise dispose of any such child to any person, in or for the vocation, occupation, service, or purpose of singing, playing on musical instruments, rope or wire-walking, dancing, begging, or peddling, or as a gymnast, contortionist, rider or acrobat, in any place whatsoever ... or who shall cause, procure, or encourage any such child; or who shall engage therein, shall be guilty of a misdemeanor.[33]

Thus, parents and guardians were liable to punishment under the new law. The statute did not affect church choirs, schools, concerts, or entertainments if the written permission of the mayor was obtained. For example, in 1888, the mayor allowed the young piano virtuoso Josef Hofmann to give a maximum of four recitals a week in the daytime only. He also gave permission to fourteen-year-old Fritz Kreisler to play the violin at the Metropolitan Opera House.[34]

As for the less gifted fiddlers and harpists on the streets, the law was unequivocal and effective. Over the next few years the *New York Times* and the annual reports of the SPCC listed numerous cases of apprehension of the children and arrests of their parents or padroni; over twenty during the first two years were singled out by the SPCC. All of the arrests but two were made under the 1876 act for using the children, "for having in charge a little girl / boy," as the SPCC reports phrased it, and for playing an instrument and / or begging. None was made under an 1874 federal act that prohibited inveigling children abroad for the purposes of employment in the United States. It was difficult to prosecute under that act, which is examined later in this chapter. The 1876 New York act provided that the fines received as a result of prosecutions initiated by the SPCC would be forfeited to the society "in aid of the purposes for which it was incorporated."[35]

In most cases, either the parents or the employer or both were fined fifty dollars or given a short jail sentence. In September 1877, for example, Domenico Pentulani, an organ-grinder, was arrested for having in his employment a seven-year-old beggar. He was found guilty, sentenced to twenty days' imprisonment or a fifty-dollar fine. In October Lorenzo Pinello was arrested when it was discovered that a twelve-year-old boy was playing the violin and begging for him in the street. He too was fined fifty dollars. In November another organ-grinder, Antonio Profili, received the same fine for the same charges, as did, one year later, Antonio Toscano, a harpist accompanied by a ten-year-old violinist. In July 1879 Francesco Nuzzo was given a much more severe sentence for using thirteen-year-old Saverio Felletti for begging purposes. Saverio had a badly deformed foot and walked with the aid of a crutch; he was considered "a good card among imported monstrosities ... a perfect bonanza in the begging trade." In this case, the master received a six-month sentence, not for his use of a child but as an example to prevent the migration of undesirables; as the presiding magistrate remarked, "it is an object of interest to the community, that the importation of human monstrosities from Italy to this country, for the purpose of mendicancy, should be promptly suppressed."[36] The SPCC was involved in all of these cases. Representatives of the society made recommendations to officers for arrests, attended the hearings, took children into custody, and publicized the cases through their reports. After all, the

SPCC had proposed the 1876 law, which, in fact proved the most effective for steering children away from undignified street occupations.

The child street musicians caused a stir in the Italian colony in New York. Until the last quarter of the nineteenth century the Italian population of the city, and indeed of the United States in general, was small. It could be divided into three basic groups. The first of these were the fuorusciti, or political exiles from the homeland. These republicans came to the United States in 1830 and especially in 1849, either directly or by way of another European country. A second group was composed of artisans, traders, and dealers, almost exclusively from the northwest of Italy. These included fruit dealers and organ-grinders from the coastal and inland towns and villages in Liguria and Parma, and artisans such as optical instrument-makers and builders from villages near Como. Finally, in the 1860s, southern Italians began arriving, especially from the Basilicata region, as cobblers, jewellers, fruit-sellers, and, of course, street violinists and harpists. The 1870 census listed 17,000 Italian natives resident in the United States, and the *New York Times* reported in 1871 that their population in the city stood at about 14,000. During the ensuing years they became much more visible in American urban centres: "for the olive features under the black slouch hat of the man, and the low-browed, Madonna-eyed face of the peasant woman of Italy are fairly ubiquitous in our cities today." The *New York Times* observed in 1874 that Americans "had been wont to associate an Italian in America with opera singers with a princely income, or with the political exile and organ-grinder with the incomes of mendicants." Now, however, they operated fruit-stalls, "they cry our newspapers, they black our boots, clean – or are supposed to clean – our streets; they sell us flowers, they cook us food, they carry burdens, they levy tribute on our coppers, their gracious gestures and musical language give animation and picturesqueness to our crowds." Among those immigrants were 1,500 to 2,000 families involved in street trades who, owing to the 1873 depression, lived in great poverty. The sight of so many poor Italian street traders may have given impetus to the campaign against child musicians.[37]

An important figure in the colony was the consul. Although his original duties under the Kingdom of the Two Sicilies were in the commercial sphere, the growing Italian population in New York required that he devote more time to the needs of the immigrants. In New York, as in London, Paris, Moscow, Rio de Janeiro, and elsewhere, the Italian consul played an important role in the emerging Italian community. Men of commerce depended on him for trade information. Labourers, pedlars, and small merchants wanted his help in bringing family members to America; he helped them obtain passports when they wanted to visit Italy, even though it was not absolutely necessary to have them in the early 1860s. Even the padroni went to the consul for passports every time they returned to the home town to indenture more children, although De Luca refused to issue the documents to any padroni.

It was only natural, then, that as the issue of the Italian white slave children's trade exploded in the late 1860s, the consul should have taken the lead in stamping out the exploitation. De Luca was not a novice: he had been preoccupied with the problem since at least 1865 as consul to New Orleans, and had even written a pamphlet on the matter in 1868.[38] By keeping an eye on the street musicians, De Luca followed precedents set by his colleagues Baron Richard Benjamin Heath in London and Luigi Cerruti in Paris.

De Luca, however, had to contend with a group of men who were jealous of his power. It seems that this problem was unique to the Italian community of New York. In London and Paris, in Moscow and Odessa, the consul had the support of the Italian business communities. But in those cities the important men of commerce had been wealthy before they left Italy; they represented established Italian manufacturing and trading companies. Similar men lived in New York, but others had made their fortune in the United States. Some professionals, or even exiles, who had left high-status occupations lost their prestige upon their arrival in New York. These men wished to assert their new prestige or to reassert their old-country status by claiming positions of leadership in the Italian community. This inevitably involved conflict with the consul.[39]

The conflict over the street musicians probably began as early as December 1872, a few months before the issue exploded in the press. Secchi de Casali published an editorial in *Eco d'Italia* defending Italian consular representatives as having been active against the trade in children in France, England, and the United

States. He felt that the finger should be pointed at the authorities in the Italian townships (comuni) rather than at Italian consuls. He also blamed the disunity in the Italian communities abroad for preventing an end to the trade: "Undoubtedly, if the Italian colonies were more in agreement, and of one sentiment, with love for their fatherland and their national name, it would not take long to wear out the speculators in this form of export, thus freeing for always the little pariah."[40]

At the top of the consul's list of adversaries was Captain Celso Caesar Moreno, the soldier of fortune whom we have already encountered. In mid-June of 1873 he published a complaint in San Francisco's *La Voce del Popolo* placing responsibility on the Italian consul-general for the trade. Another man seeking prestige within the community was H.D. Monachesi. Monachesi was not Italian, although he may have had some Italian ancestry. He was a reporter for the *New York Times*, and he was also involved with an Italian voluntary organization and the Republican party. It was this reporter who carried out the investigations into the child street musician problem in New York, and who gave Moreno his connection with the newspaper. With Moreno, Monachesi was responsible for stirring up opposition to the consul in the Italian community. In an open letter in the *Times* he asked, "What has any Italian official in this country ever done to put an end to this infamous traffic?" He felt that De Luca's briefs to the Italian government were ineffective because the Italian Parliament was unable to stop brigandage and child kidnapping within its own borders. De Luca should therefore have made representations to the American government, argued Monachesi, for the men carrying on the trade in the United States presumably were naturalized citizens.[41]

Moreno was an eccentric, but he was also an excellent publicist. He knew that he had to isolate the consul, and he understood the limitations of the consul's office. For example, De Luca had to remain non-partisan and detached from the press, whereas Moreno could use both press and political channels to promote himself. A few days after his letter was published in San Francisco (and, through Monachesi, translated and published in the *Times*) he was invited to join *New York Times* reporters to visit Joseph, who was to be interviewed in Central Park. At least at first, he was able to capture the sympathies of the editors. They charged that De Luca could "no longer deny what is declared with such minuteness, and must give his aid to the discovery of the whole truth and the application of an effective remedy." De Luca answered that he had never tried to deny the existence of the trade, and that in fact his reports to his government were an integral part of the Italian Parliament's report of 1873 on children in wandering professions.[42]

Celso Moreno again accused the consul of having done nothing to end the trade, and said that the trade had only begun in 1866, when De Luca was assigned to his post. The trade was "a relic of Bourbon misrule" and De Luca had served the Bourbon government "with pride and fidelity" as vice-consul in New Orleans before 1860." Moreno also stated that "most of these stolen children are taken from the same province in Italy that the consul comes from." He appealed to the emotions as he once again blamed the consul, along with the padroni, for having caused tears to be "shed by a thousand mothers who have been deprived of their children."[43] He did not mention that mothers often leased their children voluntarily to the padroni.

At this point, the editor of the *Eco d'Italia* came to the defence of the consul. G.F. Secchi de Casali had come to New York from Piacenza in 1843, and had established his first newspaper in 1849. A few years later he founded the *Eco*. As a liberal revolutionist he found himself out of favour with the Italian diplomatic corps until 1866, and with Mazzinian republicans. His newspaper was read by merchants and professionals, and its politics leaned towards the Republican party. De Casali exposed Moreno's contradictions and lies: the trade in Italian children was not a slave trade, for parents willingly sold or leased their children; De Luca had become consul-general to New Orleans and all the southern states in 1864, and not before; and the Italian child street musician problem had not begun in 1866, but already existed when de Casali had begun publishing his newspaper in 1849. Besides, he argued, how much more could the consul actually do? He would have to influence the New York legislature to pass a law, a formidable task. A state law, however, would only send the padroni to Pennsylvania, Connecticut, New Jersey, or elsewhere. De Luca would have to appeal to every state of the union to pass similar laws, which was obviously impossible.[44]

De Luca expanded on these and other points in a long letter of defence published in the *Times* on 23 June 1873. The most supportable charge Moreno had levelled against the consul centred on the release of passports to street musicians. De Luca exonerated himself even on this count. Over the previous four years De Luca had refused passports to street musicians and padroni, and would only grant special permits that required the bearer to go directly to his home village and register with officials there. Often he refused to release even this document if the man did not return to Italy with all the children listed in his old passport. As a result, very few padroni visited the consulate.[45]

If he was being asked to draw up a better plan for ridding the city of child street musicians, the consul said, he proposed two steps towards a solution to the problem. The first had already been suggested by Charles Loring Brace – compulsory half-day school attendance. The second was similar to the idea introduced by the Italian ambassadors to London and France: include the padroni in the extradition treaty between the United States and Italy. De Luca also felt compelled to demonstrate that he had the support of the community, perhaps to prevent Moreno or Monachesi from taking his place as leader of the Italian colony, perhaps to maintain the dignity of his office. He noted that the previous winter when New Yorkers had been worried about the great influx of south Italian immigrants, 150 Italians pledged their support to the consul in a letter; they included businessmen, the editor Secchi de Casali, an artist, and officers of three voluntary associations – the Italian Benevolent Society, the Italian Young Men's Association, and Guardia Colombo.[46]

To De Luca's chagrin, however, not all voluntary associations were on his side. One of the most prominent, the Associazione Donnarumma, met soon after the consul's statement was published. Because he had declared himself powerless to stop the trade, the association decided to take the initiative. The delegates decided on two courses: appealing to the police to arrest the children under vagrancy laws, and appealing to the courts and testing a case under one of the state civil rights acts.[47]

Secchi de Casali directed his comments mainly to this association when he noted that many people had tried to get on the bandwagon once the Italian law concerning child musicians had been passed in 1873. These societies, he complained, "only now step forward and pretending to be humanitarian [atteggiandosi ad umanitarie] claim the honour for what has already been accomplished, they gather in extraordinary councils, they make themselves judges, censors, slanderers of [him] who has the right to the respect of all his co-nationals [the consul], and they adopt resolutions and provisions which had already long ago been proposed by others." Secchi de Casali quoted the New York French-language daily *Courrier des États-Unis* and the *Commercial Advertiser*, both of which praised the consul for his efforts.[48]

One week later the Associazione Donnarumma convened for its annual picnic in Sultzer's Park at Eighty-fourth Street and the East River. During the day there was a parade to the park with music, flags, and festivities. In the evening, Filippo Donnarumma introduced Celso Moreno to the members. To allow the trade between south Italy and the United States continue would be "treason to our national dignity." Not only was this traffic "a shame to the home of Mazzini and Garibaldi, but also an insult to the country in which we live." The crowd responded with shouts of "evviva Italia." Moreno then resorted to the second part of his strategy to place himself at the helm of this movement: criticism of the consul. It was clear to whom he was referring when he wished "confusion, remorse, and contempt" on "those who have failed to do their duty in this affair." The association then passed a number of resolutions, two of which censured the consul.[49]

The Italian Republican Association of New York, headed by Roberto Prati, took immediate action the following evening – the *New York Times* claimed that De Luca had organized the meeting – at the Germania Assembly Rooms. (According to the *Times*, whose reporters were still under Moreno's sway, most of the prominent Italians in New York stayed home when they learned that the "leading spirits" of the meeting were supporters of the consul.) The resolutions bore the mark of the consul. The most important recommendation was that the United States and Italy revise their extradition treaty to allow the deportation of padroni from America. Copies of the resolutions were submitted to the American president, the lieutenant-governor of New York, the mayor of New York City, and other statesmen and politicians.[50]

The meeting of New York members of the Italian Republican Association was followed by another meeting of the Associazione Donnarumma the next evening, 3 July. Tempers flared at the assembly, which was presided over by Filippo Donnarumma. One member objected to the resolutions passed at the picnic the previous week on the grounds that they attacked the consul. He argued that the traffic in children was a matter that concerned higher powers than this voluntary association. A new resolution was passed to establish stronger links with other Italian societies in New York with a view to calling a mass meeting of Italian residents of the city on the problem of the trade (thus bypassing the consul). Another resolution called for copies of the resolutions to be mailed to all Italian immigrant societies in the United States and to the *Voce del Popolo* in San Francisco. Of course, no mention was made of the *Eco d'Italia*.[51]

A few days after this meeting Giovanni Glionna, the padrone from 45 Crosby Street, was arrested in New Haven. Although they were not often mentioned in the English-language press, De Luca and Secchi de Casali gained respect through the case. Authorities and the courts in New Haven consulted with both men, and Secchi de Casali was called as a witness at Glionna's first hearing. At the same time the editor became known to the Italian community by reporting on the case and on the problem of the traffic in Italian children in general in his newspaper. The two men were praised by Italians in New York and Italy, and even in Canada. In Montreal the Italian colony met on 18 August, and passed a resolution supporting the Italian consul in New York and praising Judge Harrison and the New Haven chief of police. The resolution was published in the *Montreal Daily Witness*. (Perhaps Secchi de Casali was being petty when he noted that no one at the meeting in Montreal had thanked "a number of Italians" who had travelled to New Haven at their own expense.)[52]

Of course, any action by the consul at this point would have appeared to be a tactical move to retain control over the Italian colony. When in late July two boys complained to the consul of cruelties suffered at the hands of their padrone, Michael Carcano of Crosby Street, De Luca had them swear affidavits. Immediately some of the prominent Italians in the city declared that the consul, having found himself unable to do anything, "has found that he should be the leader, and has therefore procured the present action to give himself prominence." According to a *New York Times* reporter, they were very bitter and felt that the consul was trying to get on the bandwagon and take all the credit for himself.[53]

During this period Moreno's supporters, in conjunction with the *New York Times*, secured the services of a lawyer, John M. Lewis, who followed up on Joseph's case and eventually arranged for

Vincenzo Motto's indictment. Riding the crest of a wave, Moreno increased his credibility by associating with the *Times* and by appearing to take decisive action with the aid of a counsel. It was at this point that Moreno's friend, H.D. Monachesi (who had publicly censured the Italian consul in a letter to the *Times*) was sworn in as a US marshal in order to arrest Motto. Moreno himself was sworn in as the Italian interpreter at the trial.[54]

Three months later, in November 1873, Moreno came up with the idea of employing the services of the famous abolitionist, Senator Charles Sumner, to end this new slave trade. He called on "the Moses of the late slaves in the Southern States" to "raise your powerful voice in behalf of oppressed and defenseless infantile humanity." In practical terms, he was asking Sumner to introduce a bill in the Senate to prohibit the trade. Moreno did not fail to mention the important role he had played since 1871 in bringing the problem to the attention of the Italian and American public. The aging senator agreed to help out and urged Moreno to pursue the matter.[55]

It is not clear whether Moreno turned to Sumner because he was losing a powerful ally, the *New York Times*, or whether Moreno's correspondence with the senator caused him to lose the support of the newspaper publisher. The *Times* felt that Sumner was rushing into the legislation without having examined the issues and facts. The paper's background article contained information that had been taken from an item written by A.E. Cerqua in the 1874 annual report of the Children's Aid Society. Cerqua in turn had gotten his information from the 1868 report of the Société Italienne de Bienfaisance. The *Times* criticized Sumner and, by association, Moreno for not having their facts straight. Sumner's proposal might have been well intentioned but it was also ineffective, more a result of his "enthusiasm for humanity" than a thorough and efficacious legislative proposal. The *Times* dealt Moreno an even stronger blow by stating that "the Italian Consul at New York has presented the strongest statements against this cruel and infamous trade in children," and that "his humane conduct in this matter has called forth warm approval from his own Government." The newspaper also endorsed De Luca's recommendations that the trade be defeated by enacting the Personal Liberty Bill, as the state of Connecticut had done in the Glionna case, and that Italy and the United States include padroni in their extradition treaty. A few weeks later, when the Italian Parliament passed the act concerning child street musicians, the editors recommended that the US Senate carefully examine the Italian law as a model.[56]

Only when Sumner, a few months before his death, introduced legislation to prevent the "inveigling, forcible kidnap and involuntary service of children" did the *New York Times* finally take a less sensational view of the problem, and begin to look more closely at the facts. Instead of colouring its texts with stories of immense cruelty, with insinuations that all padroni held their children forcibly, the *Times* presented a more sobre, accurate picture of the children: "The so-called little 'Italian slaves' are, in fact, neither 'inveigled,' nor 'forcibly kidnapped,' nor held in 'involuntary confinement,' nor 'involuntary service' ... they are not 'sold to a condition of involuntary servitude' ... Moreover, the padrone always has the free 'consent' of the child, not obtained 'by force or duress' ... The fact is, the padrone's nefarious business is a legal apprenticeship and contract, made with the full consent of the child. It becomes in its abuse a slavery, but it is doubtful if it could legally come under any of the terms of Mr Sumner's act." Thus, concluded the paper, "it will be seen that a cunning padrone, with a Tombs lawyer, could 'drive an omnibus and four right through' Mr Sumner's well-meant act."[57] The *Times* probably received its information from Secchi de Casali.

Nevertheless, in June 1874, Congress passed An Act to Protect Persons of Foreign Birth against Forcible Constraint, or Involuntary Servitude, popularly known as "the Padrone Act."[58] The law made it a felony wilfully to bring into the United States any person inveigled or forcibly kidnapped in any other country, with the intent to hold him in the United States in confinement or to any involuntary service. The felony was punishable by imprisonment for up to five years and a fine of up to $1,000.

The law and Moreno's part in it were received with mixed reactions. The *New York Dispatch* reported the act's passage, and described Moreno's elation as he returned to the city. The *Times*, however, was silent. Frederick Douglass praised Moreno in the *New National Era*, and compared his energy and zeal with that of "the Abolitionists of other days – John Brown, Lloyd Garrison, or Charles Sumner." He noted that other Italian in the United States viewed Moreno as a fanatic, but that nevertheless he had done the work that the ambassador and consular officials should have done.[59]

Moreno's fortunes changed over the next two decades. He always tried to maintain a high profile, and his opposition to Italian consular and diplomatic officials never abated. During the 1880s he waged a second battle against the padroni who imported adult Italian immigrants to work on railroads and in mines. Rightly, he saw the activities of these padroni as a continuation of the old system that had brought so many child musicians into the country. Once again Moreno charged the Italian diplomatic officials with complicity in the whole affair, especially the Italian minister in Washington, Baron Basilio Fava. Among other things he asserted that the padroni had a highly organized network, and that the ambassador and his staff acted as contacts for the network. To add fuel to the fire, Moreno said that "Fava, though he represents a Christian Catholic Nation, is a Hebrew, and so are his wife and son, and of the Semitic race; they possess in the superlative degree all their faults, such as meanness, greediness, profits, and niggardliness." Baron Fava sued Moreno, and in 1891 the aging soldier of fortune was convicted of having criminally libelled the ambassador.[60]

Throughout the late 1870s the SPCC was the catalyst behind the arrest of padroni in New York. The society had introduced the 1876 law in the New York Senate, and then had assisted police officers in identifying and locating many padroni and children. One officer of the society, Edward Chiardi, worked unceasingly on the cases, and was to a great extent successful in curbing the problem of mendicant Italian children. The philosophy of the society, much like that of the Society for the Suppression of Mendicity in London, was not to attempt to solve the problem by arresting some of the more important padroni, but rather to take each master to court, whether he had one child or ten under his command. In fact, almost all of the accused had only one child performer with them, very often their own child, which indicates the extent to which the padroni cases were sensationalized.

In 1878 the SPCC took a new path and advocated the indictment of a padrone under the US "Padrone Act" of 1874. The episode began with a telegram to Chiardi from Castle Garden, the immigrant depot on Governor's Island just off the tip of Manhattan:

"Our friends have arrived. Come immediately." Chiardi travelled to the New Street Police Station where he asked two officers to come with him to make arrests. At the depot two padroni, Raffaelo Di Grazia, aged forty-two, and Luigi Di Biase, thirty-five, had disembarked, with four children and a number of harps and violins, from the steamer *City of Montreal*. By the time the officers arrived, two of the children had already escaped. The officers arrested the two men and the two remaining boys, aged eleven and twelve, and confiscated a number of harps and violins purchased by Di Grazia in Paris.[61]

The arrest was not accidental. The SPCC had been trailing Di Grazia for the previous two years. This padrone, described by a *Times* reporter as "a swarthy, beetle-browed fellow, with an undercurrent of savagery," was alleged to have sold twenty boys in the west in November 1876, before escaping back to Italy to recruit more children. SPCC officials kept in touch with officials in Italy, and in early November 1878 the Italian consul in Le Havre telegraphed the consulate in New York to say that Di Grazia had come from his home town of Lagonegro (although the *Times* later reported his home town as Calvello) in Basilicata with six children and instruments and had embarked for Liverpool.[62] The Italian consul informed the SPCC and immigration officers at Castle Garden of the group's impending arrival.

Di Grazia was charged with cruelty to children and brought to the Tombs Police Court in Manhattan for a hearing. However, the judge released him for lack of evidence. As Di Grazia made his way down the steps from the court, a United States marshal arrested him under the federal "Padrone Act." Again the SPCC was behind the arrest; in fact, the society's counsel was an assistant to the federal prosecutor at the hearing. The examination lasted several days. The children stated that they had neither been kidnapped nor forced to work by Di Grazia. The two children were brothers from the town of Vignolo on the Calabria-Basilicata border. Their father, a charcoal-burner, borrowed money from relatives to send the boys to America, and brought his sons to Naples where he entrusted them to Di Grazia. The judge held that "there could be no moral doubt of the prisoner's guilt," but there was insufficient evidence to hold him. He was released with a warning. The children were placed in the custody first of the SPCC and then of the Italian consul-general, who sent them back to Italy two months later with four other children "rescued" by the Italian consul and the SPCC in Baltimore.[63]

The 1874 "Padrone Act" proved, on the whole, ineffective. As Secchi de Casali and the *New York Times* had warned, it was no easy matter to prove that children had actually been inveigled – that they had been forced or enticed to leave their homes in Italy; and it was also difficult to prove beyond a doubt that the children were being held against their will. The Di Grazia case demonstrated clearly the act's shortcomings and the virtual impossibility of obtaining a conviction. However, a major breakthrough occurred in 1879 in the precedent-setting case of *Ancarola v. US*.[64]

The New York Society for the Prevention of Cruelty to Children took the initiative in this case. In September 1879 officials in Italy warned the society that a padrone named Antonio Giovanni Ancarola was about to land in America with a number of children. The New York SPCC warned officials of the society in other port cities to keep an eye open for the padrone, and it also notified the commissioner of emigration. No trace of the boys or master was to be found for several weeks, until the Italian consul-general in Marseilles reported that Ancarola had left that port with seven boys. In early November the seven boys were apprehended as they disembarked in New York from a steamer that had sailed from Liverpool. All the boys had been trained to tell the same story – that they had an uncle in Montreal and were going to meet him. They admitted that the story was false, but said that they had been threatened with severe punishment for giving any other answer. The children, who ranged in age from nine to thirteen, had been indentured by their parents or guardians to Ancarola for four-year terms at a rate of sixteen to thirty-two dollars per year. Unlike many of the street children, all seven of these boys could read and write. The children's harps and violins were seized and locked up in the customs-house in the hope that Ancarola might claim them. When that manoeuvre failed, a commissioner issued a warrant for the padrone's arrest. Five days later he was discovered in a saloon in the rear of 87 Crosby Street. He was indicted on seven counts, to which he pleaded not guilty, and was ordered to stand trial before a jury in mid-December.

At trial the jury was asked to consider a number of questions regarding Ancarola's guilt. First, could it be proved that the accused had brought the children to the United States from a foreign port, in his custody, and that he had selected the mode of conveying them? Second, had the children been inveigled in Italy? Were they apprehended unlawfully in Italy for the purposes of employment in the United States as beggars or street musicians? Was it Ancarola's intent to hold them involuntarily for those purposes? Did he do so knowingly? Only if all these questions were answered in the affirmative could the accused be found guilty under the "Padrone Act."

The district attorney persuaded the judge to admit two important pieces of evidence. The first was the assertion of one of the boys that Ancarola had led him to believe that he would earn a great amount of money in the United States. This swept away one of the defence's arguments that the children had not been inveigled – that is, deceived, enticed, or allured by false representations. The second was the Italian law of 1873 prohibiting the emigration of children for the purpose of employment in street trades. Any contract by which parents leased their children to masters was rendered null and void by this act. The defence argued that that law should not be introduced to the jury because the jury might end up convicting under an Italian law. Indeed, the judge, in his final charge to the jury, warned them to beware of that danger. However, he also admitted the Italian law as evidence, and in that way the district attorney was able to prove that no contract existed between the parents and the master. This gave even stronger support to his argument that the children had been inveigled. After a short deliberation, the jury found Ancarola guilty. His counsel moved for a new trial, but the motion was denied. He was sentenced to the maximum five-year prison term, and was fined one dollar. The judge expressed his desire "to inflict a punishment that will tend to prevent violations of this law in the future, and, it may be, make this, the first conviction, also the last."[65]

Judge Benedict was correct: Ancarola's was the only conviction under the "Padrone Act." The number of Italian child street musician had certainly diminished during the 1870s; now the children had virtually disappeared. It could be that the decrease had less to do with legislation than with the improvement in the economy as the depression of 1873–8 came to an end. American nativist passions subsided, and as railroads and mines were developed the padroni began to import adult immigrants, from the same home towns as the children and from other towns and regions of Italy and beyond.⁶⁶ The abuse they poured on these new "slaves" was as great as and at times greater than that which they had inflicted on the young children. New laws, however, would deal with that problem.

CHAPTER FIVE

Italian Legislation 1868–1873

During the 1860s and 1870s Italian statesmen, bureaucrats, and diplomats were concerned with the plight of the street children. In 1868 a parliamentary commission investigated the trade (tratta) and drew up a bill sponsored by two ministries to prohibit the use of children in itinerant occupations. Over the next five years the bill was debated and modified in both houses of the Italian Parliament until it was finally passed. It seems odd that a few thousand children should have commanded the attention of so many officials at all levels of government, especially when they had other important concerns. The Ministry of Foreign Affairs, for example, which took the lead in exploring the problem, was struggling to maintain the sympathies of Louis Napoleon while attempting to annex the remaining Papal States to Italy. The Ministry of the Interior and the Ministry of Justice, which were also deeply involved in drafting the 1868 bill, were also concerned about the division of the country into administrative units, and about brigandage.[1] The plight of the children, however, required attention: it raised many important issues concerning Italy's reputation abroad, the role of the state in the family sphere, freedom of movement, the problem of emigration, and the poverty of the Italian south. The legislative process during this period shows how forces such as nationalism and liberalism introduced tensions into the quest to regulate the problem.

The history of Italian laws regarding children and youth in itinerant occupations began as far back as the pre-unification era in Naples and the Duchy of Parma. The Bourbon representative in Florence was so moved by the sight of an abandoned Neapolitan child on the streets of the Tuscan city that a law was passed in Naples in 1841 which provided that "minors could not leave the Kingdom if not accompanied by close relatives, who must assume the responsibility to feed them, to treat them well, and to return them to the Kingdom."[2] This law probably explains the care with which apprenticeship contracts were drawn up between parents and padroni in Viggiano, Laurenzana, and in other towns south of Potenza.

Three years later Parma passed a similar law. As the situation worsened and more and more children were taken from the duchy to faraway cities with street musicians and other performers, officials realized the need for a more clearly defined law. On 27 October 1852, the Bourbon duke, Charles III, issued a decree prohibiting the export of children for profit to distant places, especially children from mountain villages. Anyone entrusting or receiving a child for this purpose would be fined 100 to 1,000 lire, and would be liable to a prison sentence of one month to a year. Those holding children within Europe were obliged to return with them within six months; those holding the children elsewhere were obliged to return within a year. The edict was sent to all Parmesan consulates, which at that time were found throughout Europe and in San Francisco, New York, Montevideo, Rio de Janeiro, and Alexandria.[3] Despite the advantages of absolute rule, however, Charles III was unable to extirpate the trade. When Parma became part of the Italian kingdom, the commerce in children was at its peak.

After the Italian unification, government officials also became concerned about the problem. In the early 1860s Italian officials in various cities began to complain to their superiors in Turin about the children. The most vocal of these was the consular representative to Paris, Luigi Cerruti, whom we first encountered in chapter 2. Cerruti's 1862 report on the consular district of Paris was influential in attracting the attention of Foreign Ministry officials. New circulars emerged from that office almost immediately, and notes of caution were issued to embassies and consulates around the world concerning child cruelty and abuse of passport privileges. The Foreign Ministry warned the Ministry of the Interior, which in turn instructed provincial prefects and mayors to exercise caution in issuing passports to men who intended to leave the country with children.[4]

The most important circular, "more for its generous aims than for its practical effect," was that issued on 30 September 1864 to all diplomatic and consular officials of the kingdom. Noting that even the work of the Ministry of the Interior was to no avail, the secretary-general of the Foreign Ministry, Marcello Cerruti (Luigi Cerruti's brother), asked all consular and diplomatic officials also to exercise caution in issuing passports and travel permits to individuals suspected of using children in "mendicant trades." If children in street performing seemed to be cruelly treated, or to lack a means of livelihood, or were explicitly trying to avoid the military draft, and if they had no papers proving that they had been entrusted to their padroni, then the laws regarding passports and travel permits were to be strictly applied to them and to their padroni. Consular officals should also do their best to repatriate the children. The circular proved ineffective, and many consuls and ministry officials wondered how it was that padroni continued to leave the Basilicatan towns with passports and children.[5]

From late 1864 until 1868 neither ministry suggested new remedies for dealing with the child street performers. The occasional complaint from a consul, especially from Cerruti in Paris, caused momentary discomfort; however, the staff at the Foreign Ministry proposed no specific legislation. After all, the Public Safety (Pubblica Sicurezza) Act of 25 March 1865 contained a clause prohibiting all itinerant tradesmen or pedlars from employing individuals under the age of eighteen without the written permission of parents or guardians. In addition, there was no public pressure to deal with the children. Of course, a consul would submit the occasional letter from abroad alluding to the young mendicants, but the matter remained under the jurisdiction of the Ministry of External Affairs.[6]

In late January 1868 the Italian Parliament briefly referred to child emigrants from the kingdom, but within the context of the greater problem of the increasing emigration from Italy. This was the first time that the issue was raised in the Chamber of Deputies. The awkward topics that were raised during this question period would continue to plague Italian statesmen and bureaucrats for many decades. The first of these was the manner in which emigration wounded national pride. As one member put it: "Without doubt I am not for impeding Italian citizens from emigrating, if they so wish to. But certainly emigration is not an attractive or comforting thought, nor is it good for the political cause of the new kingdom of Italy to witness this sad sight of so many citizens being forced to emigrate. This brings grave discredit to the country which finds no possibility of an honest living for the working population."

It was significant that this deputy, Ercole Lualdi, should have begun with the premise that he was not in favour of restricting the citizen's freedom of movement. In that age of liberalism, when the citizen's rights and liberties were considered paramount by reformers, when left-wing parliamentarians especially wished to juxtapose their "freedom" with the "tyranny" of the Bourbons (who had recently been forced to relinquish power in Naples) or of the Papal States, they went to great pains to address the problem of freedom of movement. Another deputy, Carlo Arrivabene (Valenti Gonzaga), in the same sitting introduced the problem of the tratta dei bianchi, or the white slave trade. He began his intervention by recognizing that "in a country as free as ours it is very difficult to desire to stop emigration, whatever its causes, especially when in so many cases emigration is an advantage to the mother country." Yet another member warned the prime minister that he could prevent people from evading the draft, that he could protect children from cruelty and misrepresentation, but that he should "place no obstacle before the emigration of honest workmen; for if they leave their homeland they do so only because they are not fairly recompensed for their labour here."[7]

Although the issue of freedom of movement was referred to only in passing at that sitting, it would prove one of the great stumbling-blocks to legislation governing the street children. Generally, the right wing did not accept an individual's right to total freedom of movement. From a purely economic standpoint, it drove up the cost of labour and caused discontinuities in the labour market. From a social standpoint, it upset the social order in that it gave peasants, sharecroppers, and landless labourers greater freedom from the landowning classes. Emigration also threatened moral values, for emigrants far from the family and village could be vulnerable to all kinds of exploitation. The left was aware of these threats to the emigrant, but at the same time cherished the principle of freedom of movement. This presented a great quandary.[8]

It was at the sitting of 30 January 1868 that the problem of the children was first introduced to the Italian Parliament. The prime minister and minister of external affairs, General Luigi Menabrea, affirmed that the government was aware of the rising rates of child emigration and of the implications for military service, although its main concern was the cruel treatment of the children and the fact that they were being lured to other countries by false representations. The government could do only so much, argued Menabrea. Private citizens would also have to co-operate so that the impoverished classes might find work in their own country.

Although the child street musicians came up in the discussion, the need to legislate reforms affecting them was not seen as pressing. All this changed with the publication of the 1868 report of the Société Italienne de Bienfaisance. The description of the living and working conditions of "les petits italiens" shocked the Italian parliamentarians. Even more important, the document was published by an official agency. Until that time the plight of the children could be ascribed to hearsay, or at least relegated to the status of an internal matter in the Foreign Ministry. On Italian streets the children's presence was taken for granted. Now, however, the issue was in the public forum, and Parliament reacted swiftly.[9]

On 18 May 1868 two left-wing members, Giuseppe Guerzoni (whom we have already met) and Antonio Oliva, expressed their wish to question the prime minister about what the government had done or intended to do to end the trade in children described in the Société's report. Because of the press of other matters, the question was postponed until the following sitting. Three days later Guerzoni and Oliva reintroduced the matter. Guerzoni went on at some length about the children, and quoted extensively from the report. He then pressed the foreign affairs minister and the minister of the interior to say what they had done to resolve the problem.

The discussion that ensued between Guerzoni, Oliva, Menabrea and Carlo Cadorna, the minister of the interior, addressed major and minor issues. Occasional jabs arrived from the left – the child trade was a result of the repressive practices of the old regime and the clergy; protecting the children was part of the new administration's mission to redress the evils that preceded the formation of the new kingdom. Of far more import was the recurring theme of national pride. Italy had only recently been united (in fact, the Papal States had yet to join the former "geographical expression"). It was important that Italy's emigrants, who were in a sense representatives of their country, not shame the madrepatria (motherland). (In the 30 January sitting, Carlo Arrivabene, referring to the children in Paris and London, had stated that "unfortunately, because they are Italian, they in some way represent Italy.") Giuseppe Guerzoni compared the trade to a hydra's head, which had to be cut off so that "Italy would no longer be known abroad as the land of beggars and mountebanks, that it no longer be perturbed within the country by a plague which impoverishes it and makes it seem that there are no schools in Italy to educate children, no elementary schools to draw its children, no workshops to employ them." [10]

Another important issue was the shape that reform should take. Between 1868 and 1873 specific means were often proposed, discussed, and questioned. Virtually all government officials, however, seemed in agreement with the underlying philosophy of the reforms, which were liberal and utilitarian. This was best summarized by Prime Minister Menabrea at the 21 May 1868 sitting; he in turn was simply reiterating the views of various consular officials and of the Société Italienne de Bienfaisance: "The best way to promote the moralisation of the country is by inspiring love of work in our youth, by ensuring that children are educated in their own country and that they dedicate themselves to useful jobs, instead of sending them abroad to work at trades which lead to an early and miserable death, or which mark in their souls the life of the vagabond which is the immediate cause of crime."

The underlying premise was that mendicancy among children had to be eliminated because it was a useless profession. In a utilitarian world the life of the vagabond beggar had no value. Even more important, mendicancy, for the nineteenth-century liberal, was but the prelude to crime. The only way to prevent this malady was to educate the child and to ensure that he or she was trained in a useful trade. Oliva also saw education as the only long-term solution to the problem – specifically a lay education as opposed to a religious one. Only in this way, he argued could "the dignity of the Italian citizen be raised even where it lies prostrate, and could those human and civil sentiments which seem to have died out be reawakened." But since education for all would be a long time coming, short-term measures were necessary. The ultimate goal was, in Menabrea's words, the "moralization of the country." That goal would remain a foundation of all the debates on the "child slave trade" law: rarely did a legislative committee member or deputy direct his attention to the destiny of the child himself. It was always the safety, the pride, or the "moralization" of the country that was at stake.[11]

Carlo Cadorna, who had been appointed minister of the interior only a few months previously, introduced the third major issue, one that would prove a barrier to legislation over the next five years. The state was seeking a remedy to the problem of young children being sent to work abroad; but did the state have a right to intervene in the affairs of the family? If not, how could that intervention be avoided? Cadorna admitted that the matter was "extremely difficult and delicate": "if on the one hand one is dealing with the guidance of poor and innocent children, on the other hand one is attempting to avoid absolutely an illegitimate intervention in the parents' authority [patria potestà] in the family; not even for [one] who is jealous of the principles of liberty is it easy to determine these limits." The line between preventing child abuse and intruding in the family sphere was indeed a fine one, but a risk had to be taken. Cadorna felt that indirect measures, such as the denial of passports, would never solve the problem.[12]

For Cadorna, the root of the problem was the contract signed by the padrone or agent and by the father or guardian of the child; this was true for child vagabonds within and outside the kingdom. The efficacious solution would be a precisely worded law nullifying and declaring criminal some of the contracts. This would require clearing some legal hurdles. Under article 63 of the Public Safety Act, no itinerant tradesman or vendor could have working with him an individual under the age of eighteen without the written consent of the child's parents or guardians. This law implicitly acknowledged the evil that could derive from the trade, yet still sanctioned the contract because the parent or guardian was a party to it.

It was this inconsistency that Cadorna rebuked: "I believe that the law cannot allow a father the unchecked, unlimited right to speculate on the labour and work of his own child, giving him to another's authority by means of a contract. I think that the law has a right to intervene for the safeguard of these innocents, when certain facts, foreseen by the law, prove that they are denied the natural protection and guidance of their father." [13]

Cadorna's proposal seemed oversimplified – a law nullifying certain contracts could provide a comprehensive solution to the child trade. Yet eventually this idea was adopted as one of the clauses in the final legislation of 1873. In fact, in the Ancarola case in New York, the judge used this clause to prove that Ancarola's children had truly not been under contract even though a document existed, because the Italian law had nullified all such contracts.

Cadorna knew that it would be difficult to draft the law. The legislators would have to distinguish between children brought abroad by their parents and those under the care of a third party, and they would have to specify which trades minors would be allowed to practice. The minister of the interior none the less expressed his willingness to draft a bill if the House was willing.

The deputies evidently were in agreement that a bill must be passed. Carlo Cadorna lost his post in the ministerial shuffle later in the year. The ministries of Justice, External Affairs, and the Interior formed a committee to propose the most effective means of blocking and ending the trade in children. The Ministry of External Affairs unofficially took the lead in drafting the legislation, probably because the emigration of the children was the most serious aspect of the problem, and because it was the consular officials who had made the government aware of the problem. The committee sat nine times between 10 June and 23 July 1868. A first draft of legislation was prepared and submitted to the prime minister, and the committee was disbanded. Menabrea, in his other role as minister of external affairs, sent a questionnaire on 5 August to all Italian diplomatic and consular staff abroad, and to prefects within the kingdom, asking for their comments and criticisms. When most of the answers had been received, the committee was re-established and instructed to consider the diplomatic representatives' proposed changes to the legislation. This was done over three meetings between 24 November and 1 December 1868. Finally, on 16 January 1869, a supplementary session was convened to examine a few details. A review of the committee meetings and of the suggestions of the diplomats gives us an insight into the criteria behind the legislative proposals.

The legislative committee was headed by Giuseppe Maria de Mari. Other members included Cristoforo Negri, Francesco Gloria, and Filippo Ambrosoli, who had served as the royal district attorney (procuratore) in the province of Chiavari. During their first nine meetings in June and July 1968 the committee members did essentially what was expected of them. They examined all existing legislation that might have a bearing on the problem – for example, passport regulations and especially laws regarding children. This review convinced them that new legislation would be necessary. Article 63 of the Public Safety Act might prohibit anyone from keeping a child under sixteen years as an itinerant wanderer without the express permission of his parents, but in effect this law sanctified the right of parents to entrust their child to a third party. Articles 441 and 445 imposed severe penalties on anyone who gave his child to a third party for the purposes of begging, who let his child wander, or who refused his child an education: but parents could always claim that they had entrusted their children to a padrone who claimed he was taking them abroad as "little artists." The committee also addressed the difficulty of enforcing Italian laws abroad, the diligence of Italian consuls in ensuring that the law was applied to nationals living abroad, and the question of just punishment.[14]

These obstacles, however, seemed minor in comparison with the deeper questions of the nature and scope of the legislation. Committee members agreed that laws had to be extremely strong to end the trade in children; otherwise, they would be useless. But what did "end the trade" mean? A complete prohibition on child wanderers? (The term "wanderer," or "girovago," was used deliberately: it replaced the earlier term "ambulante," or "itinerant.") But this prohibition might conflict with the rights of citizens. Was the committee failing to address the more general problem of emigration from the peninsula? Francesco Gloria cautioned against confusing the two issues. The children were part of the greater Italian emigration; however, theirs was "not a true emigration but rather an ignoble commerce, a source of crime and immoral in itself."[15] But would not such a law infringe on the freedom of movement across borders, or even on the right of a father to employ his own child?

The committee agreed that it was possible that a padrone might treat his employee kindly, that a father might be benevolent towards his child while employing him abroad; however, the opposite would be true in thousands of other cases. The intentions of employers had to be put aside in constructing the law, and the effect of the trade had to be kept in mind. But what if, for example, a father was injured at his work or, even worse, in the military, and he was able to play an instrument, and could earn money by going abroad and playing on the streets? Did he not have a right to bring his own children with him? Stepping down from a theoretical possibility to reality, the legislators noted that this was an unlikely situation; in any event, the children were almost always brought abroad by a third party rather than by their parents.

There was yet another serious difficulty in the complete prohibition of children in itinerant trades: which professions should be included in the prohibition? Many itinerant trades were honourable, argued the committee members in their first report to the prime minister – tinsmiths, coppersmiths, and especially figurine-makers from Lucca. In these "honest" trades many children worked under padroni. The case was different when it came to mountebanks, charlatans, itinerant singers, exhibitors of monkeys and dancing dogs, and others of that type. These trades were "la maschera dell'accattonaggio," or "mendicancy's mask." Still, it would be difficult to distinguish precisely which trades would be included in the list.

The committee presented a draft of the legislation with fourteen articles, which closely resembled the final draft of 1873. Menabrea circulated the draft to consuls and legates around the world. The minister of the interior sent copies to prefects in the kingdom, and the minister of justice sent copies to the district attorneys of each province. The officials were asked to submit their suggestions for improvement. Many of the responses gave a short resumé of the child street musician problem in their town or cities: consuls, of course, wrote about child immigrants, while prefects reported on child emigrants. Some merely repeated the laws or what was already known about the trade. Comments ranged from brief statements to meticulous point-by-point criticisms.

Almost all the constructive comments centred on two main questions: who should be prohibited from playing music on the streets of foreign countries, and who should be responsible for administering the proposed law abroad? One official from the Ministry of Justice felt that not all street musicians should be prohibited from performing abroad, because some were respectable. He used the example of the children from Viggiano, who came from a long tradition of street performing and who were usually brought to foreign countries by their parents. The district attorney from the province of Genova wondered whether the state should be passing a law which would enter the family realm; he felt that children should be allowed to cross borders even if they were in itinerant trades, as long as they were accompanied by their parents or an older sibling. He felt that this would solve the problem of children who emigrated with family members "such as that class of emigrants which [Menabrea] referred to as *viggianesi*" (perhaps he did not know that they were from a town called Viggiano). Like the general administrator from Basilicata, he advocated the prohibition of child vagabonds within and outside the Italian state. The prefect from Genova agreed that children under sixteen should be allowed to emigrate only with their parents. He added the stipulation that parents should post a bond that would be applied to the payment of a fine and repatriation costs should the parents send the child out to beg once they were abroad.[16]

The prefect of Basilicata strongly opposed to viggianesi being made an exception "simply because they claim to be belong to a relatively respectable class of musicians, and because with the guidance of parents they are treated with love ... the so-called viggianesi, in my point of view, must not be excluded." The prefect seemed unable to distinguish between one who perceived his skill as a means of earning a living and one who had a vocation for music, between the professional performer and the worker forced to emigrate and play his instrument on the streets. He added that if these children "might wish to learn music for an artistic career, the law would not prevent that, and they could do that to their great profit in their own home towns and in public conservatories ... and as adults they could bring their talent around the world. The end result, therefore, would be to put an end to their wandering now as children, that they might as adults to their great profit tour the world with their talents."[17] The consul-general to New York, Ferdinando De Luca, seemed to have the same misunderstanding about the nature of the children's migration. He hoped that music schools might be organized so "that the young artists might be destined with time to employment in theatrical, chapel, or conservatory orchestras."[18]

The consuls were also concerned with the manner in which the law might be applied abroad. According to the draft legislation, the onus fell on the consular officials to record the names of all known padroni and children; to send the list of names to the Ministry of Foreign Affairs; to keep in contact with local authorities on the matter; to take care not to issue passports to padroni; and to arrange for repatriation of the children. Consular officials were liable to a fine if they were negligent in their duties. As might be expected, the consuls did not warm to these proposals; their attitude stemmed not from a desire to avoid work, but from a realization that the demands of the proposed bill were impractical. The consul in Berne told the prime minister that repatriation was a responsibility for consuls but that the work of stamping out the trade in each country must be left to the diplomatic missions. L.E. Melegari also questioned the wisdom of repatriation.[19] The poverty that caused the children's emigration would prevent their return. Internal reforms were necessary so that the children might have other possibilities open to them. The head of the Italian legation in Washington, Marcello Cerruti (the former secretary-general of the Ministry of Foreign Affairs) also argued against repatriation. Some of the children would be able to make a living as independent musicians (that is, they would not be tied to padroni). In America the young itinerants had become used to the free life, and if they went back to their villages, where no one could help them or give them a job, they would soon remigrate.[20]

Ferdinando De Luca thought that the consular authorities should have less responsibility for the children. Especially in London and New York – one wonders why he did not include Paris – it was difficult to get complete information about street musicians. The responsibility should lie instead with the officials in the sending villages, who should draw up lists of people in their towns to be watched carefully. These lists should then be circulated among the consular offices abroad. (Ironically, a serendipitous encounter with a viggianese allowed De Luca to submit the most nearly complete list of padroni received from any consular official three months later.) Similarly, the consular agent in Alexandria objected to drawing up lists of children for repatriation and to bearing the responsibility of repatriating the children. His consulate did not have the financial means to keep an eye on the children; in addition, he could not stay in contact with the police in his district because "in the countries of the Levant and Barbary Coast there's not one policeman on whom you can count."[21]

The prefect of Como felt that there was no need to impose fines on consular officials for neglect of duty: there already existed a code of discipline within the ministry to which officials could resort. The head of the legation in Paris, Costantino Nigra, advocated higher fines not only for accomplices in the trade but also for negligent government officials. He also stressed that greater responsibility should be allocated to the officials of the towns from which the emigrants originated.

One question that, surprisingly, never arose was whether it was within the consulate's jurisdiction to ensure that Italian nationals obeyed the laws of the country in which they lived. Traditionally, consular officials were responsible for monitoring the trade of other countries, bearing in mind Italy's interests. They also defended the interests of Italian traders and investors abroad. Because it was to the advantage of businessmen to maintain friendly relations with the consulates, the consular officials occupied positions of prestige in Italian expatriate communities. But as the number of Italian immigrants increased in the mid-nineteenth century, it became impossible for consuls to maintain face-to-face contact with all Italian nationals in their districts. Yet there was an implicit understanding that those immigrants had to be monitored. When the consuls were asked to administer the law concerning itinerant children, no one was opposed to the principle of policing; only the practicality of doing so was questioned. In fact, the consul in Hamburg objected to the proposal that consular officials assume these duties on the sole ground that ultimately the consul could resort only to threats to free the children from the padroni: "Suggestion and threats from the consuls when not followed up by coercive action will do nothing but diminish their moral authority over the Italians."[22]

Many other comments and minor objections arrived from prefects, prosecutors, and the diplomatic corps, but their concern was directed primarily to the issues described above. In late November 1868, Prime Minister Menabrea had the bill re-examined by the ministries of Justice, the Interior, and External Affairs. He asked that the legislative committee be re-established to consider all the suggestions. One of these committee members, Cristoforo Negri, who had just come back from a trip to France, Germany, and England, saw the need for radical provisions in the bill. The general objectives of the bill remained intact, though some minor but significant changes were made. For example, Baron Heath's recommendation that the qualifying phrase "of both sexes" follow "children" in article 1 was accepted, as was Nigra's call for higher fines. Francesco Gloria once again voiced his fears that the bill might infringe on civil liberties. The members also considered carefully whether the viggianesi children should be excluded from the law. In the end, they were included.

The final reading of the proposed bill in committee took place on 1 December 1868. On 16 January 1869 the committee was called together for a final supplementary meeting to re-examine some minor details. The bill was presented to the Senate a few months later. The Senate had one major objection. While the Menabrea ministry had proposed strict fines and jail sentences for anyone who might bring minors abroad as itinerants, it had not addressed the problem in the interior; that is, it did not make provision for accomplices in Italy who assisted in taking a child abroad. The Senate insisted that all those involved in getting the child from the point of origin to the destination should be liable to a penalty: the persons who forfeited the child, those who held him, those who led him across the border, and those who accepted him on the other side. In other words, the law must punish all aspects of the trade. The law applied to children employed in "wandering" trades both inside and outside Italy, argued the Senate. The upper House also voted unanimously to raise the age limit of children and youth employed in wandering trades from sixteen to eighteen. It was thought that it might be difficult to ascertain on sight that children were under sixteen, but easier to recognize that they were under eighteen.

For a number of reasons the bill was not sent back to Parliament until 19 March 1873.[23] It was preceded by a report and supporting documents prepared by a new commission. The driving force behind this seven-man committee was Giuseppe Guerzoni. He was also joined by his close friend Carlo Arrivabene (Valenti Gonzaga). Guerzoni's views were based on a liberal philosophy, on ideas of progress, and an undying faith in the state as educator. In reading the report to Parliament, Guerzoni reminded the deputies that "everything, honourable colleagues, in nature as in society is linked: no atom is left unconsidered, no force is lost. Customs, traditions, history, education, revolution, reaction, laws, everything has a place, everything works towards towards a goal, everything conspires towards one end, everything serves and helps society to climb the tiring [faticoso] spiral of human progress, and to fulfil the arcane law of their transformation."

The actual goal was ill-defined, hazy, and couched in nationalistic terms: "the Italian nation [popolo] like all young nations, desires, expects the impulse [from government] but having received it walks on its own with its own strength until it reaches the indicated goal." [24]

It was the liberal and utilitarian perspective that caused Guerzoni and others difficulty in drawing up the bill. They allowed their own preconceptions of what was useful for society to confuse the scope of the legislation – that is, the protection of children. Street performing was an unproductive trade, of no value to the nation and embarrassing when exported to other countries. The bill was aimed at children who were involved in "professioni girovaghe," in wandering trades, as opposed to "professioni ambulanti," or itinerant trades. "Wanderers" denoted anyone in street performing: mountebanks, charlatans, rope-dancers, diviners, singers, musicians, and animal exhibitors. Bootblacks, newspaper-vendors, figurine-vendors, knife-grinders, and their young assistants were all useful, productive workers, and they came under the category of itinerants. Therefore, itinerant trades should be open to children and wandering trades prohibited to them. The problem was to reconcile this distinction with the notion of personal liberty.

This problem impinged especially on the crucial question of the extent to which the state could interfere in family matters. Guerzoni defended the bill on the ground that the state must guarantee the child's rights under the civil law. The Napoleonic Code demanded that parents maintain and educate their children according to their financial circumstances, and it was thus that order in the family and safety in society were assured. Therefore, contended Guerzoni, the history of family legislation from 1800 to 1873 was one of constant effort to define precisely the duties of parents and the rights of children. "In the eyes of some people this might seem like a continuous invasion of the family sphere; in fact it was nothing but the direct and assiduous application of the law common to all: instruct, educate, support your children."[25] Guerzoni pointed out that Germany and the United States, both of which entered the family sphere with compulsory education and factory acts, were also the countries best known for the protection of human liberty.

The question of personal freedom also affected the state's intervention in the work sphere. Did the state have the right to prohibit a trade by which people were making a living? This was the case with street performing. One could even say that the performers provided a useful service to society. The performer "is fed by a need of society. The need to laugh has produced the clown. Society creates, protects, wants him." But society "has always appreciated entertainment less for the pleasure it gets out of it than for the pain suffered by the performers." If this was the case, argued Guerzoni, then the trade was immoral and should be prohibited. If the bill was passed as it stood then, was it not wrong – if the trade was immoral – to accept the trade but to prohibit the apprenticeship of the children in the trade? Was it not illogical to allow parents to perform and to forbid their children to do the same? The deputy from the left then skirted the issue, stating that only "love, charity, good works, education, foresight, savings, civilized institutions, the natural forces of progress," and time could cure this immoral trade, for at the root of this and all similar trades were poverty and ignorance.[26]

Guerzoni resolved the problem of freedom of work by asserting that adults had freedom, and that children's freedom was protected by prohibiting them from being forced into certain trades:

It is for this reason that the laws, as they have gradually clothed themselves with the new justice, stripping themselves of the ancient violence [of the old régime], have said: as much freedom as possible to adults, to those who have responsibility, to those who are perfect in the eyes of the law – a freedom without bounds other than those of freedom itself; protection and guidance of minors, of those without responsibility, of those imperfect under the law, of children. Whether an adult can read or not, whether he works at one trade or another, lives in this dwelling or that one, that to a certain extent is his business. But from now on, that a child with a right to an education should live in the darkness of ignorance; that a child who has a right to grow healthily should become entangled with a machine from dawn to dusk or in the choking air of a mine ... the state cannot tolerate this ... Freedom of work has no place in this argument: let him who wishes so be a mountebank or a ropedancer or a monkey-exhibitor; but do not force a child, who cannot have either the will or the choice and who, in addition, does not even profit from his sacrifice, to do this.[27]

Guerzoni distinguished between freedom for adults and freedom for children. He asserted, in essence, that certain trades were questionable; yet he was not clear on what grounds that was so. Were the trades immoral? Were they dangerous to society? To the child? To the adult? To the nation? What was being addressed? The fact that a trade was unproductive and therefore bad for society as well as for the individual? That children were forced to work at these unproductive trades? That they were forced to work in difficult conditions? Why did the bill not apply to children in mines and in industry, or even to children in other itinerant trades? And if street performing was unproductive and of no value to society, and therefore bad for the individual and society, why should it be permitted for the adult? Guerzoni warned that if anyone wished to "invoke the principle of freedom of work, then he would be arguing in favour of the child, because he [the child] is forced to a servile task which he has not chosen, for the benefit of others."[28] But this brings us back to the other argument: if this were true, the bill should have prohibited *all* itinerant trades, and, even more important, protected other Italian children who were exploited both within and outside Italy: sulphur miners in Sicily, brickmakers and stonemasons' labourers in Bavaria, glassmakers in Lyon, to name only a few.

The legislative committee was unable to distinguish clearly between its disdain for "useless" trades and its desire to protect children. In the end, Guerzoni's ostensible reason for the bill was the protection of the child. However, the fact that the proposed legislation barred children only from those trades that were deemed unproductive suggests that the children themselves were seen only in terms of their value to society. Children in other trades were being brought across the borders by people other than their parents, yet the proposed law would not apply to them. Children were exploited in a number of occupations within the country, yet there was little legal protection for them. In all the parliamentary and legislative committee discussions the only reference to these other children was Guerzoni's one comment on children who worked in the mines and in industry. Had the legislators truly been concerned with the welfare of the child, with the need to keep him from being forced into a job he did not choose, these issues would have been considered more seriously. As it stood, the bill implied that children in "wandering" trades offered nothing of value to society and shamed Italy's name abroad. Other children who worked in productive trades, even as itinerants, who might suffer as much as the wanderers, were to be left untouched by the law.

The commission, which had been asked to examine the law proposed by the Ministry of Justice (which in turn had received it from the original commission of 1868 with the recommendations of the Senate), submitted its report and its recommendations for modifications to the bill. In essence, it asked for two changes: that the minimum jail sentence be increased in almost all cases, and that the age limit be raised to eighteen. (The Ministry of Justice had not acted on the latter recommendation from the Senate, and had decided to keep the age limit at sixteen.)

The Chamber of Deputies began the final reading of the bill on 17 December 1873. The Ministry of Justice took into account the recommendations of both commissions, the Senate's comments, and other suggestions that came out of the debates of the Chamber of Deputies. The law forbade the participation of children under the age of eighteen in "wandering" trades, which included mountebanks, charlatans, street singers, and performers. Anyone, including parents who consigned their children to a third person for the purpose of carrying out one of these trades, either in Italy or abroad, was subject to a fine or a jail sentence or both. Employers were also subject to stiffer penalties: anyone who kidnapped or abused a child in Italy or abroad could face a prison sentence of three to ten years. The law also rendered null and void any contracts that engaged children in these trades. Parents or employers already abroad would be obliged to declare to the consul the number and names of children working with them, and consular officials would forward those lists to the Ministry of the Interior. On 18 December 1873 the law was passed by the Chamber of Deputies; the vote was 218 for and 12 against.[29] It was printed on 21 December. (For a summary of the bill, see Appendix B).

It is difficult to analyse the effect of the law, at least within Italy. I have been unable to find any of the lists of children's names that should have been deposited with the Ministry of the Interior. On 10 March 1874, almost three months after the bill became law and three months before consuls and mayors were to submit the names of children working abroad, the foreign minister, Visconti-Venosta, issued a circular reminding the officials that they must furnish the lists. He urged consuls to go in search of the children, and to ensure that the children made their way home; he also asked that they keep a separate account of their travel expenses for reimbursement. Two months later the minister of justice, G. de Falco, warned the district attorneys to co-operate in making the law effective. In November one official of the Foreign Ministry noted that many of the children who had been processed under the law and who had had their homeward voyages paid for were not reaching Italy. He asked that consuls arrange with the railways to keep the children under close observation. This is the only evidence that suggests that the lists of children were ever drawn up by consular officials and mayors. One last communiqué in 1882 affirmed that, despite its many shortcomings, the law was effective.[30] Parents, guardians, and padroni became aware of the law through the mayors of the villages, and through consular officials and word of mouth in the cities of destination. It is difficult, however, to ascertain whether the law instilled fear in them, whether they stopped employing children in wandering trades, and whether they stopped "exporting" them. As was observed in earlier chapters, the trade of the Basilicatan children in New York declined strongly after 1875; the same was true of Paris, as a result of the political situation in France. To a great extent, preventive action on the part of national and local governments and other agencies was responsible for this. The depressed economies of France and the United States and the small profits in street performing may also have urged the padroni to direct their young employees to new trades.

By the mid-1870s, when the Parmesans had largely left the street-performing trades, the street musicians, both child and adult, from Terra di Lavoro had replaced them in London and Moscow. When the Charity Organisation Society published its 1877 report on the Italian child street musicians, most of the children it examined were from that area. There, clearly, the Italian law had not put an end to the trade.

Ultimately, Ferdinando De Luca and others were correct when they asserted that Italian legislation alone would not solve the problem of the Italian children who performed in foreign cities. The consul-general to New York predicted that unless American state and local governments passed legislation the children and padroni would remain on the streets. Indeed, it was only with the passage of legislation in New York and of orders in council and circulars in Paris, and their effective implementation, that the two cities were able to tackle the problem; the Italian legislation did not suffice. In London and Moscow, where the local governments offered either no legislation or poorly designed laws that were applied only randomly, the children continued to perform on the streets until the 1880s and later. The Italian law of 1873 may have helped stem the flow of wandering children from Italy; however, it could not control the activities of children abroad who were not watched over by a consular agent, or who never intended to return to their mother country: the Italian law had no force abroad. The article in the 1873 bill that proved most useful in helping foreign governments end the exploitation of Italian children was that which nullified, both retroactively and prospectively, the contracts signed between parents or guardians and the padroni. It was this article that to a great extent helped condemn the padrone Giovanni Ancarola in New York in 1879. The judge did not accept Ancarola's contract because it had been signed in Italy, and under the terms of the 1873 law it did not exist. Thus the judge could show that the children had been inveigled and had not been party to any contract. In that sense Carlo Cadorna's intuition in 1868 – that any effective legislation would have to be directed at the contract – proved correct in the end.

CHAPTER SIX

Conclusion

The Italian child street musicians had largely disappeared from the streets of Europe and the Americas by the late 1880s. Their departure, like their arrival, was a product of the dialogue between the urban and the rural. Reformers in New York, London, Paris, and Rome responded to their presence with legislation to ban them from the streets. The street musicians, their masters, and their families responded to the social and economic climate in each city by directing the migration of the children to other trades or commerce or other towns, or simply by returning home. Adult street musicians also retreated from the scene. Generally, the decline in numbers of both the adult and the child street musicians can be attributed to three factors. Legislation was an important inducement, but not the predominant one, for if it was to be effective, the police and magistrates had to act upon it. The social and economic climates were significant. A general hostility to street musicians or to Italians, along with the stagnant economy of the late nineteenth century, also dissuaded Italians from continuing in this line of work. Closely tied to the last point are the general programs of the immigrants themselves. With the advancement of industrialization and urban growth they seized other economic opportunities that were socially more acceptable, though perhaps more difficult and onerous than street music.

By the 1880s it had become more difficult for children to continue performing on the streets. In New York, as we observed in chapter 4, the "Padrone Act" of 1874 was applied with vigour in 1878 and 1879, and resulted in the conviction of one padrone for importing children for the purposes of begging. The 1876 New

York state legislation that prohibited the use of children under the age of sixteen years in public entertainments, with the backing of the SPCC, also proved efficacious in curbing the presence of child street musicians. The New York State Penal Amendment Act of 1884 reinforced the previous act and clamped down on the use of children in all street performances and in many street trades.[1]

British legislation was late in coming. The old Vagrant Acts were implemented for a period in 1877 under the special orders of the home secretary. In 1889 the Act for the Prevention of Cruelty to Children (52 & 53 Vict., c. 44) finally provided explicit legal measures to prohibit the use of children in mendicant trades. Although the act dealt with many forms of cruelty to children, one specific clause was directed at any individual who "caused or procured" a child to beg or receive alms on the streets, even under the pretence of performing. One of the important arguments advanced in support of the act was the problem of the Italian children and their padroni, and the fact that Italy had passed legislation prohibiting the trade more than fifteen years previously.[2]

Although the legislation of the 1870s and 1880s might have been used effectively against the child street performers, it is doubtful whether it had a great influence on the decline of the trade. France had not passed any extraordinary laws concerning the problem since mid-century, and yet the trade there declined significantly from the late 1860s. In New York the press made no important references to the children from the late 1870s, except for the Di Grazia and Ancarola padroni cases. In Britain also, and particularly in London, children were less frequently mentioned in the numerous articles on Italian street musicians from the late 1870s and 1880s. Britain and some of the American states could have applied existing legislation to fight the problem. The British police, for example, might have driven the children from the streets with a strict application of the Vagrant Act or Bass's Street Music Act of 1864. In the Glionna case the state of Connecticut relied on the outdated Personal Liberty Bill. These measures, however, were time-consuming. Only in France did the prefect and police from time to time apply strictly the letter of the law, but even these were stopgap measures.

The declining presence of Italian children in the street music trade had more to do with social and economic conditions in the receiving centres, and with the migration programs of the sending towns in Italy, than with legislation. In the generally sluggish western economy of the late nineteenth century, Italian street performers looked for more lucrative possibilities. They also turned to occupations and destinations where their presence would be less conspicuous. Colonization projects in South America, particularly in Argentina and Brazil, and the large-scale transportation projects in the United States and Canada – railroad, bridge, and dam construction, as well as mining – attracted Italian labourers and agriculturalists, so that their participation in these sectors greatly overshadowed their presence in street entertainment.[3]

Some of the sending towns experimented with new occupations, while Italian street musicians concentrated in cities where the general public or at least the municipal authorities were less antagonistic towards them. We have remarked a number of times on the decline of street performing among the immigrants from Parma and Chiavari from about the mid-1860s. Former musicians either returned home or learned a new trade, although it is difficult to assess which new trades they entered. It is probable that many of the immigrants from some of the hamlets in the Val-di-Taro who might otherwise have gone into street performing joined the catering trades in London, in provision shops, in restaurants, or as ice-cream vendors. Immigrants from Chiavari probably were steered into fruit and vegetable peddling or retailing, a sector in which they had made an impact in the United States and London by the 1860s.

Immigrants from the towns near Potenza, and especially from Laurenzana, began to lay down their violins and harps in the 1870s, although the viggianesi stayed in the trade slightly longer. A combination of new opportunities and local antagonism changed the occupational profile of immigrants from these towns. The laurenzanesi and viggianesi had been numerous in Paris until the expulsions of 1867 to 1869. With the coming of the Commune they moved on to the United States and other countries. In New York and elsewhere immigrants from these towns continued in the street music trade until unfavourable newspaper reports, legislation prohibiting the use of children, and the end of the depression of the 1870s encouraged them to look elsewhere. One possibility was to continue in the music business, but off the streets. After Giovanni Glionna's arrest in New Haven in 1873, the Glionnas of New York moved to Toronto, and many laurenzanesi from both New York and the home town followed them. There they performed in dance bands, vaudeville theatres, department stores, and tea parties, or they gave music lessons. One of the original four Glionna brothers to move to Toronto, Vincenzo, had fifteen children, all of them musicians, many of whom played in the band he managed with Domenico Marsicano of Viggiano.[4]

Another Glionna brother, Francesco, was a carpenter, and after a few years' residence in Toronto he opened a labour agency and an immigrant hotel and saloon. With the development of transportation systems in North America, Italians who had established themselves on the continent were well placed to work in outdoor construction labour or to supply labourers to subcontractors. It was the latter that Francesco Glionna was able to do in Toronto. His townsman, Elia Pellettieri, had gone to Havana in the 1840s as a teenager, playing the harp. In the 1860s he went to Utica, New York, where he too opened up a saloon and an immigrant labour agency. His nephew, Rocco Perretta, also from Laurenzana, ran the saloon and labour agency later in the century. Giovanni Lapatino, another street musician, became a leading figure of the Italian colony in Oswego, New York. These men were able to direct emigrants from their home town and elsewhere into construction work. In Chicago, as in many other North American cities, the Italian presence in railroad and other construction projects increased as the presence of the street musicians declined. By the late 1870s the term "padrone" did not refer solely to those who managed child musicians; it applied increasingly to the middlemen who supplied Italian labourers to North American contractors and industries and mines; and the term still had overtones of dishonesty and slyness.[5]

The violinists, pipers, and fifers from Sora were the most intransigent of the street minstrels. They began to export this trade to the large European cities increasingly from the late 1860s. By the mid-1870s the majority of street musicians in Moscow and London, and probably Paris, were from the towns in the Ciociaria. But by the 1880s the number of child street performers even from those areas had declined drastically in most European centres, with the exception of London, although many adult musicians remained active. After the passage of the Act for the Prevention of Cruelty to Children in 1889, fewer Italian child minstrels were to be seen on the streets. Although the number of Italian adult street musicians had declined, it was estimated that there were still about 2,500 of them in Great Britain in 1892.[6] Charles Booth, in his famous survey of the labouring classes in London, noted that according to Italian government statistics, there were still about 1,000 organ-grinders in the metropolis in 1895: "A few Englishmen enter the trade ... but grinding is ... an essentially Italian industry."[7]

Throughout much of Europe and North America it became difficult to work in the street music trade by the end of the nineteenth century. In 1891 a British bill was introduced to restrict the activities of street organists and other musicians. It was not passed, but it did reflect public annoyance with the noise caused by street music. Many American states and cities restricted the activities of street musicians, and especially the participation of children in the trade. Consular reports on Italians abroad in 1893 noted few musicians and itinerant vendors in Austria-Hungary, except for food-vendors from northeastern Italy. Few musicians were left active in Russia. Many itinerants, especially musicians, were to be found in Germany; in Sweden and Norway the suonatori still made up a majority of the "colony," as they did in Belgium, along with artists' models. Brazil, Panama, and Cuba also claimed many Italian street musicians in the early 1890s. In New York, Fiorello La Guardia outlawed street organists in reaction to an embarrassing childhood incident in which he was ridiculed by schoolmates when his father invited a fellow Italian, a street organist, into his home.[8]

France was especially hostile to street musicians. Most of them had left the country by 1870, and the remainder departed, with other itinerants, in the mid-1890s. Throughout the 1880s French-Italian tensions concerning Tunisia and commercial trade filtered down to the working classes, where Italian migrants were seen as the cause of the the low wages paid to workers in many industries. Violent encounters between the two ethnic groups throughout the 1880s culminated in 1893 in the tragedy at Aigues-Mortes, near the salt-works, where 50 Italians were killed and 150 injured. The assassination of President Sadi Carnot by an Italian anarchist made Italian itinerants even more vulnerable to attacks. In 1895 an official of the Italian embassy in London remarked that "les modèles et les musiciens italiens nomades, ont presque tout disparu ... il en restait à peine quelques centaines dans ces derniers temps, en majeure partie des joueurs de harpe, de violon, des diseurs de chansonettes napolitaines, mais ils ont également quitté en masse le territoire français." In 1901 newspapers in Paris lamented an experimental city law that prohibited the playing of street organs in public.[9]

What happened to the children? Some continued playing their instruments on the streets and squares of Europe and the Americas. A thirty-seven-year-old street musician from a town near Sora was expelled from Britain in 1910, but public safety officials in Italy feared that no one in his home town would recognize his photograph, since he had left home as a child.[10] Others returned home or remained abroad and found new trades. By the 1890s, however, children had largely disappeared from the trade, although it was not unusual to see a young singer accompanying a street organist even after the turn of the century. Their disappearance was partly a result of public outcry and legislation, and partly a response to better economic opportunities elsewhere. Their plight in other trades was no better than it had been when they bore the weight of a harp on the streets late at night. By the 1890s Italian children in France were prominent as artists' models, chimney-sweeps, bootblacks, figurine-vendors, and especially as glassworkers. The majority of the models and glassworkers were from the towns in the Ciociaria that had sent so many young violinists to France, Britain, and Russia. In New York most young boys from Laurenzana were by the 1880s and 1890s directed into the bootblack trade, and they made up an important contingent of New York's one thousand Italian shoeshiners at the turn of the century.[11]

It is significant that once the young musicians moved off the streets, their plight was no longer publicized. Roberto Paulucci di Calboli, an Italian diplomat in London, was distressed that the press had largely forgotten the children from Picinisco, Roccasecca, and other small towns in the Ciociaria who toiled in the glassworks near Lyon in the 1890s. The only people who showed any concerned for them were the Barnabite priests in Lyon. Seven hundred thirty-eight of the 915 Italian children and youth recorded in the glassworks in 1902 were from that region. Although a French law of 1892 prohibited children under the age of thirteen from working in factories, the managers of the glassworks sent for younger children in Italy and had them come to work with their elder brothers' birth certificates. In many cases parents were not hired unless they brought their children to work with them. Because of the economic conditions at home, the parents succumbed to the employers' demands. Almost one-half of the Italian children and youth in the glassworks, however, arrived there not with their parents but with "incettatori" or padroni – that is, with men who served the same function and drew up the same kinds of contracts as the masters of the child street musicians. In the glassworks, the children worked in unhygienic conditions and faced the constant risk of pneumonia because of the extremely high temperatures of the works; they were continuously maligned by French workers, who accused them of keeping wages down, and maltreated by the souffleurs, or glassblowers, their immediate bosses, who traditionally were considered the roughest of glassworkers.[12]

In the large cities the Italian children and youths were ignored after they acquired more socially acceptable trades. Largely because of the attention of the Bonomelli Foundation, a Catholic agency founded by a bishop in Italy to serve Italian emigrants, the child glassworkers in the Lyon district were not completely forgotten. The newspapers and the social reformers did not seem to realize that the young bootblacks, newspaper-vendors, flour-carriers, models, and chimney-sweeps, who worked in occupations that did not carry the taint of mendicancy, were actually brought into the trade by exactly the same method as the street musicians – by a padrone who entered into a contract with the child's parents. Nor did they realize that the children in other trades also faced poor working conditions, health problems, long hours, and cruel masters to the same or even a greater extent than their counterparts who performed in the streets.

The language of liberal and utilitarian Europe camouflaged the fact that lawmakers, reformers, and philanthropists had not faced squarely the question of the children's welfare, but rather had been more concerned with adhering to an image. New York reformers wanted children in useful trades who would fit an "American" type. This was best exemplified by Horatio Alger's *Phil the Fiddler*, in which the young hero escapes from his padrone in New York to a Protestant doctor in New Jersey, and eventually makes good. Italian reformers could not stop alluding to Italy's need to maintain a good image abroad now that it had become united, and the urgency of removing the young street musicians, who were nothing but beggars. Reformers in London were at first concerned with the noise made by the musicians. Once they faced the issue of the "Italian organ boys" they became bogged down in questions about the rights of the individual. Were child musicians really beggars or did they work for a living? Did Britain have the right to interfere with the free movement of people? France was primarily concerned with law and order, and when it was decided that a law should be applied, they swiftly expelled hundreds of children with great efficiency.

The Italian itinerants and the various municipal, provincial, and national bodies carried on a dialogue over the course of the nineteenth century in which both sides obtained only partly satisfactory results. The padroni might have directed children towards different trades and different cities, but the rewards of being a master were certainly still worth the trouble. The children and youth were now in different circumstances, but their suffering was not diminished as they left the streets; indeed, they often found themselves facing even harsher working conditions. Through the efforts of European and North American reformers, police, and reporters, most of the children disappeared from the streets. If they felt they were acting in the children's best interests, however, they were not entirely correct. Indeed, it was difficult for them to distinguish between helping the children and simply trying to rid the streets of those whom they perceived as vagrants. One is more touched by the actions of a Barnabite priest or the Italian consul Luigi Cerruti, who actually befriended the children and followed them on an individual basis when reformers had long forgotten them.

APPENDIX A

Sample Contracts between a Padrone and a Parent

EXAMPLE 1

With the following, even though a private document still valid for the future, it is declared that Giuseppe P., son of the late Antonio, and Domenico B., son of the late Vito from the township of Saponara, come to the following agreement signed by them with an x. The said P., needing a lad for his street music trade, thus asked the said B. to lease him the work of his youngest son, Antonio, also a street musician; and B., having assented to P.'s request, has thus given him his son for a period of three years, counting from the day of departure, with the obligation on the part of P. to teach him to play, to buy him a harp, and to give him eight ducats in cash; and should the lad not behave well he can send him to the police without harp or cash; he is obliged to provide him with shoes, clothes and food, and at the end of the three-year period he must give him a new suit of clothes, beyond the one for daily use, according to the season; and should B. wish to flee from his master P., then his father is obliged to pay all the costs incurred to find him, and in case he should try to withold one grano [a fraction of a carlino] from P., then P. shall withhold one carlino [a fraction of a ducat] from his salary, and this proportionately; if B. should accidentally break the performing instrument, then P. shall bear the cost of repair or replacement; if the instrument is damaged owing to B.'s own negligence, then B. must pay for repairs or replacement; if B. should by chance fall sick, he shall be cured at P.'s expense, or, if the illness is self-induced, at B.'s expense. The parties have agreed that a fine of forty-nine ducats is payable by the offender to the aggrieved, so that if B. is missing to the master P., or if P. should maltreat B. without cause, they shall be subject to arrest if there is a case of reneging. Thus have they agreed upon these terms in the presence of these undersigned witnesses, the two parties having declared themselves illiterate.

Viggiano, 12 February 1861
[Followed by signatures and X's]
SOURCE: L. Cerruti, "Cenni statistici" 599–600

EXAMPLE 2

The year 1866, the 30th day of September, in Viggiano.

With the following, even if it is a private document, with two original copies: it is declared by Pasquale ... son of the late Nicola as one party, and Pietro ... as the other, both from Viggiano, that they have come to the following contract: The said Pasquale ... has in the presence of the undersigned witnesses declared that, having to travel through the kingdom [of Naples] or even outside the kingdom, in order to earn a living as a street musician and having to borrow lads in order to meet this goal, has thus asked the said Pietro ... to entrust to him his sons Francesco and Vincenzo ... also street musicians, one a violinist and the other a harpist; Pietro has happily agreed, although on the condition that Pasquale ... treat the said boys as his own children, that he provide them with shoes and clothes, and that he administer to them all the necessary food. To recompense Pietro for the service lent him during the three-year term counting from the day of departure, the padrone ... will take on the duty of handing over to the father, Pietro ... one hundred fourteen ducats for all the years, and in addition will give him some money each time Pasquale ... sends some money to his wife. Once the journey is over he must bring back the said boys with him to their family, giving them a new suit of clothes and another second-hand suit, according to the season, and a new violin and a new harp worth ten ducats, and should it be worth more he shall be refunded by Pietro for the amount over ten ducats; with the understanding that if the children should break the instruments by accident then the padrone is responsible for the costs incurred, whereas if the children break them while fooling around with them, or on purpose, then Pietro will be responsible for the costs; just as if, in the remote possibility that the children should take ill for fifteen days or for a month, it does not matter; but should they be ill for longer than that, the padrone must keep them with him none the less, but the children will lose their monthly stipend even if this is an illness sent to them by God. If they self-induce their illness then all the expenses shall be incurred by Pietro, it being understood also that the said children shall be obedient to the padrone in their work, and evening after evening they shall hand over in his own hands all the money they earn, without profiting in the least from that which they earn; and if they hold back a grano [a fraction of a carlino] the master can hold back one carlino; if they hold back one carlino, the master can withhold ten carlini, and so forth; and finally if either party reneges on any of part of this contract or on the contract as a whole, or should the boys wish to leave the master even though they have not been abused, or should the master abuse the children or abandon them, then either shall be subject to a fine of thirty ducats for damages and interest. To seal that which has been said, Pasquale has signed below along with two witnesses, because Pietro has asserted that he does not know how to write.

Signed
Pasquale ...
Giacomo ... witness
Giuseppe ... witness

[The preceding was verified as conforming to the original by Ferdinando De Luca, consul-general for Italy in New York, on 7 March 1868.]
SOURCE: *Relazione della Giunta*, 48–9.

APPENDIX B

The Italian Law to Prohibit the Employment of Children in Itinerant Trades, 21 December 1873, no. 1733 (series 11)

Article 1. Anyone, including parents, who consigns children under the age of eighteen to a third party, to be used within the kingdom for the purposes of wandering trades [professioni girovaghe], including mountebanks, charlatans, street-singers or performers, and their like, is subject to a prison sentence of one to three months and a fine of 50 to 250 lire. At the discretion of the court, parents or guardians could lose their guardianship over the children.

Article 2. Anyone in the kingdom keeping children under the age of eighteen for the purposes of employing them in wandering trades is subject to a jail sentence of three to six months and a fine of 100 to 500 lire.

Article 3. Anyone entrusting or giving away children under the age of eighteen within the kingdom, or guiding them abroad to entrust or give children to nationals or foreigners, and anyone who receives them to entrust them to another abroad for purposes of employment in wandering trades is liable to a jail sentence of six to twelve months and a fine of 100 to 500 lire.

Article 4. Nationals who keep children abroad for employment in wandering trades are liable to a jail sentence of one to two years. If the child is found to have been abused, maltreated, or undernourished, the sentence may be extended to three years, or longer if the abuse is subject to a more severe penalty under another statute.

Article 5. Anyone kidnapping a child by force or enticement (inveiglement) from parents or guardians with the intention of using the child in wandering trades, is liable, for kidnapping by force for use within the state, to a jail sentence of three to five years, and outside the state, five to seven years, and for inveiglement for use within the state, one to three years, and outside the state, three to five years.

Article 6. If the minor is abandoned, abused, raped, or undernourished, the offender is liable, for kidnapping by force within the kingdom, to a jail sentence of five to seven years, and outside the kingdom, from seven to ten years; and for inveiglement inside the kingdom, three to five years, and outside the kingdom, three to seven years.

Article 7. In the previous articles, accomplices as well as perpetrators are liable to the same sentence.

Article 8. All contracts entrusting children are theretofore and retroactively null and void.

Article 9. Parents, guardians, or whoever might entrust children for the purposes described above are required within three months of publication of the law to inform the mayor of their township or a consular / diplomatic agent that their children are abroad. They are required to register the name, age, the birthplace of the child, the name of the padrone, the overseas residence, and the overseas job. Failure to do so will result in a fine of 50 to 100 lire.

Article 10. Anyone holding children abroad is required to provide similar information within four months or face a fine of 100 to 500 lire.

Article 11. Mayors of Italian townships and consular / diplomatic representatives abroad are required to draw up lists of children employed abroad within six months of publication of the law.

Article 12. The lists of the children are to be sent to the Ministry of the Interior. Mayors and consular / diplomatic representatives will see to the return of the children to their families.

Article 13. If a child has no parents or guardians to whom he may be returned, he will be placed in a public educational institution until the age of majority or until he has learned a trade or profession.

Article 14. Sentencing is to be overseen by the ministry concerned. Sentences can be imposed in absentia. Private correspondence may be admitted as evidence at a trial.

Article 15. This law comes into effect when published. Articles 2 and 4 come into effect four months later to allow for the return of children under article 10.

AUTHOR'S NOTE: The preceding is my summary of the main points of the legislation.

Notes

INTRODUCTION

1 *New York Times* 17 June 1873.
2 Thistlethwaite, "Migration from Europe"; Taylor, *Distant Magnet*; Rosoli, ed., *Un secolo di emigrazione italiana*, and Foerster, *Italian Emigration*.
3 See, for example, Walker, *Germany and the Emigration*.
4 For a good sample of the spectrum of trades, see certificates of arrival for various English ports between 1838 and 1852 in series HO2, Home Office, London.
5 See especially Herbert Gutman, "Work, Culture, and Society in Industrializing America," *American Historical Review* 78:3 (1973) 531–88. For a review of the perspectives on immigration to the United States see John Bodnar, *The Transplanted: A History of Immigrants in Urban America* (Bloomington: Indiana University Press 1985). For Canada, see Harney, *Dalla frontiera*.
6 Curtin, *Cross-cultural Trade*; Sarti, *Long Live the Strong*; Wolf, *People without History*.
7 Woolf, *Poor in Western Europe*; Florian and Cavaglieri, *I vagabondi*; Ribton-Turner, *Vagrants and Vagrancy*; David Jones, *Crime, Protest, Community and Police in Nineteenth-Century Britain* (London: Routledge & Kegan Paul 1982); Olwen H. Hufton, *The Poor of Eighteenth-Century France 1750–1789* (Oxford: Oxford University Press 1974).
8 *Harper's Weekly*, 13 September 1873.
9 See the file of newspaper clippings on the disappearance of the hurdy-gurdy in Paris, "Chanteurs et musiciens ambulants,

Joueurs d'orgues," in Archives de la Préfecture de Police, série D, B/201.
10 Heywood, *Childhood in Nineteenth-Century France*; Weissbach, *Child Labor Reform*. On child labour legislation in the nineteenth century, see Clark Nardinelli, *Child Labour in the Industrial Revolution* (Bloomington: Indiana University Press 1990).
11 Coraggioso, *Wandering Minstrel*. I was made aware of the publication by the author's son, who informed me that part of the autobiography is fictional but the essence of the story is true.
12 See, for example, P. Ariès, *Centuries of Childhood: A Social History of Family Life*, trans. R. Baldick (New York: Vintage Books 1962); Pinchbeck and Hewitt, *Children in English Society*; E. Shorter, *The Making of the Modern Family* (New York: Basic Books 1975); L. Stone, *The Family, Sex and Marriage in England, 1500–1800* (New York: Harper and Row 1978); L. Demause, "On Writing Childhood History," *The Journal of Psychohistory* 16:2 (1988), 135–71.
13 See especially Pollock, *Forgotten Children*.
14 Pollock, *Forgotten Children*, 89ff.
15 *New York Times*, 7 July 1872.
16 Ibid., 19 June 1873; 22 July 1873; 28 June 1873; 17 June 1873; 19 June 1873; also see caricatures of children in New York Society for the Prevention of Cruelty to Children, *Annual Reports*, 1870s; Coraggioso, *Wandering Minstrel*, 38–9.
17 In Thomson, *Street Life in London*, 124; Coraggioso, *Wandering Minstrel*, 50–1.
18 George Martin, Superintendent, G Division, Metropolitan Police, Report to Home Office, 28 January 1852, HO 45/4328 (Foreign Children Brought to Beg in London), Home Office, London.
19 In Thomson, *Street Life in London*, 125.
20 Ibid.; Genoino, "Suonatori ambulanti" 75; Mayhew, *London Labour* 175; Coraggioso, *Wandering Minstrel*, 45.

CHAPTER ONE

1 Société Italienne de Bienfaisance de Paris, *Rapport sur la situation des petits italiens*.
2 "Caserta," "Terra di Lavoro," and "the Ciociaria" will be used interchangeably in this text. On Savoyards see Leppert, *Arcadia at Versailles*, Munhall, "Savoyards in French Art," and Bruchet, "L'Émigration des savoyards" and "Notes sur l'émigration."

3 American Christmas annuals contained many references to the young Savoyards. See Thompson, ed., *American Literary Annuals and Gift Books.*
4 Populations of towns are cited in Boccia's study (see note 7 below).
5 Woolf, *History of Italy,* 5, 51-54, and *Poor in Western Europe.*
6 Mariotti, "Morello."
7 Boccia, "Viaggio ai monti dello stato di Parma e Piacenza" (May 1904), 235, 26, ms. 1186, Biblioteca Palatina, Parma.
8 Artocchini, "L'emigrazione nel piacentino," 16. Casali, "Vita nella montagna piacentina," 66.
9 Mariotti, "Maria Stella," 146; Bell, *Fate and Honor,* 118ff.
10 Boccia, "Viaggio," 292, 23.
11 McFarlane, "Wandering Italians." This article first appeared in the *Penny Magazine* in 1833. See also Marchini, *Montanari,* 7.
12 Bell, *Fate and Honor,* 118ff.
13 Marchini, *Montanari,* 20-1; Carbone, *Fonti ... risorgimento,* 16.
14 Elenco di viaggiatori parmensi iscritti, 1857.
15 *New York Evening Post,* 9 July 1817, quoted in Marraro, "Italians in New York," 284.
16 McFarlane, "Italian Wanderers," 147.
17 Sarti, *Long Live the Strong,* 71-98; Bolognani, *Courageous People,* 283; Cerruti, "Cenni statistici," 579-80.
18 District Attorney, Potenza, to Ministero di Grazia, Giustizia e Culti, 19 December 1868, Suonatori Ambulanti, MAE Archivio Storico, Rome; Goffin, *Maria Pasqua.*
19 Cerruti, "Cenni statistici," 576; Carbone, *Fonti ... risorgimento;* "The Image-Boy."
20 Mariotti, "Morello," 16; McFarlane, "Ballo degli orsi," 164.
21 Cerruti, "Cenni statistici," 581, and Elenco di viaggiatori, 1857, MAE, Archivio di Stato, Parma.
22 Zguta, *Russian Minstrels,* 11, quoting A.N. Veselovskii, *Razyskaniia v oblasti russkikh Dukhovnykh Stikhov* (1879), 187.
23 Elenco di viaggiatori, 1857, MAE Archivio di Stato, Parma; McFarlane, "Italian Wanderers," 140; Interview with Sante Caramatti, May 1984, Cavignaga.
24 McFarlane, "Italian Wanderers," 140.
25 Interview with Sante Caramatti, May 1984, Cavignaga.
26 Ibid.; Curtin, *Cross-Cultural Trade,* chapter 9; Elenco di viaggiatori, 1857, MAE Archivio di Stato, Parma.

27 Ord-Hume, *Barrel-Organ*, 233, 316–21; Paulucci di Calboli, *Girovaghi italiani*, 26–7.
28 On "padrone" see Harney, "Padrone and Immigrant;" L. Iorizzo, "The Padrone and Immigrant Distribution," in *The Italian Experience in the United States*, ed. S.M. Tomasi and M.H. Engel (New York: Center for Migration Studies 1970), 43–76; and J. Koren, "The Padrone System," *Bulletin of the Department of Labor* 9 (March 1887), 112–29.
29 "Aleph," "Street Music Fifty Years Ago," 346; *Times*, 6 March 1820.
30 Elenco di viaggiatori, 1857, MAE Archivio di Stato, Parma.
31 R. Consolato d'Italia a Mosca, Registro dei connazionali residenti a Mosca, 1861–1917, MAE Archivio Storico, Rome.
32 Bracco, "Ricerche storiche," 426; Regaldi, "I viggianesi," 326. On bagpipers, see Roberto Leydi and Febo Guizzi, *Le zampogne in Italia* (Milan: Ricordi 1985) and *Strumenti musicali e tradizioni popolari in Italia* (Rome: Bolzoni 1985).
33 Bracco, "Ricerche storiche," 430–1; Regaldi, "I viggianesi," 334.
34 Parzanese, *Canti del viggianese*, 16.
35 Malpica, "Costumi – i viggianesi," 406; Robert Foerster noted that he had spoken with *viggianesi* musicians in Boston Harbor: *Italian Emigration*, 102.
36 Regaldi, "I viggianesi," 405–6; Schiro, *Americans by Choice*.
37 Parzanese, *Canti del viggianese*, 91–2 (my translations).
38 See, for example, Cerruti, "Cenni statistici"; Regaldi, "I viggianesi"; and McFarlane, "Italian Wanderers"; Genoino, "Suonatori ambulanti," 70–2.
39 Mariotti, "Morello"; Alger, *Phil the Fiddler*; Coraggioso, *Wandering Minstrel*; Zanella, *Il piccolo calabrese*; *Little Italians*. Guerzoni, *La tratta dei fanciulli*. The children also appear in *Little Men, Middlemarch, Mrs. Dorrit, House of the Seven Gables*, and Hector Malot, *Sans Famille* (Paris 1878).
40 Sommerville, *Childhood*, 168–78; G. Avery and A. Bull, *Heroes and Heroines in English Children's Stories, 1780–1900* (London: Hodder & Stoughton 1965).
41 Merello, district attorney, Genoa, to Min. di Grazia, Giustizia e Culti, 14 November 1868, Suonatori Ambulanti, MAE, Archivio Storico, Rome.
42 Prefect of Basilicata to Min. dell'Interno, 28 October 1868, Suonatori Ambulanti, MAE, Archivio Storico, Rome.

183 Notes to pages 37–42

43 Ufficio del Pubblico Ministero presso le sezioni delle corte di appello di Napoli residenti in Potenza to Min. di Grazia, Giustizia e Culti, 19 December 1868, Suonatori Ambulanti, A. Strambio to L. Cerruti, Paris, 15 December 1867, Corrispondenze ricevute, consular reports, Paris, 1861–8, MAE Archivio Storico, Rome.
44 H. Schulz to Min. Affari Esteri, 17 February 1862, Corrispondenze ricevute dal ministero, consular reports, Rio de Janeiro, St Petersburg, 1861–9, MAE Archivio Storico, Rome.
45 G. Malmusì to Visconti-Venosta, Barcelona, 11 August 1864; A. de Martino to Min. Affari Esteri, Barcelona, 16 September 1866, Corrispondenze ricevute dal ministero, consular reports, Barcelona, MAE Archivio Storico, Rome.
46 Italian Consul, Rio de Janeiro, 22 January 1864 and 1 February 1863 to Min. Affari Esteri, Corrispondenze ricevute dal ministero, consular reports, Rio de Janeiro, 1861–9, MAE Archivio Storico, Rome.
47 Appendix B to "Relazione della Giunta," 48–9, and appendix X to Cerruti, "Cenni e statistiche:" 599–600.
48 Elenco nominativo delle persone che sogliono condurre fanciulli all'estero, Suonatori Ambulanti, MAE Archivio Storico, Rome. Seconda Relazione della commissione, 23 July 1868, ibid. The source on Paris is du Camp, "Mendicité à Paris." Lucio Sponza correctly believes that their numbers in London were greatly exaggerated. He notes, for example, that an official of the Italian Benevolent Society estimated in 1881 that two to three hundred children were in the Hatton Garden area alone, whereas the census listed thirty children under the age of sixteen, twelve of whom were with their parents: *Italian Immigrants*, 160.
49 Thomson, *Street Life in London*, 125.
50 Perpère, consular agent in Paramaribo, to Min. Affari Esteri, 20 February 1866, Corrispondenze ricevute dal ministero, MAE.
51 See especially introduction to Sarti, *Long Live the Strong*, on this theme.

CHAPTER TWO

1 From posters, 12 January 1753; in Motais-Avril, *Les Voyageurs forains*, 37–9; on the broader question of popular culture in early modern Europe, see Burke, *Popular Culture*.
2 Chevalier, *Labouring Classes*, 195, 262–3.

3 Ibid., 118, 456, 147, 110ff, 231.
4 Bruchet, "L'Émigration des savoyards," 13–14.
5 *Le Temps*, 26 March 1873.
6 Leppert, *Arcadia at Versailles*, 16, 39.
7 Palmer and Palmer, *Hurdy-Gurdy*, 135, 137.
8 Munhall, "Savoyards in French Art," 92.
9 Bruchet, "L'Émigration des savoyards," 815–31.
10 Carbone, *Fonti per la storia*, 118ff.
11 Ibid., 58–61.
12 Ibid., 101; King, *McCaul: Croft: Forneri*, 161–256.
13 Carbone, *Fonti per la storia*, 16–23.
14 Ibid., 86–7.
15 Préfecture de Police de Paris, Ordonnance, 4 July 1816, Archives de la Préfecture de Police de Paris (hereinafter APPP), série D, B/201.
16 Prefect of Police to Police Commissioners, 19 January 1822, ibid.
17 Circular, Prefect of Police to Police Commissioners, 6 April 1822, ibid.
18 Ibid.
19 Memo, Prefect of Police to Police Commissioners, 22 May 1822; 6 September 1822, APPP, série D, B/201.
20 Comte de la Bourdonnage, minister of the interior, to prefects, 10 October 1829, APPP, série D, B/200; Chevalier, *Labouring Classes*, 13ff and 262ff.
21 Préfecture de Police de Paris, Ordonnance concernant les Saltimbanques, Chanteurs, avec ou sans instruments, les Bateleurs, Escamoteurs, Baladins, Joueurs d'orgues, Musiciens Ambulants et Faiseurs de Tours sur la voie publique, 14 December 1831, 17 January 1832, APPP, série D, B/201.
22 Prefect of Police to Police Commissioners, 14 August 1832, ibid.
23 Prefect of Police to Police Commissioners, 19 February 1839, Ordonnance concernant les Crieurs, Chanteurs, Vendeurs et distributeurs d'écrits, de dessins et lithographies sur la voie publique de la Capitale et des communes du ressort de la Préf. de Pol., 19 October 1839, APPP, série D, B/200.
24 See for example, two memos to Police Commissioners, 16 and 30 December 1831; the quotation is from the first of these (ibid.)
25 Prefect of Police to Police Commissioners, 19 May 1827; 17 January 1832, ibid., Corbière to prefects, 24 August 1826, ibid.

26 Du Camp, "Mendicité à Paris," 199–200; Corbière to Préfect, 24 August 1826, ibid.; 19 May 1827, APPP, série D, B/201.
27 Du Camp, "Mendicité à Paris," 200.
28 Ibid., 196–7; Carlier to Police Commissioners; 2 January and 4 April 1851, APPP, série D, B/281; ordonnance, 30 November 1853, APPP, série D, B/201. Also see F. de Persigny, secretary of state in the Department of the Interior, Instructions concernant la police des saltimbanques, bateleurs, escamoteurs, joueurs d'orgues, musiciens ambulants et chanteurs, 13 December 1853. Article 4 strictly prohibited children from accompanying performers. Children with saltimbanques had to be reported under the rules of 24 August 1826. APPP, série D, B/200.
29 Cerruti, "Cenni statistici," 584–5.
30 Ibid., 585–6.
31 This example and those that follow are from Cerruti's report, Appendix V.
32 Cerruti, "Cenni statistici," 585.
33 Guerzoni was one of the Italian parliamentary deputies to introduce a law on the children in 1868 (see chapter 5). He had been a follower of Garibaldi, joining him the year after the expedition of the "Thousand." On the route to France taken by the children, see Société Italienne de Bienfaisance, *Rapport sur la situation des petits italiens*, 2–3.
34 Correspondence between Consuls-General Caselli (Marseilles) and Cerruti (Paris), November–December 1867, in Appendix A of *Rapport*; see also *Relazione della giunta*, 6, and Appendix D.
35 *Rapport*, note G in appendix, from Cerruti to MAE, 15 June 1866. There are two versions of the report, with only slight differences, and both appear in 1868. This letter is printed in what seems to be the later of the two reports.
36 *Rapport*, 5, 3; La matrona was also mentioned in the *Relazione della giunta*.
37 The list is in the Suonatori Ambulante collection, MAE Archivio Storico, Rome.
38 *Relazione della giunta*, 6; Guerzoni, *Tratta dei Fanciulli*, 76–9. In this sentimental novel, an opportunistic and "chameleon" police commissioner under Louis Philippe falls into disgrace with all sides in 1848; he joins the underclass, where he becomes "prince" of the "association des petits italiens."

39 Du Camp, "Mendicité à Paris," 200; 698 were arrested in 1868 and 431 in 1869. Many of them probably moved to London and New York.
40 Weissbach, *Child Labor Reform*, 159–204; Heywood, *Childhood*, 260–86.
41 The Italian Consul at Nantes informed the Minister of External Affairs in Turin of this circular, 24 March 1863. Suonatori Ambulanti, MAE Archivio Storico, Rome.
42 I found only sixty-two acceptable locations listed on a sample permit. See Du Camp, "Mendicité à Paris," 193.
43 Préfecture de Police, Ordonnance, 28 February 1863, APPP, série D, B/201; *Rapport*, 5.
44 Gambarotta to La Marmora, 4 September 1865, Suonatori Ambulanti, MAE Archivio Storico, Rome.
45 *Le Temps*, 7 August 1867.
46 Cerruti to Min. Aff. Est., 29 January 1867; Nigra to Visconti-Venosta, 28 February 1867, in pacco 201, corrispondenza ricevute dal ministero, Reports of the Legation in Paris, MAE Archivio Storico, Rome.
47 Lecour to Cerruti, October 1867, quoted in *Rapport*, 14; E. Paliare, from Préfecture, to Cerruti, 6 October 1867, consular reports, Paris (1864–71), MAE Archivio Storico, Rome; Du Camp, "Mendicité," 200.
48 The petition is found in the Reports of the Legation in Paris, MAE Archivio Storico, Rome.
49 Lecour to Cerruti, 27 December 1867, ibid.
50 Nigra to Conte di Campello, Min. Aff. Est., 24 June 1867, ibid.
51 Cerruti to Min. Aff. Est., April 1867, consular reports, Paris (1864–71), MAE Archivio Storico, Rome.
52 Min. Int. to Min. Aff. Est., 20 August 1867; Cerruti to Min. Aff. Est., 18 April 1867, Report of the Legation in Paris, MAE Archivio Storico, Rome.
53 Assemblée Générale de la Société Italienne de Bienfaisance, 1868, ibid.; Nigra to Menabrea, Min. Aff. Est., 11 June 1868, ibid.
54 *Rapport*; Nigra to Min. Aff. Est., 13 February 1868, Suonatori Ambulanti, MAE; apparently he had sent earlier reports on 10 August 1866 and 24 June 1867: Reports of the Legation in Paris, MAE Archivio Storico, Rome.
55 *Rapport*, 8.
56 Ibid., 5.

57 Ibid., 7.
58 Ibid., 8.
59 Ibid., 6.
60 *Rapport* (revised version), note 6, appendix, 15; Cerruti to Min. Aff. Est., Florence, 15 June 1866, Reports of the Legation in Paris, MAE Archivio Storico, Rome.
61 *Gazette des Tribunaux*, 25 June 1868; Rossi (special agent) to Cerruti, n.d., included with letter from Cerruti to Min. Aff. Est., 6 July 1868, Reports of the Legation in Paris, MAE Archivio Storico, Rome.
62 Cerruti to Min. Aff. Est., ibid.
63 Du Camp, "Mendicité," 201; Pietri to Police Commissioners, 4 October 1869, APPP, série D, B/281.
64 Du Camp, "Mendicité," 201.
65 Leone Carpi, *Statistica illustrata della emigrazione all'estero del Triennio 1874–76*. The statistics on page 145 of Carpi's *Dell'emigrazione italiana all'estero* (1871), list the suonatori as clandestine emigrants. An article in the *Times* of 13 April 1871 noted that the Italian Benevolent Society's distribution of funds and work had more than doubled from the previous year.
66 Weissbach, *Child Labor Reform*, 219–20.
67 Lecour to Chief of Municipal Police, 14 November 1874, APPP, série D, B/281.

CHAPTER THREE

1 6 March 1820; the article also appears in the *London Register* for 1820.
2 London Mendicity Society, *Fourth Annual Report* (1822), 16, 56.
3 London Mendicity Society, *Ninth Annual Report* (1827); *Times*, 12 November 1831.
4 Grant, "Italians with White Mice."
5 *Times*, 15 January 1845.
6 J. Mazzini, *His Life*, 219.
7 Ibid., 222–3.
8 Twattle-Basket, *Note di cronaca*, 51–5.
9 Dyos and Wolff, *Victorian City*; Wohl, *Eternal Slum*; Donald J. Olsen, *The Growth of Victorian London* (Harmondsworth: Penguin 1976); Asa Briggs, *Victorian Cities* (Harmondsworth: Penguin 1968), chapter 8, "London, the World City." On leisure in nineteenth-century Britain,

see Hugh Cunningham, *Leisure in the Industrial Revolution* (New York: St Martin's Press 1980) and Peter Bailey, *Leisure and Class in Victorian England* (London: Routledge & Kegan Paul 1978).
10 Mayhew, *London Labour*, vol. 3, 159.
11 Ibid.
12 Ibid., 164.
13 Ibid., 174–7.
14 James Beresford, *The Miseries of Human Life, or the Groans of Samuel Sensitive and Timothy Testy* (London: William Miller 1807).
15 Paulucci di Calboli, *Girovaghi*, 33.
16 Bass, *Street Music*, 8, 109.
17 See, for example, *Times*, 5 September 1843.
18 Ibid., 10 November 1857, 2 May 1856.
19 Bass, *Street Music*, 3,4.
20 Ibid., 44; *Times*, 31 December 1864.
21 Babbage, *Passages from the Life*, 354–6; Bass, *Street Music*, 34–5.
22 Bass, *Street Music*, 81, 97.
23 Ibid., 97; Babbage, *Passages from the Life*, 348–9; Bass, *Street Music*, 54.
24 *Hansard*, vol. 175, 1529ff; Bass, *Street Music*, 114–5.
25 *Hansard*, vol. 176, 1073, 1367; 27 & 28 Vict., c. 55 (An Act for the Better Regulation of Street Music within the Metropolitan Police District).
26 "Mutton Hill and Clerkenwell" referred to the residences of the musicians, although the writer may have meant Saffron-Hill: Bass, *Street Music*, 26, 70–1.
27 Society for the Suppression of Mendicity, *Ninth Annual Report* (1827) appendix, 35.
28 D'Azeglio to Malmesbury, 23 July 1852; Malmesbury to Filippo Oldoini, Sardinian chargé d'affaires, London, 29 July 1852; HO 45-4342 (assuring Sardinian minister of removal of Italian mendicant boys to Italy), Home Office, London.
29 Wilkins, The "Italian Aspect," 161; Italian Benevolent Society, *Annual Reports*, in Società Italiana di Beneficenza di Londra, MAE Archivio Storico, Rome.
30 Faenza to d'Azeglio, 7 July 1861, Società Italiana di Beneficenza di Londra, MAE Archivio Storico, Rome.
31 Folder 9, folio 5: Società Italiana di Beneficenza (1861–65); *Annual Reports*, 1864–8.
32 Charity Organisation Society, *Report*, 33–5; *Times*, 30 October 1865.

33 Catalani, "Fanciulli italiani," 560–1.
34 Committee of Directors, Minutes, 4 November 1861, Società Italiana di Beneficenza, MAE Archivio Storico, Rome.
35 Faenza to d'Azeglio, 16 January 1862, ibid.
36 Melia to d'Azeglio, 22 February 1862; Melia to d'Azeglio, 4 August 1862, ibid.
37 Memo, n.d. (probably 1862), no author, ibid.; *Times*, 27 August 1853; Dr E. Passalenti, *Times*, 17 January 1879; L. Sponza, "'Quartiere italiano;'" Green, "Stability of Immigrant Communities;" Marin, *Italiani in Gran Bretagna*.
38 *Times*, 24 August 1864.
39 Medical officer of health, Holborn, 1871, quoted in Sponza, "'Quartiere italiano,'" 337; see also 321, 323.
40 18 October 1879, 590–2.
41 Sponza "'Quartiere italiano,'" 322; "Report of the Lancet Special Commission on the Sanitary Condition of the Italian Quarter" (hereinafter "Lancet"), 591.
42 McFarlane, "Wandering Italians."
43 "Lancet," 591; see also *Times*, 20 January 1879; and Booth, *Life and Labour of the People in London*, 142–6.
44 Green, "Stability of Immigrant Communities" shows that by the late 1870s most musicians were bound by godparenthood ties and were isolated from the rest of the Italian community; however, the fact that they often lived with other Italian tradesmen or leased or sold homes to them suggests that there were important links with them as well.
45 *Times*, 12 November 1831.
46 Mayhew, *London Labour*, 172.
47 Ibid., 77–9.
48 Ord-Hume, *Barrel Organ*, 428–92. Coraggioso's father and grandfather bought their barrel-organs in Leather Lane, near Eyre Street Hill, in the 1860s. See *Wandering Minstrel*, 31.
49 Charity Organisation Society, *Report*, 12.
50 Ibid., 17, 19.
51 Luciano to d'Azeglio, 1 July 1864, Società Italiana di Beneficenza, MAE Archivio Storico, Rome.
52 Charity Organisation Society, *Report*, 29.
53 *Times*, 19 November 1878.
54 Ibid., 4 January 1879; Greenwood, "Private Life," 232.
55 Prato, "Italiani in Inghilterra," 685.

56 Greenwood, "Private Life," 223.
57 23 June 1871.
58 Society for the Suppression of Mendicity, *Fifty-fifth Annual Report* (1873), iv.
59 *Chambers's Journal*, 24 January 1874, 68–70; *Times*, 5 October 1876.
60 *Times*, 3 October 1876.
61 Italian Children, HO 45/9366/36003, Home Office, London.
62 Ribton-Turner, *Vagrants and Vagrancy*, 303–4; Bosanquet, *Social Work in London*, 239–41; Charity Organisation Society, *Annual Report*, 1878. Lister to Undersecretary of State, 3 and 5 September 1877. Already in early August the Italian consul-general had noted that with stepped-up surveillance in England many Italian children had gone to Ireland. C. Cattaneo to T.H. Bucks, Undersecretary, Dublin Castle, 4 August 1877; Italian Children, HO 45, Home Office, London.
63 Charity Organisation Society, *Report*, 24–5; *Times*, 30 August 1877; Metropolitan Police, HO 46/60, Home Office, London.
64 J.R. Sandford to Undersecretary of the Home Office, 28 June 1877; C.A. Case, School Board Office, Maidstone, to the Secretary, Education Department, 9 November 1877; J.I. Ingham to A.F. Liddel, 1 January 1878, Italian Children, HO 45, Home Office, London.
65 *Times*, 21 August 1877.
66 Ibid., 3 September 1877.
67 Ibid., 21 September 1877.
68 Ibid., 1 November, 7 November, 14 November 1877.
69 Ibid., 14 and 21 December 1877.
70 Behlmer, *Child Abuse*, chapter 4.

CHAPTER FOUR

1 Brace, *Dangerous Classes*, 194–5.
2 Children's Aid Society (New York) (hereinafter CAS), *Third Annual Report* (1856), 17. Langsam, *Children West*, 11–19.
3 CAS, *Fourth Annual Report* (1857): 15–6.
4 Ibid., 16.
5 CAS, *Seventh Annual Report* (1860), 16; *Ninth Annual Report* (1862), 16. The latter were paid in kind, and they brought the flour home to their families for baking bread.
6 CAS, *Tenth Annual Report* (1863), 28.

7 CAS, *Thirteenth Annual Report* (1866), 28–9; *Twelfth Annual Report* (1865), 29.
8 *New York Times*, 24 October 1868; 1 February 1869.
9 Report of the consul-general to New York, F. De Luca, 1868, in Suonatori Ambulanti, MAE Archivio Storico, Rome. Reprinted in *Relazione della Giunta*, appendix N, 63–9.
10 *Eco d'Italia*, 17 September 1873.
11 *New York Times*, 9 November 1867; 24 October 1868; 1 February 1869; 2 September 1871. *Eco d'Italia*, 6 August 1869.
12 *New York Times*, 7 July 1872.
13 These two stories were the basis of Horatio Alger's children's novel, *Phil the Fiddler, or the Story of a Young Street Musician*. Alger was a good friend of Secchi de Casali, the editor of *Eco d'Italia*, who gave him the historical background for the book. In the story Phil was saved not by a farmer but by a doctor, who transformed the ragamuffin into a clean, well behaved, educated young man.
14 *New York Times*, 12 and 13 June 1873. See also letter from Monachesi, ibid., 15 June 1873.
15 Ibid., 19 June 1873.
16 Ibid., 18 and 19 June 1873.
17 See Seymour J. Mandelbaum, *Boss Tweed's New York* (New York: John Wiley and Sons 1965), 105–13, and Alexander B. Callow, Jr, *The Tweed Ring* (New York: Oxford University Press 1966), 262–300.
18 *New York Times*, 19 June 1873.
19 Ibid.
20 Ibid., 20 June 1873.
21 Ibid., 23 June 1873.
22 *Eco d'Italia*, 26 July 1873.
23 *New York Times*, 22 July, 24 July, 25 July 1873; *Eco d'Italia*, 6 September 1873. On laurenzanesi in Toronto, see Zucchi, *Italians in Toronto*, chapter 2.
24 *New York Times*, 1 and 2 August 1873.
25 Ibid., 18 August 1873.
26 Ibid., 20 and 27 August 1873.
27 See *Tribune*, 25 and 27 July, 15 August 1873; Vecoli, "Chicago's Italians," 57–60; *New York Herald*, 16 September 1873; *Eco d'Italia*, 20 September 1873.
28 *Eco d'Italia*, 4, 8, and 15 April 1874; An Act in Relation to Mendicant and Vagrant Children, c. 116, NY (1874); Jeremy B. Felt, *Hos-*

tages of Fortune: Child Labour Reform in New York State (Syracuse: Syracuse University Press 1965), notes that child protection legislation of 1873–4 was passed in the context of anti-Tweed sentiment.

29 *Eco d'Italia*, 13 June 1874.
30 On the placement system see Langsam, *Children West*. Langsam ascribes the discrepancy between the large Italian population in the city and the small number of children placed by the society to "clannishness" and opposition to Protestant agencies: 29–30.
31 *New York Times*, 4 and 5 June 1874; *Eco d'Italia*, 13 June 1874.
32 *Eco d'Italia*, 1 July 1874, 3 July 1874, 9 September 1874; Chargé d'Affaires, Washington, to British Foreign Office. Copy sent to Sir Richard Cross, Home Office, HO 45/4366/36003, Italian Children, 3 July 1874, Home Office, London.
33 An Act to Prevent and Punish Wrongs to Children, c. 122, NY (1876).
34 SPCC files, Mayor of New York, 15, Municipal Archives of New York, no. 39, 8 February 1888, and no. 42, 23 October 1888.
35 Supra note 33, part 5.
36 SPCC, *Annual Report* (1877), 53, 55, 57; (1879), 51; (1880), 48.
37 *New York Times*, 2 June, 6 January 1874: 2; Ernst, *Immigrant Life*; Iorizzo and Mondello, *Italian-Americans*; Pozzetta, "Mulberry District."
38 The booklet was originally printed in the Italian *Gazzetta Ufficiale*, and was also issued as a pamphlet entitled "Sulla emigrazione dei fanciulli italiani all'estero – lettera di un italiano stabilito nell' America del Nord" (15 pp, n.d.). It was then reprinted in the documentation of the Italian Senate commission of 1868 (see chapter 5). De Luca came to New York in 1866 and remained there until 1878, when he was transferred to Shanghai.
39 See, for example, the files of the Italian consular representatives in Odessa, St Petersburg, Barcelona, Lima, or Rio de Janeiro in the mid-nineteenth century, pacchi 858, 859, 895, 899 in MAE Archivio Storico, Rome.
40 *Eco d'Italia*, 28 December 1872.
41 *New York Times*, 15 June 1873; *Eco d'Italia*, 4 July 1873.
42 *New York Times*, 18 and 19 June 1873.
43 Ibid., 20 June 1873.
44 Ernst, *Immigrant Life*, 158–9. Also see Iorizzo and Mondello, *Italian-Americans*, 26; *New York Times*, 21 June 1873; *Eco d'Italia*, 25 June 1873.

45 Registro copialettere no. 177, consolato di New York, A. rico, MAE. *New York Times*, 23 June 1873.
46 *New York Times*, 23 June 1873.
47 Ibid., 25 June 1873.
48 *Eco d'Italia*, 28 June 1873. They might, in fact, have been frien͏ͅ of the Italian editor.
49 *New York Times*, 1 July 1873.
50 Ibid., 2 July 1873; *Eco d'Italia*, 4 July 1873.
51 *New York Times*, 3 July 1873.
52 *Eco d'Italia*, 23 August 1873.
53 *New York Times*, 1 August 1873.
54 Ibid., 20 and 21 August 1873.
55 Ibid., 4 December 1873.
56 Moreno had informed Sumner that seven thousand children were dispersed throughout the United States, whereas this report estimated seven thousand around the world. *New York Times*, 10 December 1873; 11 January 1874; 6 January 1874.
57 *New York Times*, 11 January 1874.
58 18 US Stat., c. 464 (23 June 1874).
59 *New York Dispatch*, 12 July 1874; *New National Era*, 25 June 1874. These are quoted in Moreno, *History of a Great Wrong*.
60 See the pamphlet published by Moreno in 1891, *History of a Great Wrong*; also see Bremner, "Children with the Organ-Man," 280–1.
61 *New York Times*, 18 November 1878.
62 Ibid., 19 November 1878.
63 Ibid., 20 and 22 November 1878; SPCC, *Annual Report* (1879), 53–5.
64 *United States v. Giovanni Ancarola*, 1. Fed. Rep. 676 (1879).
65 *New York Times*, 9 November 1879. The case was outlined in an SPCC pamphlet, *The Italian Padrone Case*. See also *New York Times*, 9 November, 16 November, 18 November, 20 November, 22 November, 10 December, 20 December 1879.
66 On American nativism in the 1870s, see John Higham, *Strangers in the Land: Patterns of American Nativism 1860–1925* (New York: Atheneum 1963).

CHAPTER FIVE

1 C. Seton-Watson, *Liberalism to Fascism*, part 1; Manzotti, *La Polemica*.
2 *Relazione della Giunta*, 13.
3 Ibid.; Artocchini, "L'Emigrazione nel Piacentino dal 1800," 22.

4 Cerruti, "Cenni statistici"; *Relazione della Giunta*, 13, 71.
5 *Relazione della Giunta*, 13, Appendix P, 72, has a copy of the circular.
6 *Relazione della Giunta*, 14; they referred to article 63 of the act.
7 Camera dei Deputati, *Sessione 1867*, 30 January 1868, 3861; 3862 Arrivabene; 3864 Castagnola.
8 Manzotti, *Polemica*, part 1.
9 *Relazione della Giunta*, 14.
10 Camera dei Deputati, *Sessione 1867*, 30 January 1868, 3862; 21 May 1868, 6143.
11 Ibid., 21 May 1868, 6149.
12 Ibid., 30 January 1868, 3862; 21 May 1868, 6146.
13 Ibid., 30 January 1868, 3862; 21 May 1868, 6143.
14 See the minutes of the committee in Suonatori Ambulanti, MAE Archivio Storico, Rome.
15 Francesco Gloria, third sitting of the committee, 19 June 1868; Report of the committee to Menabrea, 23 July 1868, ibid.
16 Ghiglieri to Procuratori Generali di Genova e Potenza, 28 August 1868; Merello, Procuratore Generale di Genova to Min. di Grazia, Giustizia, e Culti, 14 November 1868; Amaroni, Procuratore Generale di Potenza, to Min. di Grazia, Giustizia, e Culti, 19 December 1868; Prefetto di Genova to Min. dell'Interno, 5 November 1868; all in Suonatori Ambulanti, MAE Archivio Storico, Rome.
17 Prefetto di Basilicata to Min. dell'Interno, 28 October 1868, Suonatori Ambulanti, MAE Archivio Storico, Rome.
18 Marcello Cerruti to Min. Aff. Est., 26 August 1868, ibid. (quoting De Luca).
19 9 November 1868, ibid.
20 M. Cerruti to Menabrea, 26 August 1868, ibid.
21 De Luca to Min. Aff. Est., 28 August 1868, 20 November 1868; consular agent, Alexandria, to Min. Aff. Est., 15 August 1868, ibid.
22 Consul in Hamburg to Menabrea, 20 August 1868, ibid.
23 *Relazione della Giunta*, 17–18.
24 Ibid., 33.
25 Ibid., 18.
26 Ibid., 17.
27 Ibid., 23.
28 Ibid., 23.
29 Camera dei Deputati, *Sessione 1873–74*, 17 and 18 December, 629ff.
30 Emilio Visconti-Venosta to consuls, 10 March 1874; de Falco to district attorneys, 5 April 1874. The interior minister, G. Cantelli, had

done the same with prefects on 31 January 1874. A. Peiroli to consuls, November 1874; Marini to consuls, February 1882, all in Suonatori Ambulanti, MAE Archivio Storico, Rome.

CONCLUSION

1 Behlmer, *Child Abuse*, 81.
2 Ibid., 88. For debates of 19 June and 30 July 1889 see Hansard, vol. 337 (1889), 227–46, and vol. 339 (1889), 948ff.
3 Foerster. *Italian Emigration*.
4 Zucchi, *Italians in Toronto*, 79–81.
5 Iorizzo and Mondello, *Italian-Americans*, 154–6; Schiro, *Americans by Choice*; Harney, "Padrone and the Immigrant."
6 Paulucci di Calboli, *Girovaghi italiani*, 207–11; Wilkins, "Italian Aspect," indicated that there were still some padroni with children to be found in London in 1891. He attributed their presence to the uneven enforcement of the Act for the Prevention of Cruelty to Children. Most of the children were from Caserta.
7 Booth, *Life and Labour*, vol. 8, 142–6.
8 Harney, *Dalla frontiera*, 63; House of Commons Parliamentary Papers, *Reports from Her Majesty's Ambassadors in Europe and Her Majesty's Minister in the United States and the Regulations for the Control of Itinerant Street Musicians*, 5 March 1891. Paulucci di Calboli, *L'Italie vagabonde*, 27ff. He culled his information from Min. Aff. Est., *Emigrazione e colonie* (1893); A Bill to Limit the Hours of Street Organs and other Street Music in the Metropolis, Bill 63 (March 1891).
9 Paulucci di Calboli, *L'Italie vagabonde*, 30; Foerster, *Italian Emigration*, 140–3; Verdone, "Antécédents et causes des événements d'Aigues-Mortes." Newspaper clippings of reactions to the prohibition of street organs in Paris are in dossier Chanteurs et Musiciens Ambulants, Joueurs d'Orgues, APPP, série D, B/201.
10 Polizia Giudiziaria, pacco 303, busta 12200.11.13, DG di Pubblica Sicurezza, 1911, Archivio dello Stato, Rome.
11 Rossi, "Vantaggi e danni;" Paulucci di Calboli, "L'Agonie d'un métier," "L'emigrazione italiana in Francia"; Cafiero, "Tratta dei fanciulli"; Z. Ciuffoletti, "Sfruttamento della mandopera infantile italiana in Francia alla fine del sec. XIX," in Duroselle and Serra, *Emigrazione Italiana in Francia*, 249–57.
12 Paulucci di Calboli, "Traite des petits italiens," 5.

Bibliography

MANUSCRIPTS

ITALY

Parma. Archivio di Stato, Ministero degli Affari Esteri. Elenco di viaggiatori parmensi iscritti nei Registri del Regio Consolato Parmense, 1857, for Paris, Nice, Malta, Trieste, Naples, the Ottoman Gate, Genoa.
– Direzione Affari Generali. 1852.
Parma. Biblioteca Palatina. Boccia, Capitano Antonio. "Viaggio ai monti dello stato di Parma e Piacenza." (May 1804) ms. 1186.
Rome. Ministero degli Affari Esteri, Archivio Storico. Serie Seconda. Divisione "delle legazioni" e divisione "consolare" (1861–8).
– Protocolli della corrispondenza con le legazioni e consolati vari: pacco 7, Barcelona (1854–69); pacco 9, Marseilles (1857–69); pacco 10, New Orleans (1840–67); pacco 13, New York (1852–75); pacco 6, Paris (1859–69).
– Registri copialettere dei dispacci inviati dal ministero degli esteri di vari consolati nazionali all'estero: pacco 155, London (1854–70); pacco 177, New York (1854–68); pacco 183, Paris (1859–70).
– Pacchi della corrispondenza ricevuta dal ministero, 2a serie: Suonatori ambulanti ... pacco 781 (1867–9).
– Pacchi della corrispondenza ricevuta dal ministero, 3a serie: pacco 96, notes on benevolent institutes (note di istituti di beneficenza) (1861–9); pacchi 199–203, reports of the legation in Paris (rapporti della legazione) (1865, 1866, 1867, 1868, 1869–71 respectively); pacco 246, consular reports (rapporti del consolato): London (1861–9); pacco 258, New York (1861–9); pacco 260, Paris (1864–71); pacco 884, London (1861–9); pacco 895, New Orleans and Odessa (1861–9); pacco 899, Rio de Janeiro

and St Petersburg (1861-9); pacchi 850 and 859, Barcelona; pacco 890, Marseilles (1861-7); pacco 55, Moscow register of Italian nationals (registro dei connazionali residenti a Mosca) (1861-1917).
- Inventario delle rappresentanze diplomatiche Londra (1861-1950): Busta 9, fascicolo 5. Società italiana di beneficenza di Londra (Italian Benvolent Society).

FRANCE

Paris. Archives de la Préfecture de Police. Série D, B/281, Mendicité-vagabondage.
- Série D, B/201, Chanteurs et musiciens ambulants, joueurs d'orgues.
- Série D, B/200, Professions ambulantes, nomades, forains, marchands ambulants.

UNITED KINGDOM

London. Home Office Records. Assisting Sardinian Minister in Removal of Italian Mendicant Boys Back to Italy (1852) HO45/4342.
- Foreign Children Brought to Beg in London (1851-2) HO 45/4328.
- Italian Children (1874-7) HO 45/9366/36003.
- Metropolitan Police (1877) HO 46/60.

UNITED STATES

New York City. Municipal Archives of New York. Mayor of New York papers, SPCC files, file 15.

GOVERNMENT DOCUMENTS

ITALY

Camera dei Deputati. *Sessione 1867*, vols. 139, 141.
- *Sessione 1873-4*, vol. 202.
- Sessione 1871-3, vol. 7: *Relazione della Giunta ... sul progetto di legge ... Proibizione dell'impiego di fanciulli in professioni girovaghe*, 19 March 1873.

UNITED KINGDOM

Parliamentary Debates, HC, series 3 and 4, 1864 and 1889.
Parliamentary Papers. (Blue Book). *Correspondence Respecting the Introduction into and Employment in this Country of Italian Children*, 1877.
Parliamentary Papers. *Reports from Her Majesty's Ambassadors in Europe and her Majesty's Minister in the United States and the Regulations for the Control of Itinerant Street Musicians*, 5 March 1891.

BOOKS AND ARTICLES

"Aleph." "Street Music Fifty Years Ago." *London Scenes and London People.* London: W.H. Collinridge, City Press 1863, 343–52.

Alger, Horatio. *Phil the Fiddler, or the Story of a Young Street Musician.* New York: New York Book Company 1911.

Artocchini, Carmen. "L'emigrazione nel piacentino dal 1800 all'unità d'Italia." *Studi storici in onore di Emilio Nasali Rocca.* Piacenza: Deputazione di Storia Patria per le Provincie Parmensi Sezione di Piacenza 1971, 15–26.

Babbage, Charles. *Passages from the Life of a Philosopher.* London: Longman, Green 1864.

Bass, Michael Thomas. *Street Music in the Metropolis: Correspondence and Observation of the Existing Law and Proposed Amendments.* London: John Murray 1864.

Behlmer, George K. *Child Abuse and Moral Reform in England, 1870–1908.* Stanford: Stanford University Press 1982.

Bell, Rudolph M. *Fate and Honor, Family and Village: Demographic and Cultural Change in Rural Italy since 1800.* Chicago: University of Chicago Press 1979.

Bolognani, Bonifacio. *A Courageous People from the Dolomites: The Immigrants from the Trentino on USA Trails.* Trento: Edition and Patronage of the Autonomous Province of Trento 1981.

Booth, Charles. *Life and Labour of the People in London.* vol. 8. London: Macmillan and Co 1896.

Bosanquet, Helen. *Social Work in London, 1869–1912: A History of the Charity Organisation Society.* London: John Murray 1914.

Bracco, Giovanni. "Ricerche storiche intorno a una tradizione meridionale." *Clio* 15:3 (1979), 425–35.

Brace, Charles Loring. *The Dangerous Classes of New York and Twenty Years' Work among Them.* New York: Wynkoop & Hallenbeck 1872.

Bremner, Robert H. "The Children with the Organ-Man." *American Quarterly* 8 (1956), 277–82.

Bruchet, Max. "L'Émigration des savoyards de Faucigny au XVIIIe siècle." *Bulletin historique et philosophique* (du Comité des Travaux Historiques et Scientifiques) 7 (1896), 815–31.

– "Notes sur l'émigration des savoyards." *Revue savoisienne* (1894), 241–58.

Burke, Peter. *Popular Culture in Early Modern Europe.* Middlesex: Temple Smith 1978.

\tratta dei fanciulli italiani." *La riforma sociale* 11 (1901), 568–91.

atore. *Fonti per la storia del risorgimento italiano negli archivi ?arigi: I rifugiati italiani 1815–1830.* Rome: Istituto per la ...ı Risorgimento Italiano 1962.

Carpi, Leone. *Dell'emigrazione italiana all'estero nei suoi rapporti coll'agricoltura, coll'industria e col commercio.* Florence: Stabilimento Giuseppe Civelli 1871.

– *Delle colonie e dell'emigrazione d'italiani all'estero sotto l'aspetto dell' industria, commercio, agricoltura con trattazione d'importanti questioni sociali*, vol. 2. Milan: Lombarda 1874.

– *Statistica illustrata della emigrazione all'estero del Triennio 1874–76: Nei suoi rapporti coi problemi economico sociali.* Rome: Tip. del "Popolo Romano" 1878.

Casali, Giovanni. "La vita nella montagna piacentina verso la metà del secolo scorso." *Bollettino Storico Piacentino* 56:2–3 (1961), 65–72.

Catalani, Tommaso. "Fanciulli italiani in Inghilterra." *Nuova Antologia* 37 (1878), 559–86.

Cerruti, Luigi. "Cenni statistici sull'industria e sul commercio nel distretto consolare di Parigi." *Bollettino consolare* 1 (1861–2), 561–600.

Charity Organisation Society. *Report of the Committee of Charity Organisation Society appointed to inquire into the Employment of Italian Children for Mendicant and Immoral Purposes.* London: Charity Organisation Society 1877.

Chevalier, Louis. *Labouring Classes and Dangerous Classes in Paris during the First Half of the Nineteenth Century.* Trans. Frank Jellinek. New York: Howard Fertig 1973.

Children's Aid Society (New York). *Annual Reports* 1854–74, vols. 1–22.

Ciuffoletti, Z., and M. Degl'Innocenti. *L'emigrazione nella storia d'Italia 1868–1974*, vol. 1. Florence: Valecchi 1978.

Cohen, David, and Ben Greenwood. *The Buskers.* Newton Abbot: David and Charles 1981.

Coraggioso, Cagliardo. *Wandering Minstrel: The Life Story of Cagliardo Coraggioso Written by Himself.* London: Oxford University Press 1938.

Curtin, Philip D. *Cross-Cultural Trade in World History.* Cambridge: Cambridge University Press 1984.

De Bourcard, Francesco, ed. *Usi e costumi di Napoli e contorni.* Milan: Longanesi e co 1970.

Du Camp, Maxime. "La Mendicité à Paris." *Revue des deux mondes* 87 (1870), 175–212.

Duroselle, J.B., and A. Serra, eds. *L'emigrazione italiana in Francia prima del 1914*. Milan: Franco Angeli Editore 1978.

Dyos, H.J., and Wolff, M., eds. *The Victorian City: Images and Realities*. London: Routledge & Kegan Paul 1973.

Ernst, Robert. *Immigrant Life in New York City, 1825–1863*. New York: King's Crown Press, Columbia University 1949.

Fawcett, Mrs Henry. "Theatre and Pantomine Children." *Charity Organisation Review* 3 (1887), 232–6.

Ferrari, Mario Enrico. "I mercanti di fanciulli nelle campagne e la tratta dei minori. Una realtà sociale dell'Italia fra '800 e '900." *Movimento operaio e socialista* 4:1 (1983), 87–108.

Ferraris, Carlo F. "Fanciulli italiani in Inghilterra." *Saggi di economia, statistica e scienza dell'amministrazione*. Ed. Carlo Ferraris. Turin and Rome: Ermanno Loescher 1880, 456–64.

Florenzano, Giovanni. *Della emigrazione italiana in America comparata alle altre emigrazioni europee*. Naples: Giannini 1874.

Florian, Eugenio, and Guido Cavaglieri. *I vagabondi* vol. 1. Turin: Fratelli Bocca 1897.

Foerster, Robert. *The Italian Emigration of Our Times*. Cambridge, Mass: Harvard University Press 1919.

Genoino, Chiara Trara. "Suonatori ambulanti nelle province meridionali: archivio della polizia borbonica e postunitaria dell'ottocento." *La Ricerca Folklorica* 19 (April 1989), 69–75.

Goffin, Magdalen. *Maria Pasqua*. Oxford: Oxford University Press 1979.

Grant, Judith Skelton. "Italians with White Mice in *Middlemarch* and *Mrs Dorrit*." *English Language Notes* 16 (1979), 232–4.

Green, David R. "The Stability of Immigrant Communities: 'Little Italy' in Nineteenth-Century London." BA thesis, Cambridge University 1976.

Greenwood, J. "The Private Life of a Public Nuisance, London Society." *London Society* 11 (1867): 221–33.

Guerzoni, Giuseppe. *La Tratta dei fanciulli: Pagine del problema sociale in Italia*. Florence: Giovanni Polizzi e Comp. 1868.

Harney, R.F. *Dalla frontiera alle Little Italies: Gli italiani in Canada 1800–1945*. Rome: Bonacci Editore 1984.

– "The Padrone and the Immigrant." *Canadian Review of American Studies* 5: 2 (1974), 101–18.

Heywood, Colin. *Childhood in Nineteenth-Century France: Work, Health and Education among the "Classes Populaires."* Cambridge: Cambridge University Press 1988.

"Image-Boy, The" *New Monthly Magazine*, 1 January 1829.
Iorizzo, Luciano, and Salvatore Mondello. *The Italian-Americans*. New York: Twayne Publishing 1971.
"Italian Organ-Grinder, The" *Charity Organisation Review* 10 (1894), 407–13.
Jones, Gareth Steadman. *Outcast London: A Study in the Relationship between Classes in Victorian Society*. Oxford: Oxford University Press 1971.
King, John. *McCaul: Croft: Forneri: Personalities of Early University Days*. Toronto: Macmillan 1914.
Langsman, Z. Miriam. *Children West: A History of the Placing-Out System of the New York Children's Aid Society, 1853–1890*. Madison: State Historical Society of Wisconsin for the Department of History, University of Wisconsin 1964.
Leppert, Richard D. *Arcadia at Versailles: Noble Amateur Musicians and the Musettes and Hurdy-Gurdies at the French Court (c. 1660–1789): A Visual Study*. Amsterdam and Lisse: Swets & Zeitlinger BV, 1978.
Little Italians, or The Lost Children of St Bernard, The. London: James Burns n.d.
McFarlane, Charles. "Ballo Degli Orsi, Bear-Dancing, at Rome." *Popular Customs, Sports, and Recollections of the South of Italy*. London: Charles Knight & Co 1846, 163–76.
– "Wandering Italians." *Popular Customs, Sports, and Recollections of the South of Italy*. London: Charles Knight & Co. 1846, 135–51. First published in *The Penny Magazine (for the useful Diffusion of Knowledge)*, 2 and 11 February 1833.
Magraw, Roger. *France 1815–1914: The Bourgeois Century*. Oxford: Fontana 1983.
Malpica, Cesare. "I viggianesi." *Poliorama pittoresco* 1:2 (1836), 405–6.
Manzotti, Fernando. *La Polemica sull'emigrazione nell'Italia unita*. Milan: Società Editrice Dante Alighieri 1969.
Marchini, F. *Montanari all'estero*. Parma: Tip Già coop. 1938.
Marin, Umberto. *Italiani in Gran Bretagna*. Rome: Centro Studi Emigrazione 1975.
Mariotti, L (Antonio Gallenga). "Maria Stella; A Smuggler's Tale." *Blackgown Papers*, vol. 2. London: Wiley and Putnam 1864, 145–208.
– "Morello or the Organ Boy Press?" *Blackgown Papers*, vol. 2. London: Wiley and Putnam 1846, 1–144.
Marraro, Howard A. "Italians in New York during the first Half of the Nineteenth Century." *New York History* 26:3 (1945), 278–306.

Mayhew, Henry. *London Labour and the London Poor*, vol. 3, 1861–2. Reprinted New York: Dover Publications 1968.

Mazzini, Giuseppe. *Joseph Mazzini: His Life, Writings and Political Principles*. New York: Hurd and Houghton 1872.

Moreno, Celso Cæsar. *The History of a Great Wrong: Italian Slavery in America ... n.p.*, n.d. (ca 1896).

Motais-Avril, J. *Les Voyageurs forains, les saltimbanques et les bohémiens*. Angers: Lachèse et cie. 1898.

Munhall, Edgar. "Savoyards in French Eighteenth-Century Art." *Apollo* 87:1 (1968), 86–94.

Ord-Hume, Arthur W.J.G. *Barrel Organ: The Story of the Mechanical Organ and Its Repair*. New York: A.S. Barnes and Co. 1978.

Palmer, Susann, and Samuel Palmer. *The Hurdy-Gurdy*. Newton Abbott: David and Charles 1980.

Parzanese. Pietro Paolo. *I canti del viggianese*. Viggiano: Fratelli Porfidio Editore 1982.

Paulucci di Calboli, Roberto. "L'Agonie d'un métier en France (Les cireurs de bottes italiens)." *Revue des Revues*, 15 July 1902, 5–23.

– "L'emigrazione italiana in Francia. I Mestieri girovaghi ed i vetrai ambulanti." *La Riforma Sociale* 7 (1897), 558–69.

– *I girovaghi italiani in Inghilterra ed i suonatori ambulanti*. Città di Castello: S. Lapi 1893.

– *L'Italie vagabonde*. Paris: A. Davy 1895.

– "La traite des petits italiens en France." *Revue des Revues*, 1 September 1897, 5–20.

– "La tratta delle ragazze italiane." *Nuova Antologia* (April 1902).

Perrod, Enrico. "I minorenni italiani nelle industrie lionesi." *Bollettino dell'emigrazione* 2 (1902), 50–7.

Pinchbeck, Ivy, and Margaret Hewitt. *Children in English Society*, vol. 2. London: Routledge and Kegan Paul 1973.

Pollock, Linda. *Forgotten Children: Parent-Child Relations from 1500 to 1900*. Cambridge: Cambridge University Press 1983.

Porcella, Marco. *La fatica e la Merica*. Genoa: Sagep 1986.

Pozzetta, George E. "The Mulberry District of New York City: The Years Before World War I." *Little Italies in North America*. Ed. R.F. Harney and J.V. Scarpaci. Toronto: Multicultural History Society of Ontario 1981.

Prato, Giuseppe. "Gli italiani in Inghilterra." *La riforma sociale* 10 (1900), 674–703, 1095–1116.

Regaldi, G. "Il viggianese." *Poliorama pittoresco* 16:2 (1847–8), 326–7, 334–5.

"Report of the Lancet Special Commission on the Sanitary Condition of the Italian Quarter." *The Lancet* (1879), 590–2.

Ribton-Turner, C.J. *History of Vagrants and Vagrancy and Beggars and Begging*. London: Chapman and Hall 1887.

Rosoli, Gianfausto, ed. *Un secolo di emigrazione italiana, 1876–1976*. Rome: Centro Studi Emigrazione 1978.

Rossi, Adolfo. "Vantaggi e danni dell'emigrazione nel mezzogiorno d'Italia." *Bollettino dell'emigrazione* 16 (1908), 3–99.

Sarti, Roland. *Long Live the Strong: A History of Rural Society in the Appenine Mountains*. Amherst: University of Massachusetts Press 1985.

Schiro, George. *Americans by Choice: History of the Italians in Utica*. New York: Arno Press 1975.

Seton-Watson, Christopher. *Italy from Liberalism to Fascism, 1870–1925*. London: Methuen 1967.

Sitta, Pietro. "I lavoratori italiani in Francia." *La Riforma Sociale* 1 (1894), 995–1003.

Smith, Alfred, ed. *Gavarni in London*. London: David Brogue 1849.

Smith, John Thomas. *The Cries of London*. London: John Bowyer Nichols and Son 1839.

– *Vagabondiana or, Anecdotes of Mendicant Wanderers through the Streets of London*. London: J.T. Smith 1817.

– *Etchings of Remarkable Beggars: Itinerant Traders and Other Persons of Notoriety in London and Its Environs*. London: J.T. Smith 1815.

Société Italienne de Bienfaisance de Paris. *Rapport de la Société Italienne de Bienfaisance de Paris sur la situation des petits italiens*. Paris: Société Italienne de Bienfaisance de Paris 1868 (two versions).

Society for the Prevention of Cruelty to Children, New York (SPCC), *Annual Reports* 1876–83, vols. 1–8.

Society for the Suppression of Mendicity, *Annual Reports* 1819–84, vols. 1–66.

Sommerville, John C. *The Rise and Fall of Childhood*. Beverly Hills: Sage Publications 1982.

Sponza, Lucio. *Italian Immigrants in Nineteenth-Century Britain: Realities and Images*. Leicester: Leicester University Press 1988.

– "Il 'quartiere italiano' nella Londra medio-vittoriana (1851–71): Realtà e polemiche," *Risorgimento* (1982), 25–40.

Sutcliffe, Anthony. *The Autumn of Central Paris: The Defeat of Town Planning, 1850–1970*. Montreal: McGill-Queen's University Press 1971.

Taylor, P.A.M. *The Distant Magnet: European Emigration to the USA*. London: Eyre and Spottiswoode 1971.

Thistlethwaite, Frank. "Migration from Europe Overseas in the 19th and 20th Centuries." xie Congrès International des Sciences Historiques. *Rapports v: Histoire Contemporaine*. Göteborg-Stockholm-Uppsala: Almquist and Wiksell 1960, 32–60.

Thompson, Ralph, ed. *American Literary Annuals and Gift Books*. New Haven: Research Publications 1975.

Thomson, John (with Adolphe Smith). *Street Life in London*. 1877, reprint New York: B. Blom 1969.

Twattle-Basket, Prof Todear (G. Fanchiotti). *Note di cronaca ossia I giornali, gli istituti e gli uomini illustri italiani a Londra durante l'età vittoriana (1837–97)* Bergamo: F. e P. Fratelli Bolis 1897.

Vecoli, Rudolph J. "Chicago's Italians prior to World War I: A Study of Their Social and Economic Adjustment." Ph. D. thesis, University of Wisconsin 1963.

Vertone, Teodosio. "Antécédents et causes des événements d'Aigues-Mortes." In Durosell and Serra, *L'emigrazione italiana*.

Walker, Mack. *Germany and the Emigration, 1816–1885*. Cambridge: Harvard University Press 1964.

"W.C." "German and Italian Vagrants." *Chambers's Journal* 526 (June 1874), 68–70.

– "Italian Vagrant Children." *Chambers's Journal* 718 (September 1877), 614–17.

Weissbach, Lee Shai. *Child Labor Reform in Nineteenth-Century France: Assuring the Future Harvest*. Baton Rouge: Louisiana State University Press 1989.

Wilkins, W.H. "The Italian Aspect." *The Destitute Alien in Great Britain*. Ed. Arnold White. London: Sonnenschein & Co. 1892, 146–67.

Wohl, Anthony S. *The Eternal Slum: Housing and Social Policy in Victorian London*. Montreal: McGill-Queen's University Press 1977.

Wolf, Eric R. *Europe and the People without History*. Berkeley: University of California Press 1982.

Woolf, Stuart. *A History of Italy 1700–1860: The Social Constraints of Policial Change*. London: Methuen 1979.

– *The Poor in Western Europe in the Eighteenth and Nineteenth Centuries*. London: Methuen 1986.

Zanella, Giacomo. *Il piccolo calabrese*. Florence: G. Barbera 1871.

Zguta, Russel. *Russian Minstrels: A History of the "Skomorokhi."* Oxford: Oxford University Press 1978.

Zucchi, John E. *Italians in Toronto: Development of a National Identity, 1875–1935*. Montreal: McGill-Queen's University Press 1988.

Index

Aigues-Mortes (1893): clashes between Italian and French workers 169
Alger, Horatio 170
Ancarola, Antonio Giovanni 141–2, 151, 163, 165
animal exhibitors 28–30, 37, 76–7
Arrivabene, Carlo (Valenti Gonzaga) 147, 149, 157
Associazione Donnarumma (New York) 134, 135–6

Babbage, Charles 84–7, 99
Baldacconi, Rev. Angelo Maria: and Italian Catholic school in London 79
Barcelona, child street musicians in 37, 38, 40
Bardi 19, 20, 29, 32, 46, 55
Barga (Lucca) 46
Barnabites 169, 171
Barnardo, Dr Thomas 106
barrel-organ manufacturers 30, 99
Bass, Michael Thomas, MP 84–8, 99, 104
Bedonia 19, 20, 29, 32, 45, 46, 55
Behlmer, George K. 110

Boccia, Captain Antonio 20, 22
boîte-à-curiosité 43
Bonomelli Foundation 170
Booth, Charles 168
Borgotaro 19
Brace, Charles Loring 111, 114–15, 116, 119, 134

Cadorna, Carlo 107, 148, 150, 151, 163
Calvello 37, 60, 63, 73, 140
Carnot, Sadi 168
Caserta. *See* Terra di Lavoro
Cavignaga 29
Cerqua, A.E. 112, 113–14, 117, 137
Cerruti, Luigi 37, 54ff, 63, 64–5, 66, 68, 69, 71, 131, 145, 146, 171
Cerruti, Marcello 146, 155
Charity Organisation Society (UK) 10, 100, 109; and 1877 special report 100–1, 106, 107
Chiavari 19, 32, 37, 39, 55, 56, 57, 58, 60, 94, 101, 165
Chicago 40, 125
Chicago Tribune 125
childhood: history of 11, 12

Children's Aid Society (New York) 112, 116, 119, 126, 128, 137; and placement system 127
Ciociaria. *See* Terra di Lavoro
Clementi, Muzio 99
Compiano 20, 29
contracts: to lease or apprentice children 38–9
Coraggioso, Cagliardo 10, 13–14, 15, 74
de Corbière, Jacques 52–3
Corleto Perticara 37, 60, 63, 115
Cross, Sir Richard 102, 107, 108, 109, 110
cruelty to children 12–13, 71–4, 78, 92–3, 97, 122

d'Azeglio, V.E. Taparelli: correspondence with Lord Malmesbury 89; and foundation of Italian Benevolent Society 90
De Luca, Ferdinando 117, 119, 125, 126, 127, 128, 131, 132–3, 134, 135, 136, 154, 155, 162
diet, children's 14–15, 117
Di Grazia, Raffaelo 140–1, 165
Duchy of Parma 18

Index

Eco d'Italia, L' 115, 128, 131, 133, 136
Education Department (Great Britain) 108
Elementary Education Act (UK) 102
emigration: from Europe 4–6
Ethiopian serenaders 80, 84, 85

Faenza, Rev. Sebastiano S. 94
family, right of state to interfere with 150–1, 152–3, 158
Fava, Baron Basilio 139
female child musicians 93, 100, 101, 103, 109, 113
figurinai 25–6, 47, 48, 62, 95, 153
Foreign Office (Great Britain) 107

Gazzetta Italiana di Londra, La 105
German brass bands 81, 86, 88
glassworks 169–70
Glionna, Giovanni 121–3, 136, 137, 165, 166
Great Britain, street musicians in 100–2
Grezzo 19, 29, 32
Guerzoni, Giuseppe 61, 63, 148, 149, 157–8

Hammersmith, street musicians in 97, 102–3
Harper's Weekly 8, 119, 123
Havana, street musicians in 34
Heath, Baron Richard Benjamin 131, 156
Home Office (Great Britain) 107–8, 110
hurdy-gurdy 43

Ireland, street musicians in 101

Italian Benevolent Society (London) 90–4, 105, 106, 108
Italian colony (New York) 130–1
Italian Republican Association of New York 135

La Guardia, Fiorello 16
Lancet, The 96–8, 102
Laurenzana 25, 34, 36, 37, 60, 63, 67, 71, 72, 115, 118, 121, 145, 166, 167, 169
Lecour, Charles-Jérôme 66, 75
legislation and ordinances: regarding child labour 9–10; against street performing in Paris and in France 47ff, 65–7; regarding vagabondage in France 52, 74–5; regarding street music in Britain 84–5, 87–8, 165; regarding vagabondage in Britain 92, 165; Act for the Prevention of Cruelty to Children (Great Britain 1889) 165, 167; regarding Mendicant and Vagrant Children (New York 1874) 125–8; An Act to Prevent and Punish Wrongs to Children (New York 1876) 128, 129–30, 164–5; Padrone Act (US 1874) 138, 139–43, 164–5; regarding child itinerants from Kingdom of Naples (1841) 145; regarding child street performers from Duchy of Parma (1852) 145; Public Safety (Pubblica Sicurezza) Act (Italy) 146, 150, 152; Italian Law to Prohibit Employment of Children in Itinerant Trades (1873) 149–62
literature, street musicians in 36, 61, 77
living conditions 7–8, 13; in Paris 62–3; in New York 113, 116, 120–1, 123
London: street musicians' neighbourhood 95–9
Lualdi, Ercole 147
Lyon, street musicians in 61, 65–6

McFarlane, Charles 97
marmotte 43
Marsiconuovo 37, 63, 115
Marsicovetere 37, 55, 60, 62, 63, 67, 72
Mayhew, Henry: *London Labour and the London Poor* 80–2
Mazzini, Giuseppe: and Italian school in London 78–9, 95
Melia, Rev. Pio 94, 96
Menabrea, General Luigi Federico 107, 147, 148, 154, 156, 157
mendicancy 6–7
Mezzanego 19, 37, 55, 56, 60
migrant trades: of the valtaresi 22–3; of northern Italians 23ff; of the parmigiani 31–2; of Italians in London 94–5
Monachesi, H.D. 132, 134, 137
Monte Satta 20, 22
Moreno, Celso Caesar (Cesare) 117, 118, 132–3, 134, 135, 137, 138–9
Morfasso 32
Moscow, street musicians in 32, 40, 41

Nè 19, 56
New Haven, street musicians in 121–2

208   Index

New York Children's Aid Society. *See* Children's Aid Society (New York)
New York Society for the Prevention of Cruelty to Children. *See* Society for the Prevention of Cruelty (New York)
New York Times 10, 12, 13, 18, 39, 114, 115, 116, 119, 120, 124, 127, 129, 130, 132, 136, 137–8, 140
Nigra, Costantino 66, 68, 154, 156
nomenclature of child street musicians 18

Oliva, Antonio 148, 149
organ-grinding 30

padrone: his function 30–1; conveying children to Paris 61–2; as labour agent and saloon-keeper in New York 121; as labour agent 167
Paris: child street musicians in 39, 40; Italian tradesmen in 46–7; street musicians' residences 62–4; mass arrests and expulsions of street musicians 64–8
Parma, Duchy of: economic conditions 19ff
Parzanese, Rev. Pietro Paolo 34–5
Personal Liberty Bill (1854) 121, 137

Philadelphia, street musicians in 125
Picinisco 19, 41, 60, 98, 169
Potenza 25, 35, 39, 115
Prato, Giuseppe 104

refugees: from Italian states in France during Restoration 44–7
repertory of street musicians 15–16, 34–5
Ribton-Turner, Sir Charles 102
Rio de Janeiro, child street musicians in 38, 40

St Petersburg, street musicians in 32, 37
San Biagio 41
Savoyards 18, 42–4
Scherman, Senator George 125
Secchi de Casali, G.F. 115, 127, 131, 133, 134, 135, 136, 138, 141
Société Italienne de Bienfaisance 10, 55, 63, 64, 68; and *Rapport sur la situation des petits italiens* 69ff, 105, 116, 137, 148, 149
Society for the Prevention of Cruelty to Children (New York) 10, 12, 115, 126, 128–9, 139
Society for the Suppression of Mendicity (London Mendicity Society) 10, 76–7, 88–9, 90–1, 94, 104, 105, 139–41
Sponza, Lucio 96
street noise 82–4
Sumner, Senator Charles 137–8

Tammany Hall 118
Temps, Le (Paris) 9, 70
Terra di Lavoro 18, 19, 32, 39, 41, 55, 60, 91
Times, The (London) 12, 31, 76, 77, 83, 84, 95, 99, 104, 141
Toronto, laurenzanesi in 122, 166–7
Trevelyan, Sir Charles 106, 107

usefulness of street music trade 112, 113–14, 153, 158–60

vagrancy 6–7, 42, 52–3, 91, 107, 109, 110, 149
Val-di-Taro 28; economic conditions 20ff, 165
viggianesi (harpists, pipers, and fifers from Viggiano) 32–5, 40, 153, 154, 157, 166
Viggiano 32, 35, 36, 38, 40, 55, 57, 60, 63, 67, 115, 145, 154, 167
Voce del Popolo, La 117, 136

zampogna (or cornamusa) 32, 55
Zoagli 19